THE
ACTOR
SPEAKS

THE ACTOR SPEAKS

TWENTY-FOUR ACTORS TALK ABOUT PROCESS AND TECHNIQUE

JANET SONENBERG

CROWN TRADE PAPERBACKS   NEW YORK

THIS BOOK IS DEDICATED TO
BRIAN AND ANNA ROTHSCHILD,
THE MOST IMPORTANT COLLABORATORS
IN MY PROCESS.

Published by Crown Trade Paperbacks, 201 East 50th Street, New York, New York 10022. Member of the Crown Publishing Group.

Random House, Inc. New York, Toronto, London, Sydney, Auckland

CROWN TRADE PAPERBACKS and colophon are trademarks of Crown Publishers, Inc.

Printed in the United States of America

Design by June Bennett-Tantillo

Library of Congress Cataloging-in-Publication Data
Sonenberg, Janet
    The actor speaks : twenty-four actors talk about process and technique / Janet Sonenberg. — 1st pbk. ed.
        p.   cm.
    1. Acting—Psychological aspects. 2. Acting. 3. Actors—United States—Interviews. I. Title.
    PN2071.P78S66   1996
    792'.028—dc20

ISBN   0-517-88388-0

10 9 8 7 6 5 4 3 2 1

First Edition

Contents

ACKNOWLEDGMENTS

I thank the actors for generously sharing their insights into the process of acting.

I called on the knowledge, expertise, and support of many people. Among those whose brains I picked most often are Kathryn Jackson, Matthew Sussman, Katell Pleven, Irene Connelly, Jennifer Staub, William Kennedy, Ron Lagomarsino, Sam Christensen, Tony Taccone, Emily Sachar, Jane Cavolina, Dakila Divina, Sidney Feinberg, David Groff, Giselle Galdi, and Michael O'Brien. This book might not exist without Michelle Sidrane's interest in the documentation of creative processes.

I owe special gratitude to my friends and colleagues in Music and Theater Arts at Massachusetts Institute of Technology, a locus of creativity. There, Alan Brody, Michael Ouellette, and I endlessly discuss the beauty and techniques of acting and continue exploring new ways of sharing them with our students. Anne Richard helped me keep track of the paperwork and along the way learned more about acting than she ever thought she would. Watching my students omnivorously devour the lessons offered by the actors in the book, and seeing them use them to find the truth in acting moments, was almost all the encouragement I needed.

My family is small in number but huge in support. Each of them contributed in important ways to *The Actor Speaks*. My thanks to Harold, Charlotte, David, Shelley, Elizabeth, and Jenny Sonenberg for their thousand ideas and their love.

INTRODUCTION

Great acting is not magic, which is not to deny its mystery. It is not inexplicable, which is not to deny the difficulty in unraveling its many sources. Of course, anything that relies in part upon the creative application of the unconscious mind cannot be fully explained. Acting partakes of the great mysteries when the actor lends her unconscious to the creative act. But the actor who has created a great performance is not working solely with unconscious creative inspiration, the stuff of "magic." She is using acting techniques and inspiration to ply her talent, whose reciprocal action develops in time into an acting process.

A definition of terms is in order. The constant in the equation is talent, or raw ability. But ability to do what? In most theatrical forms, the actor's talent translates human behavior onto the stage or film in a way that goes beyond mere accuracy. She must have insight and an expressive language of symbol and metaphor to convey the human truth that lies beneath behavior. She must have the courage to expose that truth within herself and the desire to share it communally. Even in postmodern theaters, such as Theater of Images, which experiments with the aesthetics of bodies in space and time, these last two aspects hold true. These expressions of talent cannot be accomplished without developed material "chops": an eloquent voice and body and fine observational skills.

A technique is a systematic procedure that organizes fundamental artistic material. The actor uses this procedure, or technique, to accomplish a task that spurs her talent. That in turn opens her to her unconscious, allowing inspiration to come once more into play. When talent is stirred by inspiration, the actor's mind and emotions are stimulated to such a high degree of feeling and activity that they produce a spontaneous creative act. Without this reliable interplay of talent, techniques, and inspiration—in other words, without an acting process—all is chaos. If there is nothing to support talent when inspiration fails, fear drives the actor, taking her out of the moment of the play and into her own terror and confusion. However disorganized or tightly structured, however self-abusive or nurturing it is, each actor evolves an acting process if she intends longevity as an artist. She uses it to get herself in touch with the character, situation, and ideas of the theatrical event and to find her way to tell its story. She uses it to deliver a quality performance night after night, take after take.

A solid process assures an actor that he will not fall below a certain level of expertise; but it does more. Tapping profound emotions, taking gesture or voice beyond his ego's comfort zone, hazarding failure as he attempts to reach a moment of unguarded expression, are just a few of the risks an actor takes in exploring his creativity. These risks require courage and a process that will free and support that daring. For instance, Ruth Maleczech frequently experiments technically with both pitch and volume as part of her process. In Kroetz's *Through the Leaves* she suggested that both of the characters should speak very, very loudly. That technical choice freed one of the most startling performances of a decade, showing how we Americans fill our lonely lives with relentless noise because silence would be too dangerous. Ms. Maleczech dismisses her choice with, "Of course, that was just technical." Nevertheless, this revelatory insight might not have surfaced had that technique not been part of her process. Process touches every dimension of an actor's work; it encompasses the whole psychophysical spectrum of her being.

The purpose of *The Actor Speaks* is to investigate how these twenty-four actors work. And if they produce something we think of as magical onstage, as many of them do, to try to break it into its component parts. When these are understood, they can be practiced. They become the tools with which a young actor can implement his creativity rather than awaiting inspiration. For example, the catalyst for many inexplicable moments is in reality an image from the actor's own life that arises unbidden in his mind. He deploys it, activating the moment, without thinking about the emotional charge crowding behind it. Actors can, however, willfully begin working with imagery as a technique. In fact, several systems for doing so are described in this book. Some actors, such as Mercedes Ruehl, call upon the more traditional approaches of affective memory. Peruvian actor Teresa Ralli utilizes a strict exploration of physical structures, which allows images to arise without intentionally calling upon her emotional history. By practicing either of these techniques, the actor can increase his ability to generate saturated images, trigger them, and augment his creativity.

A contribution the actors interviewed in *The Actor Speaks* make to students of acting is in the varied language they use to discuss similar ideas. Who is to say what explanation will finally unlock an actor's understanding? While giving the same name to a technique, the actors actually describe distinctly different ways to activate it. The diverse ways in which they decode these techniques offer students fresh opportunities for understanding.

The reasons how and why an actor comes to use a specific technique and to develop a process are extraordinarily diverse. Exploring an actor's route is not only interesting but germane to both who she is and what she has to say with her art. An actor's history, weaknesses and strengths, personal and artistic, shape her process and ultimately her acting. Elizabeth Wilson began acting to flee reality by inhabiting another person's mind. While her process has developed over time to incorporate more of herself, it remains geared to "disappearing into the character." Early in his career, Alan Arkin experimented successfully with the placement of the character's center, because he felt that he didn't have one. Marcia Gay Harden says, "The personal stuff you take great pains to avoid is exactly what is going to make something exciting happen to the character." That insight is especially important to young actors reading this book. She recounts the struggle she faces in every rehearsal process to stop saying, "My character wouldn't . . ." thereby allowing her own impulses to emerge. The actor who has faith in her true voice, however ambivalent, ironic, compassionate, or analytical it is, will produce something individual. John Turturro emphasizes this by saying that he is always developing his point of view. When faith in one's viewpoint develops into an unassailable trust, then actors are free to realize their visions.

In some cases an actor will learn a whole range of techniques in classes or graduate school. Joe Seneca, who came to acting later in life, went to the Strasberg Institute to acquire actor "jargon." He found, however, that Strasberg's techniques made absolute sense to him, and he appropriated them as his process. Younger actors, such as Joe Mantello, studied in preprofessional programs with powerful master teachers whose lessons often contradicted one another. Having completed a significant enough body of work that the cutting and pasting of techniques is coming to an end, he is now beginning to work like himself, having evolved his own process. This is a powerful rite of passage for any professional. Contrast that with Dianne Wiest. She regrets her lack of preprofessional training. As a young actor she had natural, intuitive talents, such as working freely with her impulses or using props in interesting ways. She was cast in the great ingenue roles in fine regional theaters, but her process was unreliable. It did not insure her consistency or confidence. One of the ways in which she delivered a great, single performance was by exploiting her own life, a technique that faltered during the run of the play and that finally grew distasteful to her. Over twenty years Dianne Wiest built a process of her own around what she did idiosyncratically and beautifully and says, "Now I feel quite powerful in my lack of training, most of the time."

The theatrical form in which the actor works is integral to the development of her process. If, as in the case of Teresa Ralli, a member of the theater company Grupo Yuyachkani, the content of the performance is political, then the actor may look to the techniques of Barba, Brecht, and Boal. While these satisfied her early needs, she had to search out other techniques to inform her performance process and found them in tai chi, singing and the dance forms of her ancient Peruvian culture, and kathakali ritual. In Rosa Luisa Marquez's work, a site may be "the pretext" for the theatrical event. The piece is derived by ordering the results of the actors' play in response to the site. These actors require an imaginative improvisational process to meet these demands. Central to the work of the Blue Man Group is the idea that the live theater performance is a modern, communal ritual. This mandates a process that embraces the audience's unpredictable response as an element that drives the action. Ruth Maleczech's process evolved out of Mabou Mines' notion of "tracking," in which all theatrical elements could be used at any time to tell the story. In a context where the actor's psychological and emotional "tracks" are equally communicative as gesture, image, sound, or light, the actor's process is closely akin to musical composition.

Many of the actors interviewed in *The Actor Speaks* work from psychological insight and ready emotional vulnerability. They call upon themselves to be aware of the ongoing flow of their emotional, physical, and intellectual reactions. Frances Sternhagen and Lily Tomlin, for example, are blessed with this intuitive awareness. This, however, is not always an automatic process, and actors have formulated techniques to plumb their responses. Finding himself faced with something for which he has no immediate personal connections, John Turturro begins to break it down. Stephen Spinella recounts an exercise he learned from Olympia Dukakis in which he slowed down a scene so as to verify how he felt and what that made him want to do in response. This became the core of his process for the next five years.

How the actor brings herself to the character engenders many of the techniques that comprise her process. Olympia Dukakis describes first "finding the

·ballpark" of the character so that her personal history doesn't inhibit her. Having ascertained that, she makes choices within that realm, using only those aspects of herself that will animate the character. Kathleen Chalfant is often called upon to create a complete illusion of character in which her personal identity is veiled. In doing so she finds it more powerful to draw on the character's history rather than her own. Several actors first work with personalization to approach their characters. They begin by using their personal history to inform the character's behavior. When Stephen Spinella reaches a fork where his personal identity and the character's identity diverge, he finds ways to personalize even these differences. He says, "You give yourself the character's opportunity; or your opportunity is the character's life." John Turturro reads the play to "see what connects to my own experiences, or experiences I've seen people go through. Then, I try and make it as personal as it can be." Only after researching himself does he add external elements to his characterization, which he describes in detail in his construction of Barton Fink.

Other actors do not consciously look for areas of commonality between themselves and the character. Zoe Caldwell "cuts the pattern" of the character and meshes with her in a fairly elaborate preperformance process. Kathleen Turner declares, "I absolutely do not look for the similarities between my character and myself. It's none of my business whether we seem to have areas in common or not." She thinks what her character thinks as part of her process. Lily Tomlin is at her happiest when the character illusion is so complete that "everyone goes on the same trip." This involves planning activities that will outwardly speak to the character's identity while informing her inner sense as well. Vinie Burrows's first point of contact with the text is musical rather than personal; she scores the rhythms of the material and works from their tempi. Alan Arkin has always made specific, imaginative decisions about the character's mind, and from that flows the body and behavior. He describes his characterization of Aronow in *Glengarry Glen Ross* in which he created "energy fields" using a technique derived from meditation and yoga.

Creative people must tolerate a high degree of anxiety because they work toward an unknown result. In his book *Creativity and Madness,* Dr. Albert Rothenberg states that creativity arises from the anxiety experienced by the creator in his encounter with paradoxical realities. He needs to reconcile two conflicting realities into a new, unconflicted reality in order to alleviate this anxiety. Rothenberg calls this new creation the homospatial reality, in other words, one in which the conflicts come together in creative resolution. While some actors would maintain that this analysis has little to do with their work, the majority have reflected similar ideas in their interviews. In a sense, many working methods are geared to bringing the actor and her identity together with the character and her identity, creating the performance, the homospatial reality. Many working methods function as bridges over the anxiety actors experience because their products, the performances of the roles, remain unknown for a significant time. Actors who leap to early classifications of characters or to immutable choices to mitigate their discomfort may produce indicated, one-dimensional performances. All good acting processes, regardless of the kind of theater they address, allow for periods of not knowing. They supply structures the actor can imaginatively explore where the answers may be found. They give the actor the confidence to work toward the unknown result because they've proven, over time, that a moment inevitably arrives when the actor comes to know. Kathleen Chalfant describes a two-year search for her character's throughline in a scene from *Angels in America*. Despite not having found the answer that addressed all the issues, her process was solid enough to sustain her performance. Once she discovered the answer, she could immediately incorporate it into the scene and it activated every moment.

Actors often acquire a technique to bridge a gap in their ability to perform. Mercedes Ruehl cites an anxiety-provoking eleventh-hour instance when she learned to integrate her emotional underpinning in *Medea* with the technical level of control required to keep the story moving forward. That technique became a fundamental aspect of her process. Zoe Caldwell employs a frenetic, excessive exploratory process that serves as both a comprehensive reference work and a defense against the fear she experiences in bringing herself nakedly to the character's need. As a member of Charles Ludlam's Ridiculous Theatrical Company, Black Eyed Susan experienced gaping psychological discrepancies between herself and the zanies she was to play. This seemed like a chasm that could not be crossed until she freed herself of her prior training and began imaginatively basing her characters on images outside herself; for example, on a dog. Matthew Sussman, understudying two major roles in *Angels in America,* scrambled to find a way to piece together an acting process in the face of virtually no rehearsal. Fear and anxiety, coupled with desire, should not be underrated as contributing factors to the acting process for, as Mercedes Ruehl says, breakthroughs in her working method were derived from "embracing terror. Again and again and again."

Each interview affirms that the development of an

acting process is a dynamic journey. Frances McDormand recounts her personal growth as inextricably woven with the development of her acting process. She adds further that each character she played created an opportunity to realize that growth, and taught her something that enabled her to play the next. For example, when she came to play Masha in *Three Sisters,* she was ready to stop being "a shadow actor," one who supports the other actors' performances before addressing her own needs. Masha made her comfortable with "the power of the full frontal position" onstage from which she commanded the audience's, the other actors', and her own attention. Olympia Dukakis discusses the changing reasons why she acted at different stages in her life, reasons that influenced her process, performances, and even the roles she got. This journey into process and expertise happens in every field. But in an art where the creator and the product are one, these narratives of change and progress have a unique personal intensity and vigor.

I asked the actors what they had to have in place so that they felt free to act. This question opened the door directly onto a discussion of process. All of the actors strive to release the daring of their fundamental creativity. Some, like Kathleen Chalfant, call it being in the moment. Dana Ivey describes a state of unconscious engagement that she calls "riding the dragon." That sense of the wild ride is shared by John Turturro and Alan Arkin as they work toward giving something of themselves away by losing a final measure of control. Stephen Spinella gives a different insight into this by asserting his and his fellow actors' need for absolute control over the theatrical event. With that in place he can reach for "the sublime moment." However it is described, each actor affirms that being free to act is the ultimate goal. The interviews illustrate that it is only by going through a process that the actors accomplish this end.

As you read about the processes of the actors in *The Actor Speaks,* I offer one caveat in the form of the advice Stanislavsky gave to Joshua Logan when the latter came to Moscow to learn everything he could about Stanislavsky's method. "You . . . may sit in [that] chair and watch us rehearse. Perhaps you will find some things in our rehearsals that apply to your way of thinking. If something excites you, use it, apply it to yourselves. But adapt it. Do not try to copy it. Let it make you think further." Try the techniques, use them. But learn to work like yourself.

Notes on the Process of the Book

I called upon the same techniques and process I use as a director and a teacher in conducting and editing these interviews. While I researched the actors by reading their writings and interviews, by far the most important aspect of my research was in rescreening their films, watching their plays on tape at the Lincoln Center Library, and recalling past performances I'd attended. I paid attention to the moments of excitation their work stirred in me. At that point I refrained from intellectualizing that excitation. In my work, if I intellectualize too early, I come to a sterile dead end. If I allow myself to be affected and then take time to observe that effect, I achieve a more authentic analytical clarity. By experiencing these sensations, images arose: metaphors, "maps" of the actor's body delineating the source of an impulse or the center from which the actor worked, archetypal relationship symbols.

I then looked at the sum of those moments and images and analyzed them as a whole to ascertain the actor's philosophy and methodology. The final analysis I prepared was a determination of how the actor saw herself as serving the throughline of each theatrical event.

Although years of training in technique and theory add objective weight to my creative process, it is also subjective and imaginative. This book deals with a kind of intelligence that is not necessarily linear. It examines creative intelligence and it required comparable creative intelligence to engage the actors in discussion of aspects of their work that are not easily rendered in speech. By offering my own point of excitation as a starting place, we opened a window onto the creative landscape, somewhat akin to dream analysis. Stanislavsky says that it is imperative for the actor's objective to hold his interest, and out of that interest will come rich inner and external imaginative objects. The same held true in these interviews. My own inner objects offered a fertile beginning from which the actor could, in reaction, begin exploring her own, sometimes in accord and sometimes in refutation. A hundred examples of this are in the book, but I trust that they will reveal themselves without further explication.

After repeated readings of the transcribed interviews while listening to them on tape, I listed their salient points. Later, I added other issues that had come to mind. Only then did I consciously order the list. Based on an overview of these issues, I determined the throughline of the interview. Each told a story, and I set about the task of ordering the interview so its specific narrative unfolded. The results were often surprising. I found that the actors themselves were not always aware of the process they revealed. In fact, what was not fully conscious had become clear in the structuring of the narrative. This was confirmed by several actors after they read their edited interviews.

I edited the interviews in the same way I direct a play. My job as a director is to tell a story and to explicate the underlying narrative with as much clarity as the plot. That meant finding the underlying action and psychological reality of each actor's "plot" and making certain that the true meaning and the intricacies of behavior were rendered with clarity. To have the actor's voice ring out, I removed my own. So, with the exception of the dialogue with Blue Man Group, in which I included their collaborative teasing of me, my voice is implicit in the interviews.

MERCEDES RUEHL

William Hazlitt wrote, "The soul of a journey is liberty, perfect liberty, to think, feel, do just as one pleases." But what if you are on a journey and you keep yourself from doing as you please? Mercedes Ruehl discusses how she got to the point where she "could pursue, unimpeded, [her] love of acting." A "wall" had to be broken down in order to achieve "those two elements most necessary for a successful performance, relaxation and concentration." It gave way only after she learned to bring her limiting, unconscious fears into consciousness. She was then able to sense constricting influences at work, thereby giving her the command of a wider range of choices.

Mercedes Ruehl makes an articulate case for the thesis that technique is born in the face of challenge. Sometimes that challenge came in the form of humiliation or shame, sometimes as desire, sometimes in the form of fear. But whatever the source, at challenging times she "went down to the bottom of my heart and then I reached deeper, into the subbasement, and pulled out some kind of courage. Some part of me refused to be defeated." Mercedes Ruehl recounts several instances in which that courage was rewarded by a new understanding of technique.

Her interview can be read as a baseline for the divergent processes documented in The Actor Speaks. Mercedes Ruehl's working method represents the best of the American tradition of psychological acting. It is rooted in *the behavioral analysis of a role from which she derives the character's throughline and its concomitant objectives and actions. She deliberately employs emotion to fill moments. Her personal history and her research into like "outrages" that others have suffered are used to inform the character's inner and expressive life. Her sensitivity to the metaphoric content of dramatic material is deployed to physicalize and activate moments. This approach, based on Stanislavsky's method, partakes of the wellspring of the American performance process. She speaks from a place of authority being midpoint in her career, but she is close enough to its starting point to remember how, when, and why on her journey into artistry she constructed her acting process.*

"THAT WAS ANOTHER TERROR, ABSOLUTE TERROR. . . . THIS IS ALL ABOUT EMBRACING TERROR. AGAIN AND AGAIN AND AGAIN."

I
n my late twenties, playing Medea in Denver, I got a real crash course in technique. I remember feeling that I was standing at the foot of Mt. Everest, being told that everybody had decided I was the best-equipped person to climb it. "I'm the best equipped? Whoa! There mustn't be much equipment out there!" To scale the heights of tragedy is pretty awesome.

Medea's agony stems from the outrage of profound loss and the staggering blow to a pride that was not just aristocratic; she considered herself a relative of the gods, a possessor of divine blood. The pain that she suffers is caused by the loss of her husband's love and the unspeakable indignity it causes her, the utter indifference of this man for whom she's risked her own life again and again to save and to nurture, and the solitude and degradation of being a so-called barbarian woman abandoned in a Greek culture. Euripides perceived something in the heart of women as deep, prideful, destructive, and as essentially wild as anything that can be found in the heart of a man, and he set about illustrating it. He may have been illustrating something much larger historically, in terms of what was going on at that time in Athens that I'm not as well aware of. But for any tragedy, any allegory, for any story to work on more than one level, it's got to work with breathtaking precision on the fundamental, human level.

So, here you have these enormous, godlike conditions, and I am this still fairly young woman from Silver Spring, Maryland. In the modern world we've lived so little by the time we're twenty-nine. Whereas, when *Medea* was written around 430 B.C., the average age probably did not exceed forty. We can assume Medea herself was not yet out of her twenties. So at least my age was proper to the Greek experience.

The only thing you've got is the sum of your own experience, what Yeats calls "the foul rag-and-bone shop of the heart." Having located what's going on in Medea to some degree psychologically and emotionally, you then become, both consciously and unconsciously, a continual investigator of your own life, your own memories, your own outrages, your own pain, your own grief, your own loss. At the same time you are watching for indications of great grief and loss out in the world, and taking mental snapshots of it.

When you have to perform onstage a moment of

the heart's outcry, part of what you do is remember a very, very specific moment of your own life, and you cut to it immediately, quickly, and effectively. Although this may sound a little silly, I think it's not totally unlike fantasizing while making love. In other words, if you have a fantasy that's very powerful, it moves you from one plateau of arousal to the next and then to the climactic moment. *Climax*—we use the same word for it in acting. You partake of the same technique, using a mental image to access emotional, rather than sexual, arousal, and the sluice gates open so that real feeling can flow out of you. That's what I ultimately think of as technique, beyond knowing how to speak up and not bump into the furniture. The actor's passion, those sluice gates, are opened by certain techniques that are different and somewhat similar as you go from actor to actor.

At one point in the rehearsal process, Tad Danielewski, a wonderful acting teacher who was a mentor of mine, came down and saw it. He said, "It's very good, but remember the humor." I said, "Humor in *Medea*?" He went on to say that in his opinion there is no intelligence without humor. In all great tragedy, if the hero is intelligent, there is some kind of humor. He said, "Look at all the humor in Hamlet, for instance. It may be gallows humor, but it's one of the manifestations of intelligence." And indeed there was, embedded in the text, a lot of deep, ironic, dark humor.

Zoe Caldwell and her husband, Robert Whitehead, came to see rehearsals of *Medea*. It was about a year before they did their production in New York. I mentioned the gallows humor to Bob [Whitehead] and he asked me to write a letter telling them where I'd found it in *Medea*. That opened up a dialogue between us, and at one point he asked me if I would like to understudy Zoe. I was arrogant enough then at twenty-nine to ask to perform it on the matinees. He said something like, "Darling, I don't think so. We'll talk this over, of course. But I don't think it's going to happen." And of course it didn't. What did happen is that I got an offer to go back and do an interesting season in Denver. So I went back there instead of warming the bench in New York, which is always the better idea.

When Bob and Zoe came to see rehearsals, I had made my first investigation into the character and was going great guns. Right after that we went into the theater for tech rehearsals and I was resting on my laurels because I thought I really had it emotionally. Then we went into previews. After the first preview, the director came and looked at me aghast. He said, "That was like a *Rhoda* episode. I'm disgusted. I won't even talk to you," and he walked away. I cried. The next night was even worse. I remember going out with a number of people in the cast around the third preview. We had just one more preview before opening. I said, "What have I lost? What did I have before we went into techs that I've lost?" Everybody sat around very respectfully not saying anything. Finally, Tandy Cronyn, who was beautifully playing the head woman of the chorus spoke up:

"You know, I think it's all there."

"It's not all there! The audience is getting restless and—"

"No," Tandy went on, "it's all there, it's just that you're taking too long about it. When you indulge in these big emotional moments, you're giving the audience a chance to get ahead of you. You've got to keep the movement of the story one major link in the chain ahead

MERCEDES RUEHL

of them. Do exactly what you're doing, but tell the story with more authority, with more bite. Force it through like a train that's coming at a good, strong speed, taking everything else with it."

"Yeah. Yeah, faster."

"You're the central force," Tandy said. "Every character comes to you and off they go. You determine the rhythm of this tragedy's movement. It has its own music, and if the rhythm and pace of that is right, it's going to take people's breath away."

I was desperate enough to try it. So, before the next performance, I'd meditated, I'd wept, and I thought, "I'm going to do this performance for me, keeping in mind what Tandy said." I remember getting out there and saying to myself, "Tell that story, move it along, keep the lifeblood circulating, don't let it coagulate." And she was absolutely right. The audience stood and cheered. None of the interpretation had changed but I had employed another sensitivity in acting technique: I refocused on what the action of *Medea* is and not just my inner reality. When an actor indulges himself in moments of grief or pain; when he spends a lot of time choosing a word, you have time to think to yourself, "That actor is appreciating his own fabulous technique," and he loses the audience. When the grief rises and you must also deal with the other character and the new demands of the situation, then the audience feels, "When is she going to explode?" That's what I learned playing Medea, and it was a real turning point in my life.

Zoe Caldwell was one of the people who inspired me to get into this business. When I was in school, I saw her do *The Prime of Miss Jean Brodie*, on Broadway, and it just blew me away. She had such an exquisite, eccentric instrument for transmitting her love of language; the way she moved on the stage in these fabulous, big circles! When I was first let loose on the world, when I graduated from college, I was imitating the great English actresses, that sort of grand, joyous, huge, British, Maggie Smith, Zoe Caldwell, Edith Evans kind of acting. I mean, I did all my auditions with an English accent! They thought I was just so eccentric. As a result, I didn't get into any acting graduate schools. They all rejected me. Then, I couldn't get in the Neighborhood Playhouse! Couldn't get into the Actors Studio! I mean, a normal person would have gotten the message by then, but I was just arrogant enough to think that they were just not getting the magic. Or, perhaps, I wasn't somehow communicating the magic.

I had absolutely no technique, but I think you move by degrees into technique. What motivates you is some kind of love or passion or energy to get something right. As a young actor you are essentially a block of marble out of which you must discover form. You have no technique, no methodology for reaching the delicate emotional moments in a play. You have no ability to re-create a performance night after night. But something deep motivates you to persevere. This is what you either have or you don't: the feeling that you'd die if you couldn't do it. And if you possess a love of it, a deep fascination, you find a route to get to that New World. You get the money from Isabella and Ferdinand. You get the leaky ships. You go from some kind of vision and passion, and the necessary tools gather around you.

So when I got rejected by everybody, I went to the one place in the city where you can just pay your money and get an acting class: HB Studio. I studied there first with Bill Hickey and then with Uta Hagen. Bill Hickey is on the one hand a crazy, nuts madman, and on the other, a great and inspiring teacher and a wonderful actor. He started me thinking about imagery. One day, drinking his tea, smoking his endless cigarettes, all curled up, he told this story. He was doing a revue somewhere in New York, and the first scene had the whole cast entering, belting out, "New York, New York, it's a wonderful town. The Bronx is up and the Battery's down." He said, "You know, I had to do this twice a night, six nights a week, and sometimes I would come in and I'd be hungover, or I'd be tired or disinclined. Even if I was depressed, I'd have to sing, "New York, New York." He went on to tell us that as a child he had a little dog that had been a particular favorite of his. The dog was getting progressively older and sicker, and the whole family was upset about it. They loved him so much that they didn't want to euthanize him until it was clear that he was unhappy and in pain. The dog had a cool, little protected spot in the bathroom, right behind the toilet, where he'd hang out. One day, Bill went into the bathroom and he looked and the dog was there. Then he took a second look and he realized that the dog had died in his little spot. All dog, all dead. And then Bill said to us, "Now this might not work for you, but all I had to do was flash on that moment of seeing my dog dead there behind the toilet and I got everything I needed to go, 'New York, New York, it's a wonderful town!" I thought, (a) what a weird guy, and (b) I understand exactly what he's talking about so I must be weird, too. I guess he was saying he got his energy to sing that life-affirming song by engaging his grief. Later I found out that Stanislavsky had a particular name for this technique, emotional recall or affective memory.

That was the first connection I made to the power of inner imagery. I realized that there was a technique I could use to re-create the same thing night after night. It requires incredible concentration, and in order to focus it, you have to be relaxed. So that began my long struggle to be relaxed before an audience or in an audition, situations which militate against any relaxation. I needed to achieve the beautiful arrogance that said, "Nevertheless, I will be relaxed." I had to make the assumption that I had a right to be there; that there was something within my soul worthy of expression that will make time stop for the audience. Or for you judges at this audition, which at the age of twenty-three or twenty-four is primarily where you're acting. I had to get through the judges to continue.

Those two elements most necessary for a successful performance, relaxation and concentration, were on the other side of this wall. The journey to that other side is hard, and how you get there is different for every human being. For me, it did finally involve therapy. To achieve that kind of courage and self-belief took in everything I was—all the doubts that I had about myself, all the sneaking, tenacious sense of unworthiness that most of us carry around like some tinker pulling along some horrible bag of junk. That *was* the wall. Through therapy I began breaking it down. A world that was unconscious before rose up into consciousness. Then, when it seemed like the wall was thicker than I ever could have imagined possible and would not be broken down in this lifetime, came what looked like a little light, a sense that maybe I had broken through to the other side where I could begin to pursue, unimpeded, my love of acting.

Stanislavsky said the difficult must be the habitual for the habitual to become easy. And the difficult has, over a period of years, made that journey to becoming easy. When it becomes easy, you're no longer conscious of your techniques because they happen automatically. I think that probably started happening for me when I was cast to go to Denver to play Medea and Lena Shepanovska in Shaw's *Misalliance*. Suddenly, I was working in regional theater everywhere. I had gotten enough of that fuel of self-esteem going that I was able to make it on that plateau. Then I determined that it was time to act in New York.

So, I did all these auditions. Then came the audition for some Thomas Babe play at Playwrights Horizons. Babe was in the room with a casting director when I did the audition, and when it was over, they clapped. And I thought, "Wow, this is a breakthrough in auditions. I opened my heart in the presence of the enemy. I let it come out my fingertips . . . finally!" Only to discover, two days later, that not only did I not get the job, they weren't even going to give me a callback. When my agent told me this over the phone, I did something that I had never done before. I broke down and cried. I thought, "That was my best. If my best isn't even worthy of a callback, maybe I have to reassess this whole thing." By this time I was thirty-one, maybe thirty-two, and I did not want to live like a graduate student for the rest of my life. Maybe it was time to take all I'd learned and put it into something else.

I had a long talk with my father about the fact that I was at a real crossroads in my career. He said, "Well, let's look at your options." My dad knew of this woman who had been an actress who was now making in-house industrial and educational films for a big utility company in Baltimore, and she was really getting off on directing them. I thought, "Well, pick whatever comes to hand; it's a starting place." "Okay, Dad, maybe I should go and talk to this woman when I come down for Christmas." This was around Thanksgiving. I think my parents heaved a tandem sigh of relief because I'm sure they were very worried for me for those first ten years of my life out in the world. If they only knew everything I'd been through, personally and professionally, they would have not been just worried, they would have gone screaming into the night. That's probably true of all parents and children.

A couple of days before I was scheduled to go home, I got a call from Albert Innaurato. He had a play called *Coming of Age in SoHo*, at the Public Theater, and its protagonist was a woman. Joe Papp had said to him, "You know, this play has autobiographical elements, doesn't it? What would you say about taking this risk? We're in previews and the play is not really working as it is. What would you say about rewriting and making the heroine into a man?" So, he did it and the new male protagonist then had to have a female fiancée, the second lead. He was rewriting it over Christmas and would have twelve days to get it back on its feet, then preview it again in this new incarnation.

Albert called me up and he said, "Listen, I want you to come and do this. I said, 'I just want her,' so the Public is waiving the audition. Will you do it?" And I said—I, who had never done anything in New York; I, who had been trying to get a toe into the Public Theater for ten years; I, who was planning to enter the world of gal-dom and work for Baltimore Gas and Electric—I said, "Yes!" I said, "Yes, I will! Yes, I'll do that! I'll make the time to do that for you. Count me in. Is yes good enough? Yahoo, *sí, oui,* yes!"

So I go into rehearsals—scared shitless. Joe Papp's

there from the first day. This was a play where he could be really hands-on, and he loved nothing more than when real theatrical experimentation was going on. We're in final tech rehearsals and there's a big wing chair right in the center of this loftlike set. I would enter, say my lines, and then I would get behind that big chair and just stand there. I did this for about three run-throughs, and finally Joe said to me, "The stage isn't lit to focus on you behind that chair. Besides, only a third of your person is visible. So you have to figure out a way to get out from behind that chair."

All I can tell you is that I was scared enough to be on the boards in New York City, much less at the Public in a hot ticket, and it was terrifying, like attempting to walk on water! In regional theater you think, "Oh, it's all those really nice people in the audience who live in Denver suburbs who don't have a choice of all the theaters in the world, the way New York theatergoers do." No, in New York you say to yourself, "These people are the cognoscenti. They see theater on Broadway, off-Broadway, experimental theater off-off-Broadway, at the Brooklyn Academy of Music, and down at the Public. They go to Europe. They probably go to England every other week. The Berliner Ensemble? Nothing new to them! I'm not good enough yet. I'll just go back to Denver."

But I did it. The night we opened, I got a big bouquet of flowers from Joe and a card saying, "You finally got out from behind the chair. There's no place you can't go now." What got me out was the challenge. I said to myself, "I will not be a chicken." I remember in Wynn Handman's acting class, Dennis Quaid and I were doing a piece from *Cowboy Mouth*. After we did it the first time, Wynn said, "You look like a couple of has-been hippies talking some overchewed conversation. If this is the best you can do, don't bring it back." I walked through the park after the scene, the tears of anger and humiliation coming down my cheeks, saying, "I'm going to do that scene and take his breath away." And I did. I remember going out on that stage like someone had shot me out of a cannon with an energy and a will that went beyond technique or anything I ever knew before.

Each time I was challenged, I went down to the bottom of my heart, and then I reached deeper, into the subbasement, and pulled out some kind of courage. Some part of me refused to be defeated. This is where technique is born. There's a great line in a Roethke poem: "I wake to sleep and take my waking slow. I learn by going where I have to go." When I stepped out from behind the chair, I saw that I had to open out, and in that moment I realized that the audience wouldn't kill me. An owl didn't swoop down on me. In fact, when I stepped out from behind the chair, I began to realize that the audience is to the actor what the sun is to a flower. That's where the energy is coming from which enables you to continue living onstage. When you commit that line to a full-throated delivery, some meaning comes into it; emotion and life inhabit it immediately. You learn by going where you have to go. Not only is technique born there, but knowledge, comfort, and insight as well. Then you have a key moment when you realize, "Ah. *That's* how it's done."

A few years later, while I was working on *Big* for Penny Marshall, I was brought in by Howard Feuer to meet Jonathan Demme for *Married to the Mob*. And I just thought, "God, this role is so strident and unattractive, I don't really know if I want to do it. Well, I'm just going to do it with so much humanity that he's probably going to say, `You're not strident or hard enough for this role, but you've got something going for you and I'm going to remember you for my next film.' " I released myself from wanting the film, but I didn't release myself from needing to impress him. I went in and did something really grounded and emotional, different from the obvious attack on the role. Afterward, Jonathan said, "That was wonderful. Read another scene." I read the next one totally inappropriately, with great vulnerability. He said, "That's terrific." And I thought, "Does he mean that's terrific or that's terrific for the role? Because I don't think it's right for the role at all." Then we talked for a while, shook hands, and I left.

The next day, he called me and asked if I wanted the role. And I thought, "No. No. I really don't want to do this strident person." But I said, "Yes! Yes! I want this role! Are you kidding? Do I want this role?" I verbalized some of my fears; I didn't want to become a cartoon or a clown among actresses; I didn't want to just be a comedienne; I didn't even want to become a good Eve Arden type. I wanted to be an actress who portrayed full, rounded women, women who expressed the heroine aspect of a woman's journey. He said, "Listen, we're not going to make you a cartoon in this. We're not."

I was full of terror, anticipation, joy, and fear. During the next three weeks I proceeded, on a totally unconscious level, to do everything I could to lose the job. I went away to visit my best friend in Tucson for a couple of weeks. Now, in all fairness to me, no one told me that you have to stay around for three or four weeks before shooting to be available for makeup and hair tests. I didn't know anything about that. While I was in Tucson, I went to my friend's hairdresser and—this was the era of big hair—I got this huge perm. I looked like a hairdo walking a woman. Then I agreed to do a reading of a new play at the Public Theater. Just for two days, but somehow Jonathan got the idea that I had agreed to do an entire play at the same time that I was doing the film. Finally, I rented a house in the country with a couple of girlfriends, and one day, I just merrily rolled down an embankment because I was showing off and being very young and full of myself. And I got, from my feet up to my neck, a case of poison ivy. Not just little red dots. Big! All over!

Oh, yes! There was one other thing. They had a reading of the script for the backers. Michelle Pfeiffer is there, Matthew Modine and Dean Stockwell, all the producers, the casting people, the people from Columbia, the people from TriStar, the president of the United States and the entire U.N. Security Council, and I get in the worst of all possible traffic jams. To this day I say I was twenty minutes late, but Jonathan says I was forty minutes late. I have a hunch he's righter than I. So I arrive late and everybody gives me these really tensely polite stares.

After this, Jonathan calls me and says, "Mercedes, do you really want to do this role?" And by this time, my agent has called me and has said, "Listen, my dear, they are putting out calls for replacements for you, just on the off chance . . . If you really want to do it, stop sabotaging yourself." So, I said, "I'm having a little traffic jam with my subconscious here, but it's going to be worked out by day one of shooting, I absolutely promise you. Don't lose faith in me." He said all right, but he didn't sound at all convinced.

The first day of shooting, I was there on time. I got into hair and makeup immediately. I got into my costume, which entirely covered my poison ivy because there were

MERCEDES RUEHL

big shoulder pads that made me look like a linebacker and tights and crazy, high-heeled boots and chandeliers for earrings and seventeen bracelets. I go back to sit in my camper. It's ten o'clock in the morning and I'm Totally Ready, Freddy.

Five o'clock in the afternoon, they finally call me to set. I'm nervous but I'm still ready. I've sat for seven hours in such a way that nothing gets creased or smeared. In this first scene I had to drive in a convertible and come to a screeching stop. At that time, I didn't know how to drive. If anything would make me more nervous, it would be doing that. The set was out in a mall in Long Island in a kind of tacky beauty parlor. In the back of this beauty parlor, there's this little makeshift bathroom. The cameraman is setting up the lights, so I went into the bathroom, locked the door behind me, careful not to scrunch anything. I go to the bathroom, put myself together, I say, "You look fabulous!" I go to the door—and the knob doesn't work. I am locked in. There is so much noise out there, nobody can hear my cries. I looked in the mirror and said to myself, "This is it. You're an unemployed actress." And I thought, "Some of this is not my fault. This is just the gods having their way with me." Finally, some guy was able to pick the lock before Jonathan got wind of the fact that I was locked in the bathroom. And that was my first experience with a major, major role in a film. After that, I was never that frightened again. I wound up having such a marvelous time working with Jonathan. I looked forward to every day of shooting. But facing that experience was another terror, absolute terror. . . . This is all about embracing terror. Again and again and again.

Theater and film have profoundly spiritual roots no matter what the big cigar-smoking studio heads or their marketing teams think, no matter who's driving the better car to the better party. Theater came out of man's need to relate to the unseeable, the unknowable. On some level it has to relate to what is timeless and eternal that blows the breath of life into everything in the world. I see the spiritual quest as the warp and woof of this business. It totally astounds me that the largest faction of this business would laugh to hear me say it's a profoundly spiritual vocation. But I think it is. Actors are the modern-day priests who stood out on those temple steps. They have incredible power over the ideas, the emotions, the style, the aspirations, of young people. Actors have become the anima of this nation. So there is a profound moral responsibility in being an actor. I try to do material that has some kind of moral worth or truth. Then, my responsibility is always to go for the deeper truth, to look behind the cliché. Sometimes you have to use the cliché to get through it, to look behind the stereotype and explicate it, and the truth will set you free.

I've been looking at Tennessee Williams's *Rose Tattoo*. Serafina is a role that looks like a lot of fun. It's very emotional; this Italian woman who's living in the early fifties down near New Orleans in this little Italian enclave. She's big, she's sexual, and she's emotional. "Oh, what fun," I think, "I'm going to be able to chew up the scenery!" But then I think, "I have to explore, in the most painstaking and specific way, the facts of life that have brought this woman to this bank and shoal of time at the play's opening." One of the great challenges in doing Serafina is that she is a real sensualist, but she's also Roman Catholic. Moral issues always battling with her deep, almost oceanic, sensual nature. I am very cerebral and will go to a cerebral place whenever I feel a little bit scared.

But Serafina is not cerebral. I'm going to have to open up. I'm going to have to take some risks. I'm going to have to divest myself and be seen in a way that I've never allowed myself to be seen before. I have to be extremely respectful of her and of Tennessee Williams, who created her. And, I have to make sure that my ego's need to be stroked and recognized is held nicely under control so that it's only allowed to support the reality of what Tennessee Williams wrote, not to support the reality of Mercedes Ruehl's need for recognition. If you think the text and character are good enough to do, then you have to make a humble submission to the material.

At the same time, you have to have the arrogance to stand up for the truth as it manifests itself through you in the role. You can not let anybody talk you out of your interpretation of the way this character would behave at this moment if you believe that it is the best way to serve the playwright's creation. Very often inexperienced directors will have a concept to which they will try to make you conform. It's almost like a parent trying to make a child conform to her idea of how the child should mature and grow into a responsible adult. Meanwhile the child is feeling, "But there's this reality about me! I have to find a different way to integrate because I have all these wild characteristics that can't fit into your a priori vision." The child doesn't often express that, but an actor does have to learn to fight for the truth that she's discovered within herself when married to this character.

I would like to explore playing a much subtler character, a less theatrical character. A certain kind of theatricality has, so far, been a quality of mine. People don't think of me that often for the smaller, more delicate characterizations. Some of the biggest personal successes I've had, say in workshops, have been in working on characters like Laura in *The Glass Menagerie*. It's not that I find theatricality a negative. But the joy for an actor is to be able to do all kinds of roles. An actor can be said to have a certain kind of style, but what's much more fun if you're an interpretive artist is to become a seamless spokesperson for the style of whatever piece you're in.

One of the stories that I love best came from a book about Zen meditation. When you're learning Zen meditation from a master, you sit for a long time and you are focusing on the inhalation and the exhalation of your breath and a koan. Of course, you're trying to achieve satori. As you approach satori, something happens where the kundalini energy, or whatever it is, makes your whole body vibrate. The Zen master has this long rod, and when he sees somebody on the brink of enlightenment, he'll take that long stick and rap them on the shoulder or on the cheek. Sometimes that smack, that thwack on the back of the newborn infant who isn't breathing yet, that audition where you cry because they're not going to hire you after you made them applaud for you, that slap is what breaks you through into some kind of epiphany. I've always loved that idea of the Zen Tap, and I think I have experienced it a few times in my life. That's what makes you take more oxygen into your lungs than you ever have before. That's what makes your heart aspire to a leap that it's never made before. That's what makes you so suddenly single-focused on an objective that you finally reach it. That's the Zen Tap.

JOHN TURTURRO

John Turturro and I were sitting in a kitchen in New York City talking about acting. I was struck by New York's influence on his performances. This is a dramatic place where the natives see themselves theatrically. We are the heroes of our lives with an intensified sense of living in one of the largest functioning communities in the world; the Melting Pot of America (where nothing ever melts). That double sense of community and individuality are integral to John Turturro's goals as an actor. "What would make him more human?" is the question that drives his acting. The theatricality of his performances comes naturally to him. As he says, "It never scares me to be grotesque because people express themselves in the most absurd ways!" Surrounded by 12 million people, he's had ample opportunity to observe human behavior in all its manifestations.

There are other, strong roots to John Turturro's bold performances. Experiencing tremendous love from his family has left him with little need to experience it as an actor, freeing his performances of currying favor from the audience. Keeping the thread of his life connected to a sense of reality supports him as an individual, enabling him to take risks as an actor. He makes a strong case in his interview for "developing your point of view," and ultimately working like yourself.

He is clear minded about his procedure. He says things like, "The objective is the objective; it doesn't change. My choices lie in the way

in which I try and get that thing." He nails the objective with preci-
sion and experiments freely with actions—and their success or dete-
rioration in pursuing that objective. In a description of a scene
between Gabriel Byrne and himself in Miller's Crossing, *Turturro*
dynamically illustrates the way an actor activates those terms.

John Turturro is constantly inventing ways to make himself
go beyond his conscious understanding and control of a moment
and to "give something of myself away." This quality, inspiration
on demand, is unique to a very few great actors. As he says, "When
you see it, you know it's there."

"OKAY, BUT WHAT WOULD MAKE IT REALLY HUMAN?"

Someone who's a Jewish kid from suburbia can't be Laurence Olivier, but he can be a great actor. You have to find out what's special about you as a person, and you always have to be developing your point of view. As a young actor I certainly walked through stages of influence; Pacino, De Niro, Dustin Hoffman, and my work had an imitative quality. I'd see De Niro do something really subtle and I would try it in rehearsal. Then I actually came to discover who I am and what I could bring to my work that was special. I've always been struck by people who have empathy, kindness, or understanding and show it in their own way, not the way we've been programmed to see it. I am looking for the thing that makes this character most human. I can embrace any and all facets of life and explore the rich ground of complexity, good and bad, positive and not.

When I was a kid, I was inspired by Charles Laughton and Alan Arkin. I remember being thrilled watching Alan Arkin in *The Defection of Simas Kudirka* with my brother, Nicholas. We didn't know what he was going to do next. We were getting these weird body rushes. We remember those thrills. Laughton was an ugly man, a very neurotic man. But when he was on, he gave you something totally uninhibited. He'd play Quasimodo covered with makeup which took him six months to design, but there's something truly naked about his performance. He's not covered at all. These are actors who superseded who they are. They gave a part of themselves away. That's an innate quality; it's how you look at life. When an actor does that, his performance takes on a life of its own. You can see that quality in the other arts; you can find it in mothers who give away part of themselves to their child. When you've seen it, you know it's there. I aspired to that for myself. You can get beat up by the critics and the audience for that kind of acting. They say, "That person grates on my nerves," or, "He went too far." But I have to push that kind of thinking out of the way because it can inhibit me.

I don't know if you can ultimately hide what you are. I don't think so, because then you'll start indicating that "I'm kind" instead of just being kind. A lot of times I see an actor working himself into a vulnerable state, but he doesn't move me at all because he doesn't embrace life. He's a tremendously selfish person playing this tremendously vulnerable, caring person. I try to embrace the whole picture, whatever it is. I'm not afraid to be grating. That's an inherent choice which lies within my psychology. If I feel a character's human, that's what I attempt to convey. There are actors who people love, who are driven by the need to be loved, so they'll do anything to get your sympathy. They need to be in control. I feel pretty accepted as a person, so I don't have that need as an actor. It never scares me to be grotesque as an actor because people express themselves in the most absurd ways!

There are parts when you have to make a big jump, but even if I know there's a big jump to be made, I begin as myself. If I jump too soon, then a lot of times I get stuck in a rut that's result oriented. However, sometimes you've tried to do it grounded and it's dead, and you have to put yourself further into the role. You say, "Okay, let me take a jump," and you do the form and then try to piece it together. When I first started getting ready to do *Barton Fink*, there were a few elements I could relate to, but for the most part I was at a total loss for an approach. I had written some, but I had never learned to type. So I had a task: learning to type. Then I thought, "Let me read about what would have influenced someone in the 1930s, instead of just reading about the 1930s." If you're twenty-five in 1932, you grew up from 1905 and that's a whole different period. I got tapes from the Group Theatre, but I knew a lot about them to begin with. I found this book, *Jews Without Money*, by Michael Gold. It was fantastic because it's all about the turn of the century and it talked about the roots of liberal and the left-wing communist and socialist thinking. You don't really read much about that. That helped. I read about Odets, because I knew there were elements that the Coens had taken from his life. I could use his self-importance and his tirades. I used the way he talked about his work, all his passionate thoughts and outbursts. Some were based on a reality and some were based on a need to get away from his father. But his sexuality was of no use at all because he was totally promiscuous and we were going to create Barton Fink as a virgin. I also drew on some of the writers that I work with; one is collaborator on *Mac*. I like to combine elements from different people.

I needed people to guide me through *Barton Fink*, and I was lucky to be working with Joel and Ethan Coen. I went out to California a month early. We rehearsed together without any actors and explored the core of the character. Barton Fink's dilemma is that he's a full person who is trapped in his own head, and though he has feelings, he is cut off from them. I tried different physical things. "What do you think if he was sort of in a shell, like a turtle?" So I put his center in his forehead. They liked that and I used it. As the forehead goes, so goes the spine and the shoulders. Unfortunately, I wound up throwing my back out really badly, and it took me a while to recover.

In the course of that time together I suggested a couple of structural changes. I said, "You got to keep it ambiguous whether his parents were killed or not if he's still going to try and sell a script in the end. If he knows his parents are dead, he'd go back East." They went for that. But mostly what the three of us did together was hang out, read the screenplay, and rehearse. Once I started to do it, Joel told me he liked that I made him much more human so that he was that much more horrible. He was horribly human and he found it funnier.

I sort of diagnosed Barton Fink as a young person who is only the germ of the person he thinks he is. He takes all these stances. "This is who I am." Then life says, "Let's see if this is who you really are," and beats the shit out of him. By the end of the movie, he actually asks a question. This is my own interpretation, but I always thought when he asks the girl on the beach, "Are you in the movies?" he's ready to listen for the first time in his life. He's just at the beginning. Maybe his parents are dead and he's an orphan. But he's at the beginning of adulthood. I also thought that carrying around the woman's head was like carrying his own head, because he lived in his head.

Because I played so many scenes by myself in *Barton Fink*, I absolutely needed Joel and Ethan to bounce off of. We would try everything one way, and then we'd experiment, trying it another way. They were excited because I was coming up with stuff that they hadn't imagined. Because they worked very hard, I figured it was my job to truly understand what they wanted and to give them choices within their structure that they never even thought of. Like the love scene with Judy Davis. The original script called for me to kiss her. I said, "No, that's not who I am." First of all, I personally hate love scenes. I haven't done a lot of them, but I don't like them because they're not dramatic scenes anymore. They're just sort of like pornography. When you watch pornography, at least you know it's pornography. Love scenes in old films were somewhat effective because they were still scenes that represented or resolved a conflict between two people. Second of all, if Barton Fink's a virgin, she should be the initiator. He would want to initiate it but wouldn't have the means. I said, "I think the best thing by far, the most intimate thing, would be if she took my glasses off. Then I'd be totally naked." I almost look like a raccoon, or some kind of scared little animal, in the shot.

Another example is the scene in which I have to tell Lipnick, the studio head, the story of my screenplay. Actually, that was one of the hardest scenes I had in the whole film. I try and make up this whole story, but I don't know what I'm talking about. I'm talking and my brain had to be somewhere else totally, just like people do in life. There's a moment in which I space out completely. It's not the moment you would remember in that scene, but it was one of the things I liked most about my performance. The way I developed it was by getting the speech down cold, up and back, this way and that way. Then, when we shot the scene, I thought about something completely different so I had no control over what I said. In fact, I did not know what I was saying. This was one of the first scenes we shot, so I had to focus on personal things rather than something from Barton's memory. It was hard to sustain that. I'd have to go and stand on my head or do physical things or stick my finger down my throat because re-created stuff dries up after hours, and we worked twelve or fourteen hours on that one scene. When Joel saw what I was doing in the scene, he said, "That's great. Why don't you go even further?" I did, but I have no idea what I did. When I see the film, I don't know what I'm doing there, and for me that's the best feeling. I can see the idea and I can see that I filled it, but I'm just swimming around.

Joel and Ethan were getting more ideas even toward the end of shooting. For instance, Joel said, "How about if Lipnick actually makes you doubt your work?" That new idea changed everything. I thought, "I tried to make something beautiful . . . but . . . maybe . . . it's not." Just that little adjustment of self-doubt made the whole thing complete and more human for me. It made the character's journey fuller and longer. That film was a case where I really needed input from other people, whereas when I went into *Jungle Fever* after that, I knew what I wanted to do.

There's more of me as a young person in the character in *Jungle Fever* than in any other movie I've done. That's because I wrote a lot of it. Spike and I worked on the script from the beginning. We talked about experiences and feelings I had when I was a young kid, thirteen, fourteen, fifteen. So many of the feelings I wanted for that character came from my junior high school experience that I didn't have to do any research. He's someone who likes to read and who's trying to escape. I always wanted to escape from the moment we moved to Rosedale. Those are primary things. I took those feelings and put them into a man who was thirty but who's stayed emotionally at fourteen. I saw him as a man who was kept in. I wasn't really kept in, but I drew on different elements, and some of them are the ones I felt during adolescence. I didn't want to explore someone that was a generally nice guy. It didn't interest me. I wanted him to be richer. Spike wrote some and then I would rewrite. Spike approached Anthony Quinn to play my father, but he wouldn't do it. The scenes weren't working yet. Then I rewrote all those scenes because Spike was shooting. My mother and father had told me about the old-timers who instilled a tremendous amount of fear in their children. I knew a story about a teenager who was gambling and was so afraid that his father would find out that he had a heart attack and died. I wanted those feelings to be in the relationship. Spike approved my rewrites, and when Anthony Quinn read them, he said he'd do the film.

I'd conceived that character straight through: the costume, the haircut, the walk, my lines, everything. There was this basketball player, Kenny Walker, who used to play for the Knicks. He's black but we look a little bit alike. He's a very open person, the way he walks.

And his haircut. I told Spike that I was going to base my character on him physically. I knew something related. So you piece it together. The character ended up having a walk which was sort of like a bounce, half home-boy walk. The haircut was like a poodle, the sweater was soft, and the pants were baggy. He was just open. I wanted to structure it so that my character was both a son and a replacement wife to his father. He was a feminine character. I had a lot of those feelings before I could articulate them into acting. Being an outsider, being vulnerable, gawky, and not having a quick, clever response. I wasn't brutal enough. I grew up in a black neighborhood, and then we moved into a white neighborhood where I was treated like I was black. I went to a junior high school that was all black, except 10 percent Jewish, and I was totally lost. The central part of *Jungle Fever* had to do with interracial relationships and growing up. I knew relationships that could have been good, but because the kids were black and white or Puerto Rican, they couldn't be together. They wound up with someone who was their own kind but who was the worst person for them. I wanted to make sure my character was someone who was trying to look at racism a little bit differently.

I did enjoy doing that role.

You have to always be developing your point of view. You don't start out performing and say, "This is my end result," before you know the basic requirements. It takes a long time for a writer to write a play or a screenplay. An actor can't read it and suddenly embody it. Some people have the skill to go fast, but I always think it's good to take my time. Begin in the simplest way; between the two actors. I read the material a lot and see what connects to my own experiences, or experiences I've seen people go through. Then, I try and make it as personal as it can be. I see what doesn't correspond. Are there things I have to break down? *[Breaking something down is a process by which an actor takes anything, an object, a name, etc., and finds many ways he relates to it personally. This sometimes lengthy exploration yields a complex series of images the actor can use for explicating the character's journey.]*

As an actor I think I've always been good at pursuing objectives, because I'm good in life that way. It happens to be something I'm interested in. What's this guy's journey and what is the story's journey that my character supports? Does my character help someone else on their journey? I may not have much of a journey, but I find my little story. In telling that story, the objective is the objective; it doesn't change. My choices lie in the ways in which I try to get that thing. If I remember correctly, my objective in my first scene in another Coen brothers' film, *Miller's Crossing,* is to try and cut a deal. In order to do that I can be logical. Or I could make him laugh. I could try to make him understand my dilemma. I could try to bully him. If I'm trying to get what I want by being logical and it's not working, then I'll stop and shift and maybe make him laugh. If he has a problem with that, maybe I'll be a little charming. There are actors who pursue their objective by playing one action and that's it. Their work doesn't surprise me because it's too control oriented. I'd rather give something of myself away. Once the scene's dynamic is starting to occur, I'll go with it and then try to shift it, too, just like you would in life. The shifting is important. Then, if I can get to the point when that's happening and I don't know what I'm doing, that's inspiration. I've done all my work and then I try to achieve this other, living dimension, the human dimension. It ceases being my work and it becomes living.

In that same scene in *Miller's Crossing,* where I'm trying to cut the deal, I've just come back from the woods where I've been humiliated into begging for my life. In the scene I say to the protagonist, Gabriel Byrne's character, "Don't smart me!" We tried it many different ways, and then I said, "Okay, it's good, but it's not good enough. I'm not getting at the heart of the humiliation I come into the scene with. What would make it really human?" So I did the whole scene as someone who's been so humiliated that now he's going to get revenge for it. *I'm* going to be controller in that situation; I *need* that control. The added dimension which made my character, Bernie, human is that he thinks he's going to make someone else squirm. Unfortunately for me, Gabriel Byrne does not give him that satisfaction. After Bernie's total humiliation in the woods, his failure to control him is devastating. That's the take that was used, and I have to say that Joel and Ethan always use the best take, which is so great.

In the scene in which I had to beg for my life, I worked for that human dimension, telling myself, "This is as far as I can go," and then asking, "Is it? Is it?" The reality of the conditions we were working under is that we're in Louisiana, it's thirteen degrees out, and I walk backwards for most of the scene with a Steadicam and a gun trained on me. When I was a kid, a policeman put a gun to my head once by accident in a schoolyard, so I knew a little something of what it would feel like. Because I'm walking backwards, I kept tripping, falling down, falling into ditches. But I wasn't going to control myself. I said to Joel and Ethan, "Give me thirty seconds. I'll tell you when I'm ready." I needed those thirty seconds to say to myself, "This is the situation you're in," and I softened myself up to be vulnerable to that situation. That's all you can do. Then, the camera's on and you actually deal with it within that character, by being with the character.

I have always liked to work physically. When I find something physical, like a character's center, it is freeing. And I think the camera loves those kind of choices. In *Miller's Crossing* I did this thing with my shoulders like I was always waiting to be hit. To me Bernie was a hustler, a kid who grew up on the street and does everything possible to survive. I connected all his immorality to that need. I put together a picture of street kids I knew. Some kids were Jewish or Puerto Rican and they were already living by their wits. That develops a whole different being. Bernie would sleep with anybody, do whatever he had to do to live, or to live as well as he possibly could.

Actually, Bernie's body was not the first thing I developed because he operated more out of his mind, his wits. I had a lot of fun with him because Bernie is one of the few characters I've played where I could really spring my intelligence. He is quick, smart, and constantly dazzling people. He is talked about by almost everyone in the whole movie, so I knew that he had to have a presence when he finally came on. I based a lot of him on my accountant, who is actually sort of a timid guy and a very sweet man, and nothing like Bernie. But there was something I really liked about his accent, and then I found out he spoke Yiddish, which affected his English. I also loved his laugh. I tried it with Joel and Ethan and they liked it. There was something in it, big as it was, that showed he was a little afraid. My idea of Bernie was that the guy could get by and get by, but in the end he goes dry. In the last scene, I wanted him to be like a hollow actor who's trying to be emotional but can't get it up. I've had that happen to me many times onstage. When it's not there, what do you do?

My main objective as an actor is to keep people awake. I do everything possible to make them care, which they cannot do if they're sleeping. If I have a chance to make interesting choices, then as long as I'm not grandstanding, I'm willing to go that route. Who knows? I've seen people go beyond anything I would have expected of them. Life can accomplish anything, any size, any dimension—it's all human.

BLUE MAN GROUP

MATT GOLDMAN

PHILLIP B. STANTON

CHRIS WINK

Why is the Blue Man Group's interview presented as a dialogue without specific names? The answer is that it was a felicitous accident. When it came time to transcribe the interview, I could no longer tell who said what. As I culled the hours of tape, I realized that it didn't matter anyway because the fundamental creativity of this group resides in their response to each other. Their individual identities merge into a perpetually working collective. The Blue Man Group is a whirl of activity, coffee cups, ideas, and interruptions. They move circularly and rapidly in random directions, but they move together.

In the tradition of artists of the nineteenth and early twentieth century, Blue Man Group holds salons. Dissatisfied with the intense career absorption of the 1980s and its exclusionary intellectual nature, they met to discuss ideas. While they didn't necessarily fully understand these ideas, they allowed them to spark their creativity and imagination. Undaunted by what they failed to understand, they made art. This inclusionary attitude goes beyond ideas and material; a significant part of their agenda is the creation of a live theater ritual in which the audience plays an integral part in the tribal community.

A Blue Man says in the interview, "You have to have your bliss coming from the process of making the work, not from its results." While it is easier to say that when you have a hit off-Broadway show, the Blue Man Group lives that reality. They are constantly reconsidering their performance process, analyzing every show for new possibilities. "Within each piece and between two pieces there are an infinite number of moments that can be worked on, discussed, and crafted." And while they spend a tremendous amount of time refining and re-imagining, they spend even more time fostering the process of their creative relationship. In fact, they used this interview to do just that.

"WHAT WE'VE CREATED AS ARTISTS IS A RELATIONSHIP, AND THAT RELATIONSHIP IS WHAT CREATES THE WORK."

JS

Is there work that you're doing that is exo–Blue Man?

BLUE MAN 1

Well, no, all of it's Blue Man, really. I mean, it's just exo-*Tubes,* this show, but Blue Man . . .

JS

But the group . . . ?

BLUE MAN 1

Is Blue Man.

BLUE MAN 2

Even if we wrote something that didn't use bald, blue characters, we still are the Blue Man Group. We haven't finished exploring all the different areas that Blue Man can go.

BLUE MAN 3

What is your book going to be called, do you think?

JS

Damned if I know. My family is on my case to come up with a title that has commercial appeal. My sister-in-law suggested *Method to the Madness*. Not only is it incorrectly quoted, but I don't want to suggest that everyone has a process related to the Method. And I'm not exploring the link between creativity and madness, though I think a relationship exists.

BLUE MAN 2

I like that title.

BLUE MAN 3

I like *Damned If I Know* better.

JS

Damned if I know?

BLUE MAN 3

Yeah. *Damned If I Know: A Book About the Creative Process.*

BLUE MAN 2

How many artists' careers have you ruined now that they're going, "Wait a minute. I've never thought about how I do it. What's my process?"

JS

None. But perhaps some therapy sessions have been devoted to it.

BLUE MAN 2

We were attracted to your project because we talk about process all the time. In fact, Blue Man Group began as a discussion. It's a collaboration by definition, as opposed to a play where there's a clear division of labor: someone writes a script, you get together a director and a bunch of actors, designers. I know that is a collaboration as well, but sometimes it stays really clean. My old girlfriend has a theater group, and it's fascinating for me to see them try to come up with a show in a really short amount of time. They each go in with a specialized attitude of what they do: "I'm the one who does the writing." What they do is still interesting, but they are working within a tradition which assumes that each person brings something specific to the table and that makes it all work.

What we did was start talking about things, with no rules.

BLUE MAN 3

It's hard to know where to start because there is a huge sea of stuff. One of the things that we understood at our starting point is that not only this project, *Tubes,* but all of Blue Man stems from our relationship, and that the relationship is something that needs to be constantly maintained. Our ability to communicate is at the center of our process.

What we've created as artists is a relationship, and that relationship is what creates the work. So, job one is to work on the process, not just start on the work. We start with ourselves, with staying excited about our collaboration, and we don't take that for granted. Then, we get excited and play, and the work starts to happen. But it's not so goal oriented. All right, sometimes it is when we're going to go make a big show, but sometimes it's just . . .

When we started *Tubes,* we didn't have a goal. We

just wanted to have a satisfying moment-by-moment experience that we believed in. We were drawn together in the first place by a certain series of beliefs. We've talked a lot about what we like about others' work, what we think is important about it or what we hate about it. That's important because it's established a corporate culture, a spirit, and a million sets of things that eventually became tacit. We keep developing a fabric of similarity and commonality that we can always call on.

MTV wanted us to be on a new comedy/performance show called *Kamikaze*. So we went to watch it. We're sitting there watching it, and at the end of the meeting we didn't even have to talk to each other to arrive at a decision. I mean, we talked only because it was fun to talk. But we walked out knowing what we each thought based on our shared experience.

BLUE MAN 2

And we all said to the guy, "Well, that's interesting. We'll think about it." But we knew we wouldn't get involved. The problem was they had no vision. It was producer-driven work.

BLUE MAN 3

It wasn't even that. It was ratings driven: "Our stand-up comedy half hour used to be one of the highest-rated shows, now the ratings have dropped. So we're going to mix it up a little and make it faster and zanier and bring the ratings back up."

BLUE MAN 2

It was completely market driven, uncentered, and so it was a completely schizophrenic show. They'd play this really cool thing—then it would stop and all of a sudden there would be a stand-up comedian.

BLUE MAN 3

What really cool things?

BLUE MAN 2

Not really cool things.

BLUE MAN 1

Just one, Matthew Courtney, an impromptu poet, and he's really good. And they did a good job editing what he did.

BLUE MAN 2

They wanted to end the live experience of performance, poetry, and comedy like they've done to rock music.

BLUE MAN 1

One reason why we came up with our work is that when we would go to see performance art, like in the eighties, it was usually party-line politics or preaching to the converted. We were much more interested in presenting things with a nonjudgmental attitude.

BLUE MAN 3

We don't have life figured out and we feel liberated by exploring different models. The Joseph Campbell idea of mythic properties and of telling a story as a heroic journey, or the idea of following your bliss or of reinventing oneself, has been good to explore. We find some inspiration there. The fractal geometry stuff in *Tubes* is so good for us because there's so much complexity, no black and white. *[The roots of fractal geometry began in the nineteenth century as a challenge to Euclidean principles. The mathematician Mandelbrot developed a theory of fractals that was widely published in the mid-1970s. The Man-delbrot set, explicated by mathematicians Hubbard and Douady, is distinct because "the more the set is magni-fied, the more its unpredictability increases, until unpre-dictability comes to dominate the budlike shape that is the set's major element of stability." (Grollier)]* We like that model. That's how we feel. My parents taught at Co-lumbia and I grew up on the campus. As an eight-year-old they had me marching on Washington and seeing the hip-pie thing. Then we saw the punk thing and the eighties yuppie thing. Our lives seem like a series of contradic-tions and pendulum swings and complexity and fragmen-tation in a huge cultural kaleidoscope. And it feels that way just in our short lifetime! Fractal geometry offers so many different ways to look at things and no single an-swer. When we first read about it and saw it, we didn't even understand the mathematics of it. We didn't care.

BLUE MAN 2

The first thing Blue Man did was getting a bunch of peo-ple together in little rooms for a salon. That's where we read about fractals. Blue Man was born out of show-and-tell. We'd say, "Here's a cool idea," and we'd kick it around. We accidentally started a "follow your bliss" type of scenario. We accidentally kick-started a life that wasn't just mental but became visceral because we weren't just talking about career-oriented things. And there was no goal, you see? That excitement, "Oh, fractal science is really interesting," created a place from which you could talk about anything even though you weren't "qualified."

People are so often directed at their goals that they don't give themselves time to just pick up a book outside of their field—like the Gleick book on chaos theory. They think, "It would be nice, but . . ." They don't have a context for free learning. Their heads get shut and they specialize; they focus on their careers.

BLUE MAN 1

You've got to read about the industry. You've got to learn all the names of all the important agents.

BLUE MAN 2

You gotta network.

BLUE MAN 3

Techniques and sources.

BLUE MAN 1

Strategies for weaving in and out of the system. And finally, you look around and you say, "I wasn't involved in planning this system. I wasn't one of the founding fathers. I don't even remember agreeing that I thought it was a good system."

BLUE MAN 2

In the goal-oriented eighties you weren't hanging out and going to happenings. You were pursuing your thing. Artists were just as much into that as the Wall Streeters. And so, it was really nice to have a respite from all that by having an afternoon discussion.

BLUE MAN 3

We're having a salon this Sunday night. It was really important to us that if we were trying to have an off-Broadway show, we wouldn't have to stop looking at chaos theory.

BLUE MAN 2

It represents a chance to get away from the logical things you think you need to get ahead or to achieve a goal. We also go to see all kinds of different things; some just because they seem cool. We sew in all this stuff we get interested in. Like, we got fed up with all the hype around virtual reality because it seemed to be just another excuse to be alone. We intend virtual reality to seem pathetic as it is portrayed in *Tubes*. There are probably some great applications for virtual reality, but we wanted to throw a little bit of cynicism at it without getting preachy.

BLUE MAN 3

Can you imagine what virtual reality can do for quadriplegics?

BLUE MAN 2

Of course. It's just the hype that was annoying.

So does any of this seem interesting to you? Then do you care that your tape recorder hasn't been on all this time?

JS

Oh my God!

BLUE MAN 3

One of the things we talk a lot about is the spirit of the show.

BLUE MAN 1

Even before we opened we were concerned that the spirit of the Blue Man be bigger than the props and the costumes and the technology and the blue. Not that we're really doing a narrative, but we wanted the feeling that there was something underneath all of it which was the equivalent of a good story. Something inside of us that wanted to come out. By the end there is a sense of communication or a tacit relationship or love between us and the audience.

BLUE MAN 2

When we put the pieces together, we talked about the overarching action of each of them. We wrote the music to create an emotional throughline. "Tension Song," which recurs a couple of times, keeps up the tension while we do these very mundane things, like catching stuff in our mouths. We could have had comedy music, like Spike Jones music the whole time, but we wanted this show to have mysterious music; minor keys but still very melodic. We worked really hard on it. The "Tension Song" is *ching ching ching ching,* and the beat keeps propelling us forward so that people are wondering what's going to happen next. Out of the feeling of the music we develop mental constructs for ourselves, images. A bit has ended and another bit's going to begin, and there's really nothing going on for a few seconds, but we still have to be connected to the show's purpose, which is to give this audience an experience of and a belief in the communal experience. It's a nice, humbling thing to know that in live performance, a strong performance is not guaranteed. But on a strong night there's a real connection between us and to our commitment to our superordinate goal, which is the exalted moment, and that this work is a possible vehicle for achieving that.

BLUE MAN 3

That's a term we use a lot, and it's a real good term. I think it came from a passage where someone is talking about people wasting sex by keeping loneliness at bay rather than collaborating to achieve the exalted moment. Early on we knew we had to have an exalted moment—

you know, a moment of vital force. Jean Gianno, the poet, calls the exalted moment "uninterrupted fire," *feu continu,* or something in French. It's that thing that you see in a Pollock painting or—

BLUE MAN 1
But also something that happens with a lot of people together.

BLUE MAN 2
It doesn't happen when you're watching TV. Or maybe it does. We don't know. But it's great to make people laugh. It's great to do something weird.

BLUE MAN 1
What we were interested in is making it obvious to a live audience that something can happen with a lot of people together that can't happen when you're alone watching your VCR or . . .

BLUE MAN 3
It's a tribal thing. There's something about the live experience that's unique and special that will never go away no matter what technology comes along. People are still going to need to congregate. That's who we are. The council meeting, the tribal gathering around the fire, this is a ritual that's being reinvented. When there is a lack of it, it manifests as the loneliness of living in the city.

BLUE MAN 1
The experience is visceral.

BLUE MAN 2
Definitely visceral.

BLUE MAN 3
Endocrinal.

BLUE MAN 2

It's like it's triple overtime. They've been playing for two hours and fifty minutes and a soccer player scores a goal. He's run the equivalent of twenty miles at that point, and he's dead tired. But he sprints down the field with his hands up, kicking his legs higher. It's something that transcends any kind of physicality, any kind of control.

BLUE MAN 3

Do you find other people talking about that feeling when they're performing? When you study Meisner technique, which we did, you hear about getting out of your head and losing yourself by really paying attention to the other person.

BLUE MAN 2

You want some sugar for your coffee?

JS

I've got it right here.

BLUE MAN 2

One's enough? Or would you like six?

JS

No, six is a little too much. I'm not a Blue Man.

BLUE MAN 2

We actually eat very healthfully.

BLUE MAN 1

I didn't get a coffee, did I?

BLUE MAN 2

No, would you like a cappuccino?

BLUE MAN 3

I'll take a cappuccino.

BLUE MAN 2

Caffeine and everything?

BLUE MAN 3

But I have Dairy Ease now, so even the whole milk in cappuccinos doesn't scare me.

BLUE MAN 2

What do you do when you call the take-out place, say, "Hey, can you make it with Dairy Ease?"

BLUE MAN 3

You have to have your bliss coming from the process of making the work, not from its results. Then you don't have to worry about anything.

BLUE MAN 2

We don't know anything about management theories either, really, but we like the way a lot of it sounds. The basic model of Japanese management is the idea of continually working on something because it's never done. We try to do that, too. Within each piece and between two pieces there are an infinite number of moments that can be worked on, discussed, and crafted. Every night, based on our notes, we can potentially rewrite the show. It's up for grabs. I feel sorry for people doing a play. The other day I made a mistake but I got a huge laugh . . .

BLUE MAN 1

Most of our acts are mistakes.

BLUE MAN 2

We've made mistakes that have led to reworking a whole piece. Like sitting down at "The Feast" with a woman. She didn't always take the Twinkie, and so our first idea was to have a crudité for her. You know, like, "Oh, you

don't want this Twinkie? All right, we also have crudité."
And that's kind of funny, celery and carrots. But it's not
really funny. And then . . .

BLUE MAN 3

Then came an accident. Someone got a Twinkies Lite box
instead of a real Twinkies box.

BLUE MAN 1

We were pissed. But, that night the woman didn't take it,
and then Chris pointed out that they were "lite," so she
shouldn't feel so bad because it's "health food."

BLUE MAN 2

When you point out that it's "lite," they feel like they
have to accept it.

BLUE MAN 3

So, if in one show we do something just a little bit different from five hundred times of going like this and like
this, then . . .

BLUE MAN 1

Chaos theory.

BLUE MAN 2

You know that bald guy, Peter Garrett, the singer in Mid-
night Oil? He's totally committed to something bigger
than himself. That's also what we like. He's not narcissis-
tically driven, although he's got some autoeroticism and
that's important, too. You get off on yourself a little bit in
front of people. But he goes back and forth from within,
to the audience. It's very vulnerable to have a moment of
spiritual solitude in front of other people. So he's creating
for himself, then he checks in and has a radius of awareness that includes the whole building.

When we did Lincoln Center, we talked about starting with our radius of awareness as big as the room we played in.

BLUE MAN 1

That would command the room, so to speak.

BLUE MAN 2

It is presumptuous and scary. It's scary! Who am I to take on that big a . . .

BLUE MAN 1

. . . command the attention of an entire room so they will follow you on the emotional journey you want to take them on?

BLUE MAN 2

And that's why being a Blue Man makes it easier. Brando can do it by himself. Vanessa Redgrave can just do it herself. It's who she is. She fills the entire space, no matter how big. I wonder what those huge people are like in their private lives. It must be a problem to be huge all the time, you have to come down. But they are alone, not part of an organism like we are.

BLUE MAN 3

The three of us will take this one thing away from this experience, no matter what happens: in fifteen years, we could find ourselves with an acting job alone somewhere, but after over five hundred Blue Man performances, and equal responsibility for every aspect of the entire show, we know absolutely that there's a place we should be shooting for. We'll never want to settle for a "fine" performance. Some people don't know that they weren't Vanessa because they've never felt what it was like.

Knowing what it's like to be Vanessa together gives you the courage to just go out and do it. On the nights when that Vanessa Redgrave stuff happens, when we come out and we have the courage to be that big, we can tell that it's different. We'll always be able to know how to go forward.

BLUE MAN 2

I like *Method to the Madness*.

BLUE MAN 3

Obviously, we wouldn't mind your book referring to madness, but other people . . .

BLUE MAN 2

I mean, it is kind of madness.

BLUE MAN 3

Talk to us about the show last night. What can you teach us?

ALAN ARKIN

Even an enormously talented actor can take a long time to achieve his performance goals. Many issues can militate against the realization of a satisfying vision, from an insufficiency of technique to a lack of personal experience with which to inform a character or situation. In Alan Arkin's case, his life and process were at odds with his goal of experiencing and expressing onstage something about the joy of living. As a young actor he felt that every time he went onstage, his life was at stake. His acting process was ferocious. It enabled him to create characters that were "like laser beams." He thought about the character endlessly, jamming himself into his skin with a high, almost punitive, degree of empathy and imagination that left little room for the man himself. He realized that his life was an improvisation for his characters. At that point he made many critical changes. His interview takes us on a journey through his evolving personal awareness and its effects on his acting.

The contrast between his early working methodology and philosophy and his current goals and process is dramatic; from consuming himself for his acting to giving life its primacy; from mastering artistic agendas to systematically breaking them with glee. His work, once painstaking and intense, now has the looseness and sureness of a Picasso sketch. He says, "Working without any preconceived idea of where you are can be the most exciting way to work." I wonder, can an actor work success-

fully, reliably, and with such abandon without internalizing years of technique?

Of particular interest in his interview is his delineation of the mind of his character. This has been a constant in his work, but it has reached a point of exceptional imagination and sophisticated technical elegance. As the mind goes, so goes the character's body, the way he listens, acts, and reacts. In his characterization of Aranow in the film Glengarry Glen Ross, *he sets up an "energy field" of anxious thinking that plays itself out as the character's throughline. His description of the imagery he employed to create the father in* Edward Scissorhands *demonstrates a remarkable imagination at work.*

In an apocryphal story, a disciple asked the Dalai Lama, "Master, how long does it take to achieve enlightenment?" The Dalai Lama replied, "Five minutes, if you do everything right." Alan Arkin's current process has an enlightened sense of ease, but his journey to this point took much longer than five minutes. The captivating simplicity and joy in the way he works now communicates itself to every character he creates.

"HOW DID I ACHIEVE THAT JOY ONSTAGE? THAT'S A FORTY-YEAR ODYSSEY."

I murdered myself studying acting. I started at the Brooklyn Academy of Music. By the time I was five it was the only thing I wanted. I dragged my mother around—the opposite of a stage mother—to acting schools. I didn't feel like I had a window onto real life. Real life was an intrusion on my fantasy life where I was locked up. Music, drawing, writing stories, acting. I was never terribly interested in reality. In fact, I felt like an outsider to reality.

I remember being about eight years old and listening to a woman talking to my mother and crying about some event that had taken place. I didn't feel sorry for her. Why? I analyzed her delivery from a performance standpoint. I came to the conclusion that she was feeling so sorry for herself that she didn't leave me any room to get in.

As a kid I once went to a film and I was bored with it. I pretended for a minute that I was hiding in a closet watching the event through a keyhole. All of a sudden the entire reality of the film changed. Up until that point my imagination made the film a real event, I wasn't watching a performance. The minute I watched it through the keyhole, certain performances became interesting and real and others became patently false. I felt that they were currying favor from an audience. My feeling was, "They don't know I'm out here so why are they acting for me?" That gave me my first gauge, my first ethos, for good and bad work.

Acting was all I wanted to do. And yet, I always had this terrible dissatisfaction with what I did on the stage. I was very good at manipulating an audience even when I was very young. I could get the reaction I wanted from them, but I would come offstage feeling very empty and very angry. I felt that I cheated the audience.

Then I met an acting teacher in L.A. named Benjamin Zemach. He had studied with Stanislavsky and used Stanislavsky's psychological approach. He believed the actor had to engage the audience, and he wanted joy on the stage. There's a confusion about Stanislavsky's method in this country. When people say Method, they really mean Lee Strasberg, but he changed the Method. Lee Strasberg's version is tortured psychiatry as far as I'm concerned. He took the joy out of acting for a whole generation of actors and turned it into some kind of subterranean digging for garbage and hoping to come up with a pearl. Yeah, I know that the emotional life is a real thing, but I think it's made infinitely too much of in acting. I think it's something that Lee Strasberg, God rest his soul, foisted on the American people, by way of his frustration that he didn't have a degree in psychiatry. I think if you need work on your emotional life, if you have trouble expressing yourself emotionally, you go to a damned doctor, you don't become an actor. Go into another field until you have some contact with your emotions.

Zemach opened everything for me. He would ask simple things like, "Why are you coming onstage?" I'd say, "Because that's where the character has to be." And he'd ask, "But why is the character coming onstage?" I didn't have any answers for that. He introduced me to the idea that the character has motivations—all the things that everybody knows about now. You've got to have some sense of the character's life and relationship to the events offstage—who were you yesterday; who were you last year; were you ever married; do you have kids; is it hot out? All the things that are second nature now.

At the same time I was studying with Zemach, there was work that fed me profoundly. I revered these actors not just for entertaining me but feeding me, giving me tangible values to live by; a whole school of French actors in the thirties that nobody knows anymore: Raimu, Harry Bauer, Louis Jouvet, Michel Simone, Marcel Dario, and Jean Gabin. These were, as much as anybody, my idols. Later, when I became famous, people would come up to me and say, "I like your work. You're good." I didn't care. I wanted to affect people the way I had been affected by Jouvet or by people in our country like Walter Huston, Spencer Tracy, and then later by people like Montgomery Clift. I was deeply affected by the work of these people; changed.

In the best of them I got a sense of pervasive joy—like Walter Huston's work in *Treasure of the Sierra Madre* and *The Devil and Daniel Webster*. These were as good a pair of performances as anybody's ever given. He gave me a sense of security in his work, a psychological understanding of why he was doing what he was, and on top of that, a boundless joy—at living! That was something that I wanted. I wanted to be able to experience that and express it. And I learned a lot from Spencer Tracy about the complexity of goodness. Most people think of goodness as something namby-pamby, easy to aspire to. They picture saints going around with their hands clasped in prayer as they do good deeds. But Spencer Tracy shows what a complex area goodness is. He was able to coat a lot of his work in a kind of sly exuberance, but there was a moral fervor in the serious work.

Huston and Tracy had a better time than I was able to have. The only time I was able to have a good time was when I got to the point when the role was playing me. When I wasn't acting anymore. It happened to me for the first time when I was nineteen, and I became a junkie for that experience. The driving force, not only of my work but of my life, is that experience. When you're not doing it anymore, it's just happening. You're just off somewhere in the sidelines going, "Go, go! Don't stop! It's okay!" And you're doing fifty things you never did before and you'll never do again. It's playing you. The first time it happened was in a play that Benjamin Zemach was doing. I was playing something that I had no understanding of at all, a soldier home on leave, a husband and a father—none of which I had ever experienced. I killed myself on the production trying to work Zemach's way. Then, in one of the dress rehearsals, I went onstage and I was no longer there. The character was there and I just had to get out of the way. It was like downhill skiing on an endless, perfect run, or surfing a perfect wave in Hawaii. Somebody once asked me if it was an out-of-body experience. It never occurred to me that it was, but the way people describe it, it feels that way. I felt like I was forty feet away watching the performance. All my critical faculties were off with my observer, but onstage there was nothing but the character. Both of those people were me.

What took me years and years to find out was that this experience could happen to anybody in any walk of life. I became a junkie for acting because I felt that the power of that experience lay in acting. It took years to discover that it didn't lay in acting, it lay in me. Experiences like that do not happen unless you are deeply devoted to whatever you're pursuing. I studied with Zemach just a couple of years, but enormously intensely. I lived it, breathed it, slept it.

Shortly after that I got an extraordinary scholarship to Bennington: room, board, tuition, and maid service! In an all-girls school. I was one of five guys on campus in those days because they expected the girls in the theater and dance departments to go on and work professionally and they needed guys to work with. There's a movie in there somewhere except nobody would believe it. It was unbelievable!

At Bennington I studied with another great teacher, named Larry Arrick. He pushed me into a lot of places I didn't get to with Zemach. He dug deeper into that New York, angst-ridden, psychological approach, which was very helpful to me at the time because it gave me more armor to go onstage with. I was so terrified of being onstage that it was a perfect gauge of whether I was doing good work or not. If I was afraid and aware of the audience, then I knew I wasn't doing good work. If my armor was sufficient so that I was just relating to the other character, then my guard would come down and I would relax.

I always had the ability to put myself into other people. I could look at somebody for a couple of days and then I could start imitating them and feel like I could be them. I would know what they were thinking. It was kind of odd, almost like ESP, in a way. I knew what people were doing and from where they were doing it. I didn't know why about anything. I don't know if anybody knows why about anything. I always felt that I just became the person. It was not a statement *about,* which I think art, ultimately, has to be, in order to be valid. It's not the thing itself. It's a symbol.

I didn't feel like I had any particular center myself, but I could find the center of somebody else and play it. It would change from character to character. It was a very important insight for me. Was it Michael Chekhov's? I had done it instinctively, and then when I read him, I said, "Yeah!" Then I started doing it consciously. But the only time I was centered was when I was acting. Until I was in my thirties, every time I went onstage my life was at stake. I don't know that it's necessarily the best work, but it's always interesting to watch. If it was a bad performance, I felt I was lucky to be alive—that the acting god didn't come down and strike me dead. It was completely nuts.

Through a college friend at Bennington, I did a summer of improvisation in St. Louis. I had to kill myself learning how to be funny. I could be funny in a play periodically, but to be funny in improvisation was not something that came naturally to me. I was very awkward, stumbling. Paul Sills came down and saw that show and said, "We're starting a thing called Second City in Chicago, and if you want to join, there's a position for you." And I said, "Thank you very much." Inside I was saying, "Fat chance! I'm going to have a big career and I'm not going to bury myself in Chicago for a hundred bucks a week." So, I went back to New York and starved for another year. My first marriage fell apart. And I said, "Well, I'm going to throw my life away. Nothing is keeping me here. Nothing. I'll go to Chicago and spend the rest of my life earning $125 a week in an obscure company."

I played a very great range of characters at Second City, but the further away I worked from me the happier I was. I went there to find an identity. I felt that this body didn't have one, didn't have a shape to it. What do you learn if you're driving a car 140 miles per hour on a track? It's not as if that kind of learning experience is reflective. The learning experience has two parts to it: one is when you gather the material and the other when you're throwing yourself into it. Each has its own rules. The Second City experience put twenty-five years of thinking and planning and plotting and rehearsing and seething into practice.

I thought I was going to get fired in the first couple of months because I could not be funny. One day I played a character I had been fooling around with all my life, from my library of characters, and that was funny. So everything I did for a while I did as that character. And then I pulled out another character. When a scene came up, I would go through my index file of characters and pick the one that seemed closest. Somewhere in me I found these characters amusing even though they weren't necessarily comic. The minute I'd open my mouth as one of these people, audiences would laugh. I could almost do no wrong with these six or eight characters, and I developed more after a while. I could have known everything about these characters if I had wanted to. If somebody had asked me to talk about one of them for four hours, I could have done so. I knew I had found the character when I was comfortable onstage doing absolutely nothing. It was a kind of gyroscopic sensation: where is he when he is at rest? Armed with the character and the action, I could go onstage. Without those two things I was dead, it was like I wasn't there. I didn't know who I was.

I was a year in Chicago and then another year in New York with Second City. Two years that felt like twenty. Two shows a night, six days a week. If it could have been seven, I'd have found a way of making it seven. Playing twenty, thirty characters a night and three shows on Friday and Saturday nights, I learned so much. How to conserve energy, for one thing. If you have to work five hours onstage, you know you can't work in the same way you would if you have twenty minutes in a play. By the end of those two years I felt like I had dried myself out.

When I went on Broadway in *Enter Laughing*, I had to relearn how to work on a part over a long period of time. Slowing down from the rapid improvisational process was tough. It almost didn't work at all. I treated the role with an almost sacrosanct seriousness, which was a mistake, and so I didn't really find the character until we were out of town in previews. The play wasn't working and they were on the verge of firing me. I was in every scene and I hadn't found the character. I went to Gene Sachs, the director, and asked, "It's not working. Can I take it a whole other way? Can I try something that has nothing to do with what we have been talking about?" I did it that night and poof, the whole play came together.

Carl Reiner wrote *Enter Laughing,* and it was autobiographical to a certain extent. I think Carl Reiner would have liked me to be paying homage to Carl Reiner, but I was paying a little too much homage to Carl Reiner. So I took out all of the homage and I just treated it, in my mind, frivolously. I turned it into an outright farce, where up to that point they were treating it as a warmhearted human comedy about someone with aspirations who finally makes it in the world. That night I played it as a farce about an insane, ambitious kid from the Bronx. I made him a total naïf, not wildly bright. I don't know how Carl ever felt about it, but it worked.

I went into *Luv,* which Mike Nichols directed with Anne Jackson and Eli Wallach, for a year. It is hard to believe, but I did a year with those two people and there was never one moment of difficulty or unpleasantness, which was a wonderful experience. Unfortunately, the character in *Luv* was what I was, an outsider who had to fight to get heard. Lonely, with a lot of feelings about the way the world should be and no hope that it was ever going to be like that. He was the most angst-ridden person who ever walked. It's a wonderful play, but it became painful to play him. I didn't like being that guy. I tried to distance myself, but I couldn't do that forever. It started seeping through, and the more it seeped through the unhappier I got. I tried to remove myself from feeling anything for him by commenting, "What he's feeling is stupid." The pain and also the comment ended up on the stage. My character became a kind of an objective view of that character; comic objectivity. I don't think Mike Nichols knew. He had just begun his meteoric rise and he didn't mind it if he saw it. Actually, to a large extent, his work was like that, so I don't think it would bother him. It wasn't intentional, I just couldn't stand being this guy for that length of time. My performance ended up looking Brechtian. I think that "Brechtian" came out of that: Brecht didn't want to really face what he was talking about. People talk about his work as an intellectual idea. I think that's nonsense. You don't become an artist with an intellectual idea. The intellectual idea comes from a deep need, and you give it a name so you think it's an intellectual idea. I think Brecht's ideas of detached theater were because he was really on two sides of the street. He didn't want to admit it to himself, let alone anybody else, so he tried to objectify himself and his work.

Then I did *The Russians Are Coming!* and I lived happily ever after. The end.

No. Not the end. The first four or five years I was in film, acting was kind of a reflex for me. Thinking is something you do when something's not working. When it's working, you stop thinking. For that period I didn't have to think about acting much at all. My work was filled with a lot of reality and a lot of colors. However, it was also filled with turbulence, anger, and unfulfilled longing. When it came time to do *Catch-22*, which was four or five years after Second City, I said to Mike Nichols, "Who is this guy? What should I do with him?"

He says, "It's you." "Me?" I didn't say it to him, but my internal monologue was, "Me? I haven't got a me. There is no me. There's going to be a blank hole in the screen." I really felt that if I just walked and talked like me, there wouldn't be anything on the screen. When I watched the dailies, I breathed a sigh of relief because my fear did not materialize. There are a couple of scenes I like, but to this day I can't see much of anything in Yossarian.

My way of working started changing when I started becoming preoccupied with life. I realized in my middle thirties that I had achieved everything I ever dreamed. I had promised myself that everything would be taken care of when I got to that point. I had the rude awakening that nothing had been taken care of. I was still as unhappy as I ever was. Unless I was acting, I felt like my life had virtually no meaning, but I could no longer devote eighteen hours each day to it. I felt lost and unhappy. I wasn't really doing very much for my wife or my kids because I didn't have anything to bring them. I had no joy to give them. No center. I had put my life on hold. When problems came up, I held a subconscious dialogue with myself saying, "That will all be taken care of when I'm famous and successful. I don't have to worry about that now." One of the things that bothered me when I was a kid was that nobody listened to me at all. My parents were wonderful people, but their way of relating was to lecture constantly, in stereo. I defended myself with the thought, "When I become a successful actor, everyone will listen to me." Now I was really successful and everything got worse instead of getting better—I said to myself, "Hey, wait a minute. There's something wrong here. I've either got to get myself a bunch of sycophants and have an imaginary life like a lot of actors do—just pay people to feed my fantasies until I'm on the stage and can live my own fantasies—or, I've got to recognize that there's a real world out there that needs some attention." The sanest part of me recognized that sooner or later my work would dry up.

I went into analysis, and that was interesting and exciting. It was a revelation that I wasn't just this mass rolling down a hill that I had to watch helplessly until I crashed into a rock. I actually had something to do with why it was rolling down the hill, impelling it in the first place and changing its direction. I thought I was pretty smart, I'd done an enormous amount of reading. However, I'm embarrassed to say that the fact that there was such a powerful dynamic working inside of me came as a complete revelation.

It's insane not to admit that there is a direct correlation between one's life and one's work. If you think you are separating your life from your work, you're conning yourself. You're robbing one hand to feed the other, and they will both suffer for it. The alternative to not admitting it is saying, "The thing that has made my work good is that my life is a mess. So, therefore, I'd better keep my life a mess so my work stays exactly the way it is." Maybe the acting has reached some kind of high level, but in order to substantiate this level of mess I'd have to intensify it because it's feeding on itself. Sooner or later it will consume itself. Then, in order to feed the mess of your life and in order to not have everything shrivel up, you become an addict of one kind or another. The alternative is to say, "My life is not dog food for my art. This insanity will end up feeding nobody. The reason I'm an artist, to begin with, is not because I woke up in the middle of the night at the age of three and said, 'This is my mission, to become an artist,' but because someone fed me through their art and gave me a sense of what life is all about."

Well, in order to do that you have to be alive. Art must be a celebration in order for it to be art, otherwise it's therapy. Somewhere along the line I had a conscious recognition of the fact that I wanted my life to serve people, and I wanted it to be a celebration. The problem was I had nothing to serve anybody anymore. My life was, in fact, the dog food for my work, and it was killing me and killing everybody around me.

I worked my rear end off at analysis, too. However, you come to the point in analysis, if you've worked hard enough, when the doctor finally gives you that most wonderful of cop-outs: "Well, I never promised you a rose garden." I said to myself, "Bullshit! There is a rose garden out there. There are people who have it and I want it, too." So I started thinking about metaphysics. There was no where else to go. I started working with somebody and I'm still working with him.

My work started changing again as a result of that journey; first in analysis and then in my work in yoga. During the shooting of *The In-Laws* something happened. What was really taking place was that up to *The In-Laws,* my acting was a way of substantiating my existence, a way of giving me license to be alive. Acting was my way of confessing, apologizing. That was why my life really was at stake with every appearance onstage or in front of the camera. As a result of the work I did in analysis and the continuing work I did in yoga, I was no longer expiating in my acting whatever crimes I felt I had committed in my life. Acting was no longer this confession booth, and it was no longer the only place where I found identity. I was starting to have a sense that I had an identity offstage and off-camera. But I wasn't conscious of that at the time. So when it came time to do *The In-Laws,* I was having fun. I'd tell my wife, "I know I'm going to get canned. I know it because I'm not working. I'm not doing anything."

I used to think about my parts endlessly, not what I was going to do with them, but what the background was from a sociological, psychological standpoint. Where they were centered. That was my obsession. I used to try and jam myself into their skin. It was a process of constantly jamming: walking down the street—how does he look at this building? The past-history stuff, what they were like when they were four years old, never did me any good. I had to be them in whatever moment, in my own life. I had to be them in my life in order for them to have any reality. And once I could do that and then be silent with them, I could be them anytime, anyplace. My life became the improvisation for my characters.

For *The In-Laws,* however, I didn't prepare at all. I knew immediately who he was and how I wanted to play him. And that was it. He was somewhat anal retentive. Seeing my character unravel is the situation, the developing idea of the film. Unless he's a tight-ass to begin with, then there's nothing to see unravel. It was so obvious I didn't even have to say it to myself. I stopped having to think about that. I could have let go years ago and whatever abilities I had would have been there. Everything. I didn't have to hang on so tightly. That was the beginning of the change. And the event was joyous from the first moment to the last moment in spite of Peter Falk's first week. He'd admit this. He was grousing and bitching and complaining the whole first week. I got friendly with his secretary and finally asked her, "What the hell is the matter? Everything's great. Everything is going wonderfully. What is wrong?" And she said, "He's miserable because he has nothing to complain about." And I said, "Oh, God!" It was like looking at myself the year before. The next week or two I spent breaking that down, forcing him to give up that stance, and he finally did and started having a good time. One of the great joys in my life is when people come up and say about that movie, and maybe three or four other films, "God, it looked like you were having a good time when you made that film, did you?" And with great joy I answer, "Yes!"

For several years whenever I got a part, particularly parts I liked playing, I was terrified that I was going to get fired because I didn't have to climb any mountain. I thought they were going to fire me in *Wait Until Dark,* for example, because I didn't want to do anything until the first time I pulled the knife on Richard Crenna about a half hour into the film. I didn't want anybody to know who I was—or that I was anybody. I didn't know it at the time, but what I was playing has ultimately become a definition of evil for me, which is centerlessness. Yeats talks about that: "The center cannot hold." I wanted him to be something that was not present. My first introduction into the world of drugs was during Second City in Chicago. I wasn't involved in it to any great degree, but I had had enough experience with people on drugs of various denominations. The character was drawn from a lot of people I knew back then, pushed together. I played him as on every drug he could possibly be under. I thought that his "not being" would be more frightening than violence. I always found it terrifying to be around someone whom you can't know and can't figure out what they're doing.

The first film that I tried with an agenda that made me feel like I was an an acting criminal was *Hearts of the West*. It was a nice film. I played a lousy director, a wonderful part. I said to myself, "It's too good to waste on just one director. I'm going to play a different director I've hated in every scene." So I did fifteen different forms of incompetence, one for each scene. I felt it was very brazen and that it would look like fifteen different people. But to my surprise, it looked like one person with fifteen different aspects. It was a totally unorthodox way of working that had nothing to do with the religious way I had studied. I thought I was doing something sacrilegious. I won the New York Critics Prize for it. That was a step on my dangerous path of trying to destroy all agendas.

Something else changed in my work and it terrified me. I used to have the absolute ability to have the scene I was playing be my only existence. You've seen actors like that, they're kind of drunk when their scene is over? I could not do that anymore. I had to relate to the reality outside the scene. I didn't know what to do about it. Finally I recognized that since I couldn't do anything about it, then it was just the way I was going to have to work. It's still the way I work. I cannot shut out anything anymore. I can't shut out the camera, the director. I can't do that kind of focus anymore. My characters are not myopic anymore. They're not laser beams. They're more diffuse, they're capable of going in more directions than the earlier characters. They're better listeners. They don't take themselves as seriously.

There are a few new ways I have of working which I feel create the loosest and most abandoned work I've ever done. One I learned from Renoir's rehearsal techniques. He rehearsed his actors by asking them to read scripts as if they were the phone book, investing absolutely nothing in it. My wife, Barbara, and I tried that in our living room with nobody around with a thing we did for PBS. It scared the hell out of us. I wondered, "Why is this so frightening?" I realized that it's because every actor wants to go into a project with the assurance that he can act the role and not get fired. As a result, we bring to the project our bag of tricks, clichés, and the expertise from the past we know will delight the audience and keep us hired. What Renoir's method does is rob you of those security blankets. It forces you into the soil, which is the script.

The script itself is what you must grow from: the situation and the rhythm of the words, which has more impact, I think, than people ever talk about. The rhythm has an enormous amount to do with its style. Adjusting to that rhythm teaches you something about the script, the characters, and what they are trying to say. What is moving about Chekhov is Chekhov, not the words. The thing that makes it an entity and gives it unity is the power of his voice and the integrity of his own personality or soul. His method of getting there is random. In his daily life he recorded fragments of conversations all the time. I think, to a great extent, he composed his plays that way. In order to play Chekhov correctly you must consider what he brought to it himself. I can't use the classical acting standpoint anymore. Knocking my brains out until I found some central, core idea for the character and then working from that doesn't work for me. You have to abandon traditional methods of characterization altogether. I think he wrote that way, not from characterization so much as bits and pieces and fragments—he was like a pointillist. Chekhov makes sense in some total way, but if you break it down to small pieces, it won't hold water anywhere. I mean, what is the main action of Lopakhin? It seems to vary from line to line. There are certain themes that keep playing over and over again, but to try to define it in terms of one idea is to rob it of its looking like a cascading garden of ideas and a multitude of feelings, all of which add up to something.

For ten years I've thought about this on a daily basis: What the hell was Chekhov trying to do with "Moo"? In *The Cherry Orchard,* the character Lopakhin comes onstage once in a while and says, "Moo." What does he mean by that? How do you play that? I've seen fifteen people do it, and it always stinks. I finally say that the way to do it is to just say it. Not give it any weight whatsoever. Just have the guy come in and say, "Moo," and then go on. Or, "I'm in mourning for my life." What is "I'm in mourning for my life?" What does she mean? I think you just say it!

"Why do you always wear black?"

"I'm in mourning for my life."

And you're on to the next thing. Just saying it and seeing what happens without any plan, without any preconceived idea of where you are going, can also be the most exciting way to work. I want to be daring and find out if I have anything to say or not. To do that I've stopped concerning myself with how I'm saying it.

The other thing I do now, which is one of the most frightening things I've ever done, is that when I know exactly what I want to do with a scene, what I want to accomplish, I force myself to think about something completely different just before they shout, "Action." I trick myself into not knowing what's going to happen. It's not like I'm pretending, it's like I really don't know. Doing this makes me the happiest I've ever been. I don't know what comes next, but all those things that I've been working on for fifty years are still there.

I loved working on *Edward Scissorhands*. It was a wonderful experience from beginning to end. It has got to start with the director, who's the leader. Tim Burton is terrific to work with, and I took that role to work with him. Better to work with a director you want to work with and a script you don't understand than with a script you think is terrific and a director you don't. When I first read it, I didn't have a clue as to what that script was about. Then Tim made reference to an obscure book of photographs, *Suburbia*, by Bill Owens. I was shocked that he knew it and he was shocked that I knew it. And he said, "I want the movie to have that tone." Immediately, I had a clue how to play the part. That was the key for both of us that we could be on the same track.

When I first arrived on the set, I saw the town that he had built, and Johnny Depp had just come out of makeup and he had his costume and makeup on. I said, "Oh, yes!" I understood everything, everything I needed to know about my character. What I wanted to play was a person who wasn't real. I wanted to play somebody who wasn't really there. But acting is an absolutely concrete thing. If you want to do a fantasy, then you have to give actors something very real to do, and then what we see can be a fantasy. So I gave myself concrete ways of doing that.

The two things I focused on were: one, he *really* wanted to be in the basement getting plastered out of his mind, just far enough so nobody would know; and two, whatever there was of him, which was not much, desperately wanted to be a good father. However, since it wasn't in him, the only way he knew how to be a good father was to do imitations of Robert Young in *Father Knows Best*. He needed constant reference to that television program. So, he was a guy who couldn't act at all, doing an imitation of Robert Young, and what he really wanted was to be in the basement getting plastered. It sounds complicated, but it was really rather easy to play. Nothing shocked him much because when he let things into his mind, they would hit stainless steel. The end product was a guy who was kind of not present, not really alive, an imaginary person. That role was one of the two things I've ever done where I see him and think, "Who the hell is that?" I don't recognize myself.

I didn't have to do much preparation for *Glengarry Glen Ross*, but learning those lines was the hardest task of my career. Usually an action will take you through a whole scene. With this material the action would change every word. That happens in life, but it doesn't happen in show business. I have a three-page scene after I'm interrogated by the cops, and I have a minibreakdown in front of the guys. It took me six weeks to learn that three-page scene. It drove me nuts. Everything is a broken speech, and every word, virtually, has another action. From a technical standpoint it was very difficult. I had to concretely plan which action to play on what phrase. It didn't leave a lot of spaces in the performance.

I had an instinct for what was tacitly written into the part, and I was hell-bent not to do it. I felt that Mamet thought my character, Aronow, was a kind of joke. Mamet likes operators; I think he identifies with them. Aronow is the counterpoint to that, the patsy. I feel like Mamet was slightly embarrassed about having to write this guy because Aronow is in a place Mamet does not want to be. It was probably perverse on my part, and I guess in a sense I didn't have the right to do it, but I felt that my purposes were better than Mamet's. I wanted to take the schmuck out of him and turn it into decency. I wanted to find ways to take what Mamet was squirming over about this guy and turn it into something that was decent and maybe naive, but not a jerk. Aronow says virtually the only decent thing in the script, which is that "up until a few years ago your concern was for the customer, doing something decent for the customer." Part of the reason Aronow's a bad salesman is because he knows he's dealing in crap and it's sticking in his throat.

I found a way to love him by giving him a past that made me care about him. I decided that he had not been a salesman his entire life. Until a few years ago he had been a grammar-school teacher, and he didn't have tenure when the school shut down. Selling real estate was something he didn't want to do. This choice gave substance to something that the audience didn't necessarily see but they would feel. He was not a very good salesman. He is naive about the nature of the work. Aronow wants out but doesn't know how to get out. It's hard to find one governing action for a person who has reached a dead end in his life and wants out. A lot of his actions are internal, looking for the answer.

I'll tell you what I played for most of the film. I played the internal idea that if I nag myself inside long enough, if I press enough internal buttons, an equation will come up that will get me out of this rat trap. Aronow's questioning in every moment of his life: "Where did I screw up, and how can I get out of this?" Reality would constantly intrude upon that inner place where he was trying to figure everything out.

The past six or seven years I've stopped looking at people as potential for imitation. I don't look at people anymore. I feel them. It's energy fields as much as anything else. I wish I could explain it in a human language, but I can't. Getting better and better at anything means fine-tuning your instrument, getting more keenly aware about finer and finer things that you're doing. Getting better as an actor means becoming more and more aware of subtler things within your system. The finer, the more subtly aware you become of something, the more subtle the vibrations you feel. People get embarrassed talking about vibrations as if it's some 1960s thing. The truth of the matter is that everything we experience, everything we see and hear, comes to us through vibration. It's all basically the same energy, just different gradations of that energy. I've reached a point now where I can feel that impact when I'm around people. Anybody can do it if they just decide they're going to do it, but most people have such an agenda—that word comes up a lot, but I think it's important—an agenda of things they want to get across that they don't just sit back and watch and listen and feel what messages people are presenting to them. That's what I mean by energy fields.

I used it in my work by recognizing that when Aronow is searching for an answer in his head, it creates everything else I need in the character. I set up an energy field. As Aronow, when I try and figure out what the answer to my life is, it instantly depresses me. My emotional reaction in my heart is depression, and the constant worrying of the problem in my head is a desperate desire to counteract the depression in my heart. These two things are at war with each other. The polarities start producing a struggle that has a lot of physical manifestations, one of which is to pay enormous attention to what someone else is saying because they might have the answer that will antidote this war that's going on between my heart and mind. If they do, then I'll listen with more and more attention. If they don't, I am completely uninterested and just drop out of the conversation. I go back into the confusion within me and continue trying to find a way out of the war.

Does that make any sense? Then you should nod.

On-screen, even though there is not much reason to feel that way, there's a kind of tenuous dignity about Aronow. It's interesting. The kinds of parts I'm getting recently are different than I used to get. I used to get someone who was the outsider. Now I've even gotten some reviews in which people talk about my being "the heart" of the project, the decent, the good person. It's not anything I'm trying for or asking for or even looking for in the scripts I'm getting, but that seems to be what I'm bringing on-screen.

I want to play people better than me. I want to play somebody that I have to reach for, that I have to struggle to find. That's what engages and interests me. Most people want to expose their innermost horrors. I'm not interested in that. You're going to tell me to go onstage and play Shakespeare. I don't want to go onstage; I hate the endless repetition. My son, Tony, and I did a play together a few years ago in a local theater. He was maddeningly brilliant because he looked like somebody who had been on the stage for fifty years and was now doing it just for the fun of it. He'd come offstage every night at intermission and say to me, "Why did you ask me that question again? I answered it last night and the night before. I thought I answered it very well. Why do you continue to plague me with the same question?" And that's exactly how I feel. I don't want to continue to be plagued with the same questions in the theater night after night.

The atmosphere on the set is increasingly important to me. If I get a sense that people there are curing cancer, I know that two-thirds of my work will be to try and counteract that attitude, so that I can ultimately do my work. I no longer feel I am the character. Now I only feel I'm playing the character and I am capable of enjoying it. When I see directors and actors taking the work more seriously than anything in human life, even if the piece is painful, I work to force the atmosphere to change for the better. That's what energy fields means to me. It's insisting that the workplace be a place where we can joyously do something together and maybe contribute some joy to the audience's life.

Life is always ... Wait a minute ... Life is never ...

RUTH MALECZECH

Ruth Maleczech's interview begins with the multidimensional idea of tracking. She will explain in some detail, but let me just state that it utilizes all of the theater's elements as ways of communicating the narrative. When an actor feels free to claim any of the theatrical elements as part of her process, her palette is very rich. It also decentralizes emotion and psychology as the actor's primary tools. Ruth says of psychology, "That's one of my tracks." It is not the one she uses most often.

Recalling her performances, both with Mabou Mines, which she cofounded, and in more traditional roles in plays, I see her solid, still form, and then, with no discernible transition, I see her breaking into an utterly surprising sequence of images, lifting me out of comfort and into breathtaking, disturbing poetry. I hear the shocking manipulation of her none too beautiful voice. She is free of a hundred restrictions and conventions within which other actors unconsciously or consciously operate.

In part, what enables that freedom is her agenda. She neither thinks about being the character nor seeming to be the character. What is important to Ruth Maleczech is her judgment of the character. That is what she performs. This is wildly contradictory to the lessons inculcated into psychologically oriented actors. In fact, I have often heard colleagues say that actors must not, can not judge their characters. Nevertheless, this is precisely *what Ruth Maleczech does. It is a Brechtian idea, but applied by her for her own ends, which vary with the circumstance.*

Ruth Maleczech is, perhaps, the most important actor of the avant-garde theater in the United States. What ultimately makes her acting avant-garde is not only the material she chooses, but her fundamental approach. It is highly technical. But what distinguishes her work primarily from the mainstream is that it is not driven by objectives, emotions, and desires, but by images. She generously attempts to break down a sequence in Lear *to illustrate this process. The attempt can not possibly convey the startling effect onstage. However, that scene in* Lear *is indelibly etched in my mind. Read this section carefully. It delineates a unique process that should become one of every actor's "tracks."*

"OF COURSE, THAT WAS JUST TECHNICAL."

In the early days of Mabou Mines, in the late sixties, we expanded the way we worked by enlarging our sense of narrative. We decentralized the actor speaking the text, in an emotional and psychologically revelatory way, as the primary way of conveying the narrative. Instead, any element could carry the story, and we referred to these as tracks. Picture gesture, sound, movement, psychology, pitch, rhythm, music, tableau, shifts in lighting, etc., as individual racetracks running concurrently as the story unfolds. All of these tracks are available at all times, and at any given moment, you can "jump the track" you're on and use another. For example, you can tell the story by performing a gesture, followed by an amplified sound and then a shift in lighting. All the theatrical elements are up for grabs at all times, as you move quickly from one to the other. This performance structure is more akin to musical composition than to traditional theater. When a whole group of people understands this way of telling a story, it makes for a very broad, creative canvas. And from the years of working with Mabou Mines, I've completely internalized this process.

It manifests itself in many different ways. People comment on my being very still onstage and then moving very quickly to another moment entirely. They find it surprising because they don't see the psychological transition. Well, the reason they don't see the transitions is because I just go from one moment to the other without transitions. I don't like the moments between. I like to be someplace, so I am transitionless. That's not to say I am not dealing with psychology. It's very psychological. It's just that I jump the track into the next moment instead of going through the process of getting there. Actually, for me the process *is* the jump.

My work is not driven by objectives or desires. It's primarily driven by images, and I intend the audience to sense that drive. I use rehearsals to set up the images I will use. Then, in performance, I literally jump from one image to the next. If I see myself doing something in my mind's eye, then I just go to that place. I am actually jumping from picture to picture. Performing is like running a marathon to me. My performance is always slightly ahead of me. So, I am trying to catch up with what I see ahead. I don't have any time to check to see how it's all working. If I'm running a race, I have to keep on going, I can't pay attention to what's already gone by. There's no time for that.

Sometimes I find the images on the stage in the present, and sometimes they come from my past. Of course, my response to them is in the present. I don't "go away" to respond. I like to respond in front of the other actors and the audience because I get to share it and be part of the human experience of the stage. That's the exciting part. The other actors are, for me, like the bumpers in a pinball machine. I shoot my pinball, my image, and it goes *tch, tch, tch,* bouncing off those bumpers, each hit having its repercussion. Often the next image will come directly from the response of the other actor.

I'll try to give an example of a sequence, but it will be difficult for me to come up with all of the images I used. In 1990, I played Lear in Lee Breuer's adaptation, produced by Mabou Mines, of Shakespeare's play *King Lear.* We reversed the gender of all the roles. Act III, scene iv, in *Lear* started with me hanging on to Kent, played by Lola Pashalinski, and ended with my hanging on to the Fool, played by Greg Mehrten. Lee just gives a pictorial outline of the space when he blocks, as opposed to JoAnne Akalaitis, who likes to block gesture. He wanted me to get to my knees on the ground on:

> *Thou think'st 'tis much that this con-*
> *tentious storm*
> *Invades us to the skin; so 'tis to thee;*
> *But where the greater malady is fix'd,*
> *The lesser is scarcely felt. Thou'dst shun a*
> *bear,*
> *But if thy flight lay toward the roaring sea,*
> *Thou'dst meet the bear i' th' mouth.*

When the mind's free,
The body's delicate;

So, to get there I slunk down along Lola's body and used as an image a dog I used to have. That got me to all fours on the floor.

It was one of the storm scenes, so when I was down on the ground, I would be fully in the mud. There, I used an image from my childhood. When I was very young, we had a victory garden and each of the kids was responsible for the vegetables in a single row. I was the youngest, so my row was onions. The image I used was being down in the dirt of the garden, picking the weeds around the onions on the lines:

> *This tempest in my mind*
> *Doth from my senses take all feeling else,*
> *Save what beats there. Filial ingratitude!*
> *Is it not as this mouth should tear this*
> *   hand*
> *For lifting food to't? But I will punish*
> *   home.*
> *No, I will weep no more. In such a night*
> *To shut me out? Pour on, I will endure.*
> *In such a night as this? O Regan, Goneril!*
> *Your old kind mother, whose frank heart*
> *   gave all—*

Then I used an image of reaching into a tunnel and trying to pull something out of it on the lines:

> *O, that way madness lies, let me shun that!*
> *No more of that.*

That part of the sequence ended with me on my knees. Then I got back on all fours, stretched my back, and used my old dog again. When she had to make a choice—where to lie down, where to piss, anything—she would walk in a circle first. So I walked in a circle on all fours on:

> Prithee go in thyself; seek thine own ease.
> This tempest will not give me leave to
>   ponder
> On things would hurt me more,

The sequence ended by my grabbing hold of Greg's leg as if I were standing on my hind legs. It sounds so stupid, but anyway, that's it.

I don't work "on character." I wouldn't know how to do that. I do try to perform my judgment of the character. It's very closely tied to Brecht, but actually it feels like a mixture of Brecht and Artaud. I can't objectify something about which I have no information. I don't get the information unless I'm acutely tuned in. So, to find out something, I have to go inside myself and experience it. That's the Artaud part. When I come out with the information, it gets Brechtian, except not for Brecht's agenda. Political education is not always my purpose. Sometimes my purpose is to trick the audience, sometimes it's to move the audience, sometimes it's to educate, sometimes it's to become immersed in working with the other actor, and sometimes my purpose is to put forward a political agenda of my own. My agenda is very changeable and Brecht's is not, but the technique is relatively the same.

I try to hear the voice of the writer, actually, rather than "knowing the character." I'm listening for the little, secret voice that the writer heard in her head when she wrote the play. Finding the voice is a part of the process that comes out of Artaud. I don't think about realizing the writer's intentions per se, I just try to hear the writer's voice. I think if I can get a handle on that, I can come close to what other people call character.

I don't spend a lot of time investigating the background history of the character. When we worked on Kroetz's *Through the Leaves,* which we did in 1984, I took certain generalizations from the script. She's a butcher and she loves it and is very proud of her business. She's a very self-sufficient, independent person. She's fascinated by Victor. He's the biggest event to come down the pike and she doesn't want him to go away. On the other hand, she doesn't want to do things to make him stay. After I put these facts together and look for the voice—that's real important—then I think about what I, Ruth, think about what Annette does. My opinion of her is what eventually constitutes my performance. It would be hard for me to do a performance in which that wasn't part of the work. I want that to be there even if the writer didn't write it there, and in the case of *Through the Leaves,* Kroetz didn't. Technically, it has to do with little distances I take in relationship to the behavior of the person I'm playing.

I'll give you an example. Throughout the play Annette is so out of control and her manner can be ferocious! She's a monster in her own way, just as Victor is in his. So, when Annette puts on the Eliza Doolittle costume, that *might* constitute a very feminine, pretty, delicate, fairy-tale sequence in which she suddenly becomes an unthreatening person to Victor. I didn't want to do it that way. I considered that the costume made her, or me, more powerful. When I flapped those clothes like wings, beating him about his body, I was marking him with my power, subjugating him as part of the image *I* was creating. I allowed the romantic side of Annette—well, romantic and stupid—to emerge in the dance sequence afterwards. But I didn't show it in the dress-up part because I judged that this was not the value I wanted the audience to experience.

As I mentioned, finding the voice is instrumental in my process. Annette's voice in *Through the Leaves* actually came from a very realistic, accurate place, so it's easy to talk about. Fred Neumann, who played Victor, and JoAnne Akalaitis, the director, and I discussed the fact that the characters were supposed to be shy of each other, shy of everything. We also knew that most productions of the play were long, some taking two hours and more. None of us had ever seen a production of the play, but we figured since the play is just forty-five pages long and the language is pretty spare that other actors must have spoken quietly and taken a lot of pauses. I mean, forty-five pages and it takes two hours—that's a lot of pauses. We puzzled over that a little bit.

At the time, my son was playing Little League ball and we used to ride in the van to the games with the other parents and their kids. The kids were very rough and tumble, and my son was excited to be around them and I was, too, because they, and their parents, were not people that I would otherwise encounter. Most of them lived in Queens or the Bronx, and it was great being with them, especially the van ride. We all sat in the back and the adults talked over the noise of the kids and the radio and the traffic. It struck me how loud they were talking! They had normal conversations, but they were talking really loud and I just loved the sound of it. Then, even at the game, someone would turn to somebody else and talk very loud. I thought, "These people conduct their lives in a very—well, they're loud! They're not arguing or fighting, but they're talking loud."

It made me feel that they were disconnected from one another. That was like Annette and Victor in the play. At a great distance from each other, they needed these loud voices to connect. JoAnne, Fred, and I were meeting, and I told them about these people who were from a similar place in New York in which JoAnne was setting the play. I wondered if this was characteristic of the locale, and perhaps of Victor and Annette. So we tried it out. Fred talked really loud. I talked really loud. Even when we were right next to each other, we talked really loud. It produced an odd kind of humor. We all liked it.

Then JoAnne had the idea that the pace should be really fast, without pauses. These were people who couldn't afford to have a pause between them because the other might read something into it. So we spoke very fast and very loud without pausing, and it lifted the play. It was quite technical, of course, but our first impulse had nothing to do with motivation, justification, or character. It was just a way to get at the idea that these two people say these words to one another but they don't communicate. Our play was very short. Our version of *Through the Leaves* took an hour and ten minutes. Then JoAnne added blackouts and unbelievably loud music between the scenes. It all worked in a mysterious way. The lights bombed on, the language, bombast, bombed out, and two people kept passing, always passing one another, never connecting.

Friends of the playwright came to see the play and they all said, "You know, that this is the wrong way to do this. You are supposed to speak quietly, and there are supposed to be long pauses and you're just to sit and look at each other and not know what to say." I think we found a truthful American equivalent to what people do when they don't know what to say to each other. One of the things that people definitely do in New York is talk.

I look first for the voice, but if I don't have success in finding it, I go for physical things. The physical came first in *Lear* after a long, unsuccessful search for the voice. The opening of the play had a fairy-tale quality, and I wanted my voice to reflect that throughout. I experimented with a high-pitched, fragile vocal quality, but the events of the play were so varied and demanding that I couldn't maintain it. My second idea was to drop to a growly, animal-like, ferocious level. That didn't work for the same reasons. Since I didn't usually play "roles," I was confronted by demands I hadn't encountered before. The most painful one was finding that my own range of being, my vocal and physical range, wasn't enough. I liked *King Lear* very, very much, but I didn't know anything about playing Shakespeare, except my sense that the acting is inextricably connected to the language. I tried to hear it and sometimes I was successful, but basically I wasn't. At that point I turned to physical things. It wasn't until much later on that my voice fell into place.

I found just one simple physical thing: bend my knees. It made me feel smaller. I'm pretty short, but I felt smaller still, and I liked that. In fact, it made everyone on the stage, except the dogs, bigger than me. It made my confrontations with all the other people in the play more important by contrasting my diminutive size and my fading power against the height and power of the taller actors. It spoke of age, which stressed the lack of time Lear has left to her, from the moment when she divests herself of her property to her death. Just as King Lear gives up his royalty with the expectation that he will still be regarded as king, Lear in this production expects to be regarded as the matriarch even though she has given up the accoutrements of the matriarchy. She is landless and dependent, like a person who makes a disastrous living will. However, I didn't have to deal with the other technicalities of age because, in order to maintain that shortness, I couldn't pick my feet up much as I walked. I could focus on simply bending my knees, and that took care of it. That was a big relief.

We didn't intend the audience to like her. A lot of men play Lear as pettish, volatile, and spoiled, and we tried to find parallels. But first you have to figure out why she gives up her property. Why would anybody do that? We opted for Lear to have the veneer of a fairy-tale-grandmother-pretend-person, with something quite different underneath. She is everybody's darling grandmother until something goes wrong, at which point she turns into a Fury. She's a bee, busybodying her way into her children's lives. She has no understanding of their needs. She doesn't comprehend that her sons' wives want commitments from them. She expects to be her sons' first commitment. In the course of the play this invulnerable selfishness is partially healed through her progressive deterioration, and some understanding is tapped.

I wanted to do *Lear* because I wanted to say those words. Not because I thought it was a great play about age or that it could be a great contemporary vision of old people losing their footing in this country, though those things are true. If there were a way to say the words and not do the play, that would be preferable. But as soon as you say them, you're stuck with the play. I knew them very well. I was a dresser in Herb Blau's production of

King Lear in San Francisco, a long time ago. I stood in the wings and watched all fifty-two performances done by Michael O'Sullivan, a wonderful, wonderful actor. He was only twenty-seven when he played Lear, but he had been so self-abusive that he was like a ravaged, eighty-year-old man. So I knew all the words and I never forgot them. I felt the language was so great that speaking it would transform me. And it did. All the other discoveries I made about how the play feels when women play the men's roles; and how men feel about women stealing their roles; and dealing with multiculturalism within a Shakespearean context; or raising my consciousness regarding the deprivation of the old in this country; all of that was the reward for taking the chance to say the words.

We worked on *Lear* for about three and a half years, and it was finally, after the New York performances, when we went out on tour, that I found that my first instinct about the voice was right. The vocal fragility has to be sustained throughout the play, but in order to do that it had to be more deeply grounded in me. The choice that I originally made was very thin, without much play in it at all. My voice was dying! What I tried on tour was to go just a couple of notches lower than that and to work more with breathing and less with pitch. Playing with combinations of pitch and volume is very characteristic of my work. I usually leave breathing entirely out of the picture, letting it come with physical movement. But in the case of *Lear*, I began to pay a lot of attention to my breathing, and then it was easier to make certain my pitch had enough play in it to satisfy the variations and demands of the evening. Classically trained actors probably know that. I'd love another crack at *Lear*!

Right now I'm working on a piece called *Mother*

that Patricia Jones is writing. It's inspired by Gorky's novel *Mother* and Brecht's play *The Mother*. In the Gorky novel the character is a battered woman, and we're going to keep that even though Brecht got rid of that little detail in his play. Very intelligent ideas about the theater Brecht had, but he was screwed up and he left that detail out. In *Mother* the woman has a son who is involved in some kind of revolutionary activity, like Act-Up. She's worried about his going to jail, so she takes over his position to protect him and realizes that she's a better revolutionary than he is. There are circumstances that she can get away with because she's this little old lady. The novel and the play set that up; but in both those works, she continues his fight and becomes the hero of the revolution. She becomes a "figure" rather than a person. She is dehumanized. It's really quite shocking. She has no sex, no anger. So, we're putting those things back in. We want to explore what women in America do to survive.

One of the reasons that I have decided to work on this piece, and actually, it began with *The Screens,* is that I have been a mother to two people for twenty-four years. I know something about the event of mothering; not a lot, don't get me wrong. But I feel like I know something, and it will be interesting to see what knowledge I can bring to bear on the work. So I am doing a series that explores that issue, with *The Screens* being the first, *Lear* being the second, and *Mother* the third. JoAnne Akalaitis wants to redo *The Screens* soon. We did it at the Guthrie, but we didn't get it quite right, so I'm delighted to have another crack at it.

KATHLEEN CHALFANT

Kathleen Chalfant identifies herself as a character actor. The character actor is expected to create an illusion of character that is more complete than the leading lady's. While the leading lady may be hired to externally show some aspect of herself that the audience finds identifiable, the character actor is hired to seem to be the character.

We should look at her interview in that light to gain insight into her process. Apart from the obvious techniques and devices that go into creating the artifice of character—wigs, physical stance, accents, etc.—there are more subtle rules that guide her work. Fundamental to Kathleen Chalfant's process is refraining from drawing on her own experiences to emotionalize a moment. She prefers to draw on the character's past history rather than her own, finding that it keeps her in the scene by not deflecting her attention to herself. Does the actor's preferred way of working create a character actor or do the requirements of character acting necessitate those choices?

Throughout her interview she invokes this caveat: beware of anything that is comfortable or emotionally satisfying. Whether artifice is central to a performance or not, vigilance is essential. A beard (she discusses three men she played in Angels in America) or an accent or even an internal choice can generalize the actor's primary responsibility, the moment by moment communication of the character in the situation.

She has created the roles of Virginia Woolf and Georgia O'Keeffe in one-woman shows. Her film work includes performances in Bob Roberts, Miss Firecracker, *and* Five Corners. *She has appeared in innumerable plays in regional theater, off-Broadway, and on Broadway. Nominated for a Tony for her work in* Angels in America *on Broadway, she has been a long-standing member of that company in several of its productions.*

Kathleen Chalfant explains her acting process with wonderful lucidity. In doing so she illustrates how an actor maximizes her opportunity to "be in the moment." This state, which all actors hope to achieve, can only be reached after a tremendous amount of preparation. Kathleen Chalfant does this work with respectful attentiveness. Then she is free to act.

"TO MAKE A CHARACTER IS ACTING."

As I get older, I begin to understand the things people used to tell me about acting that seemed impossible at the time. Trust the text, trust yourself, get out of the way; all of these things were like voodoo chants when I was a young actor. Now they are true. Somehow or other I convinced myself that I know something about acting and how to do it at some basic level. There's a level below which I will not fall.

In order to learn to act you must take apart something that happens faster than thought, break it into its component parts, and then put it back together. That's also what rehearsal is, breaking down a speech or a reaction, and then getting it close to the speed at which a human being actually does it. Quite often, plays are just a little slower than life because you've added a step—the breaking down. The trick is to act as quickly as you think, which is not necessarily a function of speed. When you're doing it properly, it often feels as though you have all the time in the world. Then you can allow yourself to be entirely taken, with no conscious control. That's what being in the moment means. In order to be prepared to give yourself over to the moment, you have to have done all the work beforehand: knowing the words backwards and forwards, knowing where you're supposed to stand, and more importantly, knowing what the character is doing at every turn and why she does it.

There's another trick to it which is a difficult one: you cannot play both parts. That's a very common problem, and all of us do it at some time. When you're playing both parts, you respond to what you think the other person *should* be doing or what *you* would do if you were the other person. It instantly takes you out of the moment and out of the reality of the play. It is sometimes difficult to refrain from negating what the other actor is doing because we are all so critical. And in fact, sometimes it seems that you ought to do it because the other person isn't playing his part properly. The great discipline is to respond solely to what they are doing. If they are giving you nothing, well, then the scene or perhaps the whole enterprise will fail. But nothing is solved by playing both parts because the audience sees what's really there, not what's in your head.

The other day I was talking about this to George Wolfe, the director of the New York production of *Angels in America*. We were meeting for the first time and were chatting away about a million things, and at one point he said, "You know, when I read this play, I knew how to do

103 KATHLEEN CHALFANT

the whole thing right away." And then he said, "I guess I always do that." I realized how true that is. Often at first readings, you experience the phenomenon in which everybody's performance is right there. Then it's gone, for weeks and weeks! The nadir of the process is about the third week of rehearsal. You spend your rehearsal time honestly trying to get back to your first impulses, what you did in that magical first reading. That phenomenon happens, in part, because you only have time to bring your own character to it, and you're hearing everybody else for the first time. You go into each scene with some basic knowledge of who your character is on the page, maybe of your objective at the beginning of the play; you're looking for your name to come up and you find your way through the play as innocently as people find their way through life. After that, you are never as innocent again.

Then you add all of the baggage. Quite often you play the end of the scene at the beginning. You test the emotional waters to see whether you really can be moved. By that I mean, you know that halfway through the scene you're going to have to be in a rage or cry or be hurt, or you're going to have to do terrible damage to someone else, and you "practice your emotion" because you distrust that your own emotional life will be there when it needs to arise in the scene. You come in from the get go as if every single member of your family has just been wiped out in an accident on the grounds that you probably won't, given the information in the scene, be able to cry, because after all it's Wednesday and everybody's tired.

Of course, ultimately it doesn't matter if you can really cry. What matters is whether you communicate to the audience what it means to cry. Acting is not about you. It's not about the ready emotionality that everybody identified as acting through the fifties and the sixties, or the great question in acting schools, "But can you really cry?" Acting is about the communication of the word, not a form of therapy. The actor's purpose is to communicate the text. I think actors and acting are like an orchestra. Actors are both the horn player and the horn. The primary creative document is the text, or the score, and actors, the horn players, are only creative in the moment. Our creative moment is very fleeting, and you have to get so many people together to make it happen, including the audience.

As I said, I didn't always understand this, and I certainly didn't really understand about being in the moment. I knew that it was an ideal. I had flashes of the experience. I could tell when things were false or forced. But the first time that I was neither ahead nor behind, trying to make it happen, was amazing. I remember when it occurred, and let me tell you, it was real late in the day. I was in a play at the Milwaukee Rep. called *The Splintered Wood*. There were whole sections of time when I wasn't controlling, when I wasn't testing the emotional waters, when I didn't worry about what the next thing that was going to happen was. I was—this magical thing—in the moment. I also knew as soon as it stopped. So my task then became to make the whole play be in the moment. I never did get all the way through from the beginning to the end, but it was then that I realized that it was something over which I had control. It wasn't magic. There was a way in which I could prepare myself for it to happen. All the basic work had been done. The other actors in the play were very good so I didn't call upon myself to play all the other parts. I trusted the situation. I believed the director's vision. I understood the play completely.

The character was very familiar to me. She was a middle-aged woman who ran a boarding house. The greater part of my life from the sixth grade through college was spent in my parents' fifty-room boardinghouse in Oakland, California, so I understood the milieu of this play. I had been doing a lot of Southern plays, and although I'm not a Southerner, my father is from Iowa and has roots in West Virginia, and the sound of the language was familiar to my ear. I felt comfortable in the world of the play, and unconsciously at first, I got out of the way. Then I made it a task. I said to myself, I will go into each of these scenes at the beginning of the scene and will make no other decisions until the end. I gave the rest of myself, which is the horn and the horn player part, to living in the moment through the scenes and trusted that I had everything in place. It felt great!

Of course, you also have to be wary of stuff that feels great because the job is not for you to feel good, it's for the audience to get it. I had a wonderful example of this danger in the movies because only in film can you have objective proof if something works or not. In the film *Five Corners,* I played the mother of a young man who was thinking about going to Mississippi as a freedom fighter. The central event in the scene was that I, the mother, was going to turn on the television and see a real interview of a mother of someone who had been killed in 1964. It was to be a very emotional moment. The director and I agreed—it was one of those movie things, right?—that I wouldn't see the tape until they played it for the shot. So we set up the scene, which was quite complicated technically, and when we began shooting, they turned on the tape on the television. It was completely devastating! I felt great compassion for this woman. I really felt like a mother whose son was about to go, and I understood the danger. Tears were streaming down my face and I thought, "Oh, wow! Isn't this great? This is what movie acting's all about! You do it in the moment." And I wept!

Then there was a technical error so we had to reshoot the scene. I thought to myself, "Oh, well, I'll never achieve that again." I did the whole scene again and it was hard and it was acting. Afterwards I was curious and I went to see the dailies. The second take was better. There was a certain amount of craft at work; it was focused. It seemed, oddly, more real because its purpose was to communicate the situation. It was a good lesson to have because how it feels is so compelling that you get fooled by it. You get so caught up in it that you begin to indulge it—"My God, I can cry!" It's very seductive. It happens all the time in rehearsal, too. Before you get to that nadir in the third week, there's this nice part in the second week where you're really getting it and you come in and this amazing stuff happens, and you weep and laugh and you just feel great, and then it all goes away and you despair.

This acting business is a very delicate thing because of that clarity that's required for the audience to receive the communication. Everybody has a different way of going about it. Some actors, in order to accomplish the task, must believe that they really are the character, that they really don't hear anybody crumpling cellophane in the front row. Other people need to have a strong technical underpinning, or armature, before they can even begin. They have to know every inch of the terrain in a very technical way and can't even begin to jump into it until they have all of that down. I think I'm like the armature people. Then I get to a point at which I challenge myself to believe that the armature is in place, and I try to walk into the scene new.

I am a character actor. That's a descriptive term and it ends up finally conveying the kind of work that I do as I get older and older. For years it meant an actor who was not pretty, but even that's not necessarily true. In the simplest terms it means that you don't play leading roles, unless the leading role is old and peculiar and from the South. What it means more importantly from the actor's point of view is that you are hired by people who are not interested in who you are—you are hired to play a character. To make a character is acting. It's not me. Acting is not being. I can walk and talk so that after a while you believe that I am an old Jewish man with a beard. It's acting, it's not real life. I don't know that I, as Kathleen, have all that much to offer, and I'm not hired to do that. I am hired to play fairly extreme characters who are far from me, or at least I think are far from me. My impulse is to turn into someone else. I don't know that I'd be very good at being me, whoever that is. If I were hired to be me, I would be terrified by being put face-to-face with who someone imagined I was.

In *Angels in America,* for instance, I play six characters. Two are women, Ethel Rosenberg and Hannah, a Mormon woman; three are men; and one of them is the Continental Principality of Asia, which is an angel. Two of the guys are old and peculiar with European accents— this is very actorly analysis!—and the third is a doctor who's about my age. The old peculiar guys are a very old rabbi and the world's oldest Bolshevik, and the other is a very Waspy Park Avenue doctor. The Waspy male doctor, Henry, is closer to me on paper than any of the other six characters, and he was the hardest one to play.

First of all, Henry is not extreme in any way. He is a handsome, successful, confident, competent, Park Avenue doctor who is comfortable with scary, powerful people. He is used to swimming with the sharks and knows that he belongs there. However, he never expects to have the shark turn on him. Playing him continues to be a fascinating investigation into making a guy. He is in a scene with another man, played by a male actor, and not just any man, the most powerful sort of testosterone-ridden figure in the play, Roy Cohn. So already the illusion is challenged just by being onstage with a real man. I am almost always physically smaller, so the illusion is challenged further. Henry doesn't have an accent. For a while he did have a Southern accent, but that seemed to soften the character and make him seem more feminine to people, though it didn't feel like that to me. That was another example of how something which felt good to me was entirely wrong. I thought I was playing him like some kind of hardscrabble, mean guy, but apparently I sounded like Belle Starr. Anyway, it was wrong. So, now he talks the way I do in this kind of affected Waspy way! But the real guy on the stage has a real man's voice and I don't have one, though I've lowered mine a bit. Most people know it's a woman playing a man. The question is, do I spend a lot of time trying to make the people believe I'm a man or do I just play the character of Henry and the devil take the hindmost?

First I did all of the physical things that you do. I looked at men to see how they sat and saw how they pull up their trousers. Men cross their legs in a different way than women. There were lots of men around in the play, and I'd ask them, "What do you do? Be a guy. Let me watch." Then I had to also figure out how men fight, as opposed to women. I would be fighting in an absolutely authentic way, but it was as a woman, which meant that I'd give ground emotionally and physically as well. When it got really scary, instead of moving forward to engage the other person, I'd back off to a safe place and hide as far away from the assailant as I possibly could, feeling all the time as though I were entirely in control of the situation, as women do, by keeping my own counsel. I'd listen to the other character. What it looked like was a man retreating. There'd be notes and notes and notes about that, and I couldn't understand them because I didn't feel like I was giving ground. But I was told by the guys that powerful men of that generation would move forward and engage in the battle, because if you back off, the other person would kill you. I had to learn to do that, and it was hard because it felt dangerous and unnatural. The "girl notes" I asked for and got made me immensely self-conscious for a long time. As a result, Henry was rather rigid physically because I never quite believed it. I wonder if all these technical things went into Henry because I wasn't convinced about the way the scene was being played and looked to fix it in these other ways. I finally realized that I didn't have much control over the illusion, but I did have control over making the scene work. However, it took me three years to figure out what the scene was actually about!

It's the last scene in act 1 when Roy Cohn is diagnosed with AIDS. The scene begins with the doctor's long monologue describing the horrors of AIDS. You think, "What kind of person would say this to someone who had been his patient for years?" All of us went at it from the point of view that Henry felt a subterranean hatred and contempt for Roy Cohn as a Jew and a homosexual. I kept trying to play that, and I could make it happen, but it was never quite satisfying. It was hard coming into the scene with all that, and the first moment always felt wrong. So we said that the scene opened in medias res, but even that was never quite right. Sometimes we would reach the battle for life and death in the middle when Cohn turns to Henry and says, "If you call me a homosexual, I'll destroy your career," and that part of the scene would play out right, but then we'd have to force the ending into place. The doctor's response is—well, you see, and here was the problem. It felt like there was one beat too many in the scene because the doctor doesn't respond immediately. When he does, he says, "Roy, we've known each other for all of these years . . . ," and he tries to smooth over Roy's mortal insult and make it okay. Then Roy comes back, "So say it, say it," and the doctor starts to say, "Roy Cohn, you are a homosexual," then stops in the middle and backs off. That whole little section was always very hard to play. Why exactly does Henry do that?

Well, I finally figured out what it was. I was backstage at *Angels in America* in Los Angeles, thinking about the scene for the umpteenth-thousandth time. All of a sudden, as I was about to go on, I figured out where it began. The doctor isn't going in there hating Roy, full of homophobia and anti-Semitism. It is 1985 and AZT was an experimental drug being used on only twelve patients in the program at Bethesda. Henry's first impulse is to frighten Roy so that he will pull all the strings he has in order to be put on AZT. To do that Roy is going to have to expose himself as a homosexual to Nancy Reagan, because there is only one reason to be on AZT and it's not because you have liver cancer. So the doctor thinks the encounter will end with Roy, who has been his patient for thirty years, putting aside all other concerns in order to save his life if he says, "This disease is really a son of a bitch and there's no fucking around here." Roy then derails Henry's plan, and the doctor unexpectedly finds himself in a battle for his life. Making that choice enabled us to play that scene from beginning to end. But it's one of those times where you bash away at it forever and ever—all the best minds bashing away—and what do you find? You're playing the end at the beginning!

The other men I play are very extreme for the most part. Luckily, with one of them, I even get to wear a beard, so that helps. Generally speaking, if I want to disappear into a character, the more physical characteristics he or she has that are distinct from mine, the more successful the illusion. The rabbi is eighty-six years old. As it happened, my father-in-law had Parkinson's disease at the time I was working on the character and I watched how he moved. Parkinson's disease affects balance in a characteristic way. In general, old people try to find walking strategies that concretize their centers of balance and gravity. They tend to bend their knees slightly and sit into their behinds. Therefore, the rabbi looked shorter than I. Because he's wearing what is essentially a habit (a long beard, *payess,* glasses, a hat, a big black coat, and *tzitsis*), and he's giving a eulogy at a funeral, he's immediately identifiable. He's a rabbi with an Eastern European, Yiddish accent. The audience brings its own emotional baggage to this particularly iconographic circumstance, habit, and accent.

You've heard the story a million times about Laurence Olivier saying first he had to get the nose? There's a lot of truth in that. You've got to get something to begin with. I had the way the rabbi talks and could do him from the neck up before I knew anything about his physical life, the way he thinks or what he does in the scene. He came to me like channeling or something. Tony asked me to do a reading of *Angels in America,* in New York in 1988. I sat down and he said, Kathy, you're Hannah and Ethel Rosenberg and would you read the doctor and the rabbi? The rabbi simply came right out of my mouth, and I have no clue to the source of that impulse. You probably don't have any control over your first impulse, but if you have one, go with it. If you don't have any first impulse, then you set to work.

The rabbi's first scene begins in a perfectly ordinary way. He's an old guy, hired to do a eulogy, which he knows how to do in his sleep. He doesn't know the family. He vaguely knew the deceased in the Home for Aged Hebrews. He's willing to do a job, get through it, and go home. He's tired. He's got everybody's information written down on a card, and as he starts reading, he notices that they have strange names like Maria, Luke, and Eric. He admonishes them for their gentile names—and he's not such a nice man. This is his territory so he doesn't feel that he has to behave. He's annoyed. He is not self-conscious about expressing the thoughts coming into his head. He makes two attempts at beginning the eulogy, but finds he's on the wrong path. Then, in the middle of a perfectly ordinary situation, the muse strikes. I suppose he's experienced this before, because when it strikes, he's off. Then he goes out into the graveyard to wait for his wife.

In his next scene, the rabbi doesn't want to talk anymore, he wants to go home. Louis finds him and goes into a long justification of his abandonment of his grandmother, and the rabbi begins to suspect that he's laying the groundwork to abandon somebody else, too, and seems to want his permission to do so. Louis asks what the Holy Scriptures say about a person who abandons another person at a time of great need. The rabbi says, "The Holy Scriptures have nothing to say about such a person." He is not the kind of person who would be overwhelmed with compassion for someone about to abandon someone after he's left his grandmother alone in the Bronx Home for Aged Hebrews. He does give Louis an answer, he tells him the truth, but he doesn't offer him the kind of forgiveness Louis is after. He says, "Jews believe in guilt."

I saw that the rabbi was not a nice man, but I didn't see that this was necessarily a bad thing. You decide in an entirely objective way whether the character is a nice person or not. Having done that, you have to make that judgment go away. "What does this person think about himself?" is the question you must answer in the playing. The danger that all actors fall into at some time is wanting to be liked, and then they try to justify their characters to make people love them. What I need to do is to tell the truth about the character as written. The character is on the piece of paper, and the possibility of playing its song is available to anyone who reads it. All you have to do is show up with your horn and blow. Let the audience decide whether he's nice or not.

Hannah, the Mormon mother, is very difficult, and many people don't like her in part one of *Angels, Millennium Approaches*. She doesn't have lots of available emotion. Paradoxically, I have to be on guard, because every once in a while I burst into tears for reasons that I don't understand. Her first scene is when her son, Joe, calls her on the telephone in the middle of the night to tell her that he's gay. She does not respond sympathetically. What she says to him is you're old enough to understand that your father didn't love you without being ridiculous about it. Joe hangs up the phone shortly after, and Hannah immediately sells her house and flies to New York to be with him. It's not true that she didn't respond to Joe, but the audience doesn't like her because she doesn't cry or yell. She's very contained and difficult. Sometimes when I'm confronted with people's negative reactions, I think, "Oh, God! Is there some way that I can play Hannah so people would feel about Hannah the way I do?" Of course, that way madness lies, or bad acting due to sentimentalizing a character whose great power is that she's not sentimental. Hannah isn't awful at all to me in any way. But it's not my business.

What sorts of decisions did I make about Hannah? Hannah has a sense of humor. She's contained in all ways. She's doesn't talk very much, and when she does, it's in short sentences. In a play where people talk for pages, Hannah's longest speech is maybe six or seven lines long. She is a woman of deep religious feeling. She's a Mormon but not an orthodox one, so she's aware that she's out of step with Salt Lake City. She doesn't have very many friends. Her intelligence makes her very curious. She seems to make judgments about people because she's so stern, but that's just part of her containment. That containment led me to stand like this, protecting myself with my arms and standing quite stern and straight. After the orgasm she has with the angel, I open the front of my body for the first time in my life; I open my arms and thighs. After the orgasm my body is round.

How she stood came to me first. I could always go back to the way that Hannah stood when there were scenes that I didn't quite get. I have to be careful about it because I can get to be very rigid and I have to realize that people are people, and they don't solely stand in a characteristic way. I have to be sure that it's the character that's doing it and not the actor who's indicating the character.

Her contained physical life is reflected in the way she speaks. She has an accent, which is in the rhythm of the text. Accents can be dangerous because you always can play the accent and not the action. It's always good to test the accent by getting rid of it, especially in something you've played for a long time. You see what's revealed if you drop it. You see what's sensitive there. If it works, bring it back. Hannah just doesn't talk the way I do.

Because of the evolution of the script over these three years, I have specific information about Hannah that doesn't appear in the lines. Some of the stuff I know about her is useful because I can utilize it to make scenes come alive. I can remember something that happened to Hannah. I find that more useful than remembering something that happened to me. Emotional substitution is a very dangerous technique for me because it almost always takes me out of the play and off on some track about myself. I used to try and use it in rehearsal, but I never was very good at it. It's easier for me to make up somebody else's life.

The last man I play is Alexi. He is the world's oldest living Bolshevik. He is a very sexy number, pretty great looking, very old, but he's blind, too. He has a different physical life than the rabbi. He's stunning, he has a really cool hairdo. He's very erect and he's very, very angry, enraged. I think he was probably a White Russian who became a bolshie, and no one is angrier than Alexi. The original structure of *Perestroika,* part two of *Angels,* was five acts each preceded by a kind of satyr play, that consisted of a little scene in front of the Supreme Soviet in 1985. There are eight actors in *Angels in America* and we each played an old bolshie. When it became clear that *Perestroika* was too long, the easy way to cut forty minutes was to lose all the bolshie scenes. This was very painful to everybody because they were really wonderful, had a lot of truth in them, and they were to be played in a very broad, comic way. We all talked in these hot-dog Russian accents. But, all the scenes were cut except Alexi, my bolshie, and he now opens *Perestroika*.

Because Alexi is vestigial, I made an actor's error. And this is an instance in which I took an acting note from a critic! I continued to play him broadly with all the stuff that points to a comic character. I thought that I was playing him with deep seriousness and conviction, but that it was funny. I was conscious of the function of Alexi's speech and how it set up the angel's speeches later in the play. People liked it. I try not to read the notices for a play until it closes. But people always call when you get *not* such a good notice. So my sister-in-law called me up and said, "Oh, I just read the notices in *Newsweek*. You got one nice notice and one not so nice notice." Being an actor, I didn't even ask about the nice one. "What was the not so nice one?" She said, "Well, it could be a directorial thing. Jack Kroll said that he thought that Alexi's speech was very important, and he lamented that it was being done in a comic and less than serious way." And I went, "Oh, well, he doesn't get it. He doesn't understand that what Alexi is saying is a red herring and it's wrong." But I was wrong. Jack Kroll caught me acting. His review said it was the director's error, but it wasn't. I was convinced that I was playing it honestly, as it was written. I wasn't. I was performing it in a way that would get laughs. I had not quite understood that the context in which the speech was now being made had changed. Jack Kroll showed me that I had gone three-quarters of the way, but I was not there yet. I then started playing the scene as though I were in front of the Supreme Soviet with something urgent to say. Alexi is filled with contempt for his audience, and he doesn't care if he destroys them. He wants them to stop the madness of living without a doctrine. I removed a layer of performance. Now I play the character, not an idea of the character.

The character of Ethel Rosenberg, the last human character I play in *Angels,* is not the historical Ethel Rosenberg. She is an idea of Nemesis in the same way that the Roy Cohn in the play is closer to the devil than he is to the historical Roy Cohn. And she's scary. She's Ethel Rosenberg as she would be after being dead for twenty years having watched Roy Cohn's ascent in the world. Now she comes to watch Roy Cohn die. It took a long time to reach that because the scenes are written so that she can be played in an obvious, slightly comic way as a nice little Jewish lady, holding her purse. But she is somewhere between the nice little Jewish lady transformed by tragedy and the monster, a mythical villainess, created by the people who destroyed her as the mastermind of a spy ring.

There is a lot of historical information that we have now about her—both her sons spoke—and a wonderful biography which is out of print. Tony read all the books he could find. He kept the historical parts that were important to him. I realized when I came to do the play that I didn't know anything very specific about Ethel Rosenberg. So, I, too, read all the books, and they were helpful in some ways and confusing in others. She was immensely complex but no mastermind of a spy ring. I had all that information and I went through stages of using it and taking it out. With all the historical baggage, Ethel has been hard to find. But more difficult than finding the character of Ethel was finding the structure of the scenes and the emotional throughline. Because Ethel is a ghost, she can do anything—so we played it a lot of ways and finally struck on the Nemesis solution as her dramatic function.

I took her relationship to Roy Cohn from the text of the play so that Ethel knew he was personally responsible for her execution. That forms a special bond between them, very personal. I took that she was a first-generation Jewish immigrant, not entirely assimilated, from the Lower East Side. This shaped her accent. I made her my age and not her age; she was in her early thirties when she died. As she was written, she seemed to be older, not a young mother.

Ethel has come because she's heard in heaven that Roy's in Big Trouble and she wants to see this. She wants him to know that she's there, watching. He's about to be disbarred, and Ethel wants very, very, very, very much for him to survive until he's suffered that shame. She doesn't want him to die now. Soon, and horribly, but not now. That's the part of Ethel that's driven by rage and revenge. Somewhere, there is a part of Ethel who is somebody's mother, someone who knows what it's like to die alone, in pain, reviled by the world. She rides along the knife's edge of revenge and compassion. Either one or the other of those things is a clear objective and easy to play. The trick here is to show both. The one that's the obstacle and the one that's the objective change in the course of the play. It's a balance because revenge and compassion are both

KATHLEEN CHALFANT

119

very strong currents in human emotion which are instantly identifiable by the audience. You have to be careful that one doesn't overwhelm the other.

I'll give a concrete example of this balancing of the objective and the obstacle, but it's with Hannah, not Ethel. In the whole of the play there is only one moment when Hannah is onstage with her son, Joe. When she's arrived in New York, he's disappeared and his wife has had a psychotic breakdown, and Hannah and she are both staying at the Mormon Visitors Center. Joe has not communicated with either of them for three weeks. He walks into the Mormon Visitors Center out of the blue to ask for compassion, and his mother doesn't give it to him. The scene is twenty lines long and represents their entire relationship. You can play it in any way. She can be cold. She can be fighting with every fiber of her being to keep herself from throwing her arms about her son. She can be so horrified by what he's done that she tries to destroy him. You could play the moment after he asks for compassion with an instant response of "You have no right to ask for compassion because of all the harm you've done." Or—and this is the way of dealing with the obstacle—when he asks for compassion, you can let the possibility arise that something might happen between them—for this long—and then reject it. The obvious obstacle in the scene is that neither can show his feelings for the other. You have to be careful when using the obstacle not to make the scene about *not* showing compassion for one another. It is what's happening, but that's not what they are actively doing.

The last character I play is an angel. Tony's notion of heaven is that it's organized into a huge bureaucracy, kind of like the United Nations. God has left and the angels are in charge. The problem with the angels is that they are extremely sexual beings whose essence is adoration, but the object of their adoration has gone. They have no imaginations. We catch them at a moment of crisis. They are in deep mourning because with God gone, the world is coming apart. So acting it is not just going to be how to play an angel, but how to play an angel in crisis.

I don't know how we'll approach them. We are going to have another go at it here in New York.

TERESA RALLI

The Peruvian theater company Grupo Yuyachkani comprises an extraordinary collection of talents, but rising to the top in that context, or in any theatrical context, is Teresa Ralli. The first time I watched her act, she sourced herself in ways that were either unfamiliar to me or from which I had previously seen only confusing acting emerge. She was breathtaking. To say any less would deny the transcendence of her work. Teresa Ralli is among the best actors I will ever see. Her process both inspires and manages a mighty flow of creativity.

As a company dedicated to political and social theater, Grupo Yuyachkani was logically drawn to the work of masters such as Grotowski, Barba, and Brecht. As their work developed, they began to draw on performance techniques that would enable them to engage audiences in public settings, like streets and squares. Tai chi, kathakali and Balinese dance forms, and the music and dance of their Peruvian culture informed this work. Each member of the company strove to become a "multiple actor: a thinking actor who sings, dances, and plays musical instruments."

Her interview offers a detailed way of harnessing creativity, focusing energy, working with the voice, body, and imagination and imagery as a powerful unit, without reliance on emotions. She is vigilant about the limitations she experiences when she allows either her emotions or the spoken word tyrannical reign

*in shaping her acting. To work away from this, she developed com-
plex strategies that she practices daily.*

*From the stringent rules of subjective and objective re-
search that Teresa Ralli describes in this interview comes work that
is open to all of the voices within the actor. An astonishing array of
clear human expression emerges. She stresses her need to explore
structures with hard and fast rules. Out of this comes mastery; out
of mastery flows unleashed creativity and true expression; out of
unfettered creativity and expression grows the master's ability to
redefine the rules.*

"I RESPECTED THE RULES THAT I PLACED ON MYSELF; I PRACTICED THEM SO MUCH THAT THEY ALLOWED ME TO GO BEYOND. ONCE I FIND THE ANSWER BEHIND THE RULES, I CAN BEGIN TO CONSTRUCT NEW RULES."

When I started as an actress in the company
Grupo Yuyachkani, I didn't know anything. I didn't study in a theater school. Our
first work sprang from themes, messages we wanted to
give to the audience. As we matured as a group, we realized we needed technique. That first, highly charged approach to technique was directed toward the need to
explain issues clearly in performance. As our lives and
our study as a group became more complex, we realized
that we had to go deeper into the handling of theater
tools, and we opened ourselves to other influences. We
took principles of training from the great masters, like

Grotowski and Barba, and began the long task of translating those into our own group reality. Our other research investigations into techniques, like exploring kathakali or Balinese dancing, proved that, at their core, they had the same principles as the dance expressions of our Peruvian culture. We wanted to reinforce the cultural linkage with our audience, and we became conscious that if we constructed images with universal meaning, the ways to link with the culture of our audience would emerge.

The search for audiences outside of the traditional theatrical space led Yuyachkani to new themes and new ideas. As actors, we had to prepare ourselves technically for the new challenges of ideas and space. We needed to be actors capable of projecting our presence in a square, on the street, to a whole community. We developed the concept of a multiple actor; a thinking actor who sings, dances, and plays musical instruments. This is not a unique idea; people in theater in other parts of the world have used it also. Our continued existence as a group has allowed us to research and study permanently. Our ongoing relationship and encounters with great teachers have given us fundamental ideas that we have processed into our group reality. In addition, the research and knowledge of our own culture, the Peruvian culture, has created an identity for us as a group at work. Nevertheless, within this group, each one of us has his or her own vision of what it is to be a multiple actor.

If I am to open my private world to share some of the aspects that constitute my training as an actress, I would divide it in two parts: the general training and the applied training. Applied training is the way in which all the general training functions when I engage myself in the work of a show.

I always start by recognizing my own body, and I try to work on a continuous line. I look for a physical exercise with a fixed structure. By that I mean an exercise unit with a beginning, a development, and an end. When I work with exercises that have fixed structures, I feel like my body has a real, concrete job to do in space. That has helped me a lot because at first my energy was not harnessed or focused. Working with these structured physical exercises, I was able to experience the sequence of movement, which was something new in my work. For the first time I felt, with my body, what it meant to be fully alive in space and time.

The imposition of rules on my training has been critical. The structure of each exercise is its rule. Kids are very free in their play, but for each game they invent, they also invent rules, then they are free to play intensively. You are the doctor, I am the nurse. You throw the ball from there and I'll catch it. If it falls, I lose and you win a point. In theater we need rules as well, even to do free improvisation. There are occasions when one applies rules in order to overcome rules or to invent new rules. Finally, theater is a game of conventions, and that means rules. In time, I discover the soul of the exercise. Only at that point do I allow myself to lead the exercise. Through tai chi, I explored energy in movement. My body and my corporeal memory stored these discoveries. When I go to a new period of research, these lessons in energy in movement emerge as I need them. When I'm faced with a new work, my body starts composing, applying the general technique to the demands of the new idea.

I work with these exercises slowly but intensely. People accept their physical actions; they do them quickly without realizing what they're doing. The complexity involved in learning to go up the stairs is astonishing, but human beings have lost contact with this marvelous complexity. My goal in these exercises is to stop my mind to allow my body to think! In order to do that I have to lower my speed. I've always been fascinated by slow-motion films of runners. They are not actors, they're not representing anything. Nevertheless, they are communicating to me everything that the body is feeling and doing because of their heightened physical awareness.

I've worked with this idea in many ways. For a long time I researched putting on and taking off clothes, slowly and quickly. At first I did it with technical precision, using the least amount of movement. Then I worked slowly but intensely to allow the images that existed behind the movements to appear. Very strong things emerged. Through the absolute concentration of my mind on one thing, the movement, I fully recognized the parts of my body and began traveling into my own history. Images crouch behind each action when I work slowly but intensely.

This research into slowness has two effects. The first is that it provokes in me a state of total alertness in body and mind. The other aspect has to do with performance. When I am inside the process of creation of a piece, creating a character, if I suddenly introduce a moment of slowness but intenseness while doing an everyday action, I allow the spectator a magnifying glass on the action. I reveal an image behind this everyday action, allowing the audience to perceive something deeper.

When we are creating a piece, we always start from the location of an idea. In *Against the Wind*, which is a very powerful show, we started from the idea of the war and violence in my country. But the word in which all of that was concretized was *violence*. We began working in two parallel lines, two tasks. Miguel Rubio, our director, gave us each the task of training onstage around the idea of violence. We were to explore this individually, working side by side onstage. The other task was reading and researching on the societal events pertaining to violence. We call this part of the process of creation "sensitive accumulation" or "accumulation of sensation." When we begin, we don't know what we are going to achieve. We observe all types of information. A book, an article, or subjective information; what you feel on the street when you see a face, information from your own secret box, the personal images that come to you when you are working. All that is processed onstage when we are rehearsing. That's where I get my images, and they turn into surfboards on which I glide.

In the process of *Against the Wind* one image that arose for me was the image of traveling; feet that were always walking, always running; people running away from war; searching for a safe place to stay; people constantly migrating inside their own country. Along with the feet came the image of a piece of cloth, and I couldn't let go of it. At the beginning, it was the cloth where women bundled everything, even their kids. Then I began exploring cloths of larger sizes. That cloth became a black hole in which I hid, but ultimately drowned. It became the piece of earth that I took with me from my home. It was a mountain to traverse. It was my piece of house. It was a thousand things. What happens at that point is that I made connections between these images. And of course Miguel was always watching and, later, sequencing the images. Another image that arose was one we saw on television and on newspapers: plastic bags containing the bodies of the dead. It wove a bridge between our contemporary world and the way ancient Peruvians enfolded people in funerary shrouds. A huge cloth appeared that turned into the image of the mountains of Peru, and from them the dead emerged, returning to the living to speak. What I'm trying to say is that this process by which one image turns into a gesture or into an object or into a repeated action is not orderly. Images which intuitively come forward in the first task begin establishing connections with the conscious, logical task.

Certain images carry with them a strong emotional charge. But there are images that, without losing their power to communicate, are only images. I work more with images than emotions, because I believe that with a complex image the emotion will surface. I do not search for emotion. I learned that it was better to work with images because when I used to work my voice through emotions, the adrenaline did not allow me to manage my sonic riverbanks. That doesn't mean that I regret my emotions when they come. I allow them to be there. I allow them to go out to the audience. I just don't use my emotions to produce my work. As an audience member, I have watched actors suffering onstage, and that provoked in me a very strong sense of distancing. I asked myself, "Why is he crying so much? What is the problem?" If the actor gives himself over to his emotions, it doesn't allow any room for the audience. It takes away all possibility of their being moved. Instead, I try to achieve poetry. What is poetry? Discourse over the abstraction and the unity of images in a very simple way. That is what I'm searching for onstage.

I think that I am very intuitive. I have, inside myself, a fight between the path of logic and the path of sensitivity, but always the sensitive path is the winner. It has cost me a lot to come to terms with this. In the first stage of my work and life, it was critical to have the message absolutely clear. Therefore, all my motivating images had a very strong social accent. Over time that has changed. That doesn't mean that I exclude the social or political now. Still, for me, the most important aspect of a show is its idea. But there is more for me now. I like to provoke in any spectator the sense that it is marvelous to be human, and that it is possible to know oneself with others. It is possible to learn to give and receive affection. That is at the foundation as to why I will always do theater. But I also have very secret images that sometimes even I cannot understand. They are very subjective. It's as if I have a lot of people inside me who need their moment to come out. My childhood seems to be stimulating me a lot lately, and I don't know why. Images that hide strong emotional charges are always coming up as I work now. I allow them to come out just a little bit, then I put them back again. I don't regret them, but I care for them and protect them. I tend to be more hermetic in my everyday life than onstage. Onstage I'm another person. As time goes by, I'll be able to set these images and experiences of my life in their proper place.

The vocal training works in more or less the same stages as the physical. I can search for voice in two modes: organic voice and vocal interpretation. Before I can interpret vocally I first have to find my true voice, which is part of my body. Throughout our lives our voice has dominion over our body. Everything that we say, from very simplest to the biggest concepts, has the body at its service. Sometimes its tyranny is so complete that it turns the body off completely and we exist as talking heads. Our job in theater is to create a strong impression with both the voice and the body. I have tried to find techniques that contradict the patterns of real life, in other words, where the body simulates the voice.

Voice is the most profound expression of our being. If I don't breathe, I don't live. Sound is breath. The true voice emerges from the deepest part of our body and moves us back to our farthest subconscious. That's why I believe that in order to work the voice, we have to be really cold and set strict rules for ourselves. At the beginning I had to engage in a cold, technical exploration to work my voice without allowing my emotions to stifle it. Respecting those rules allowed me to know my own body's sound, a voice unbound by emotion and convention. Only then could I allow myself the freedom to improvise with words, allowing my images and emotions to emerge vocally.

I gave myself rules and a structure in order to confront the sound of my voice with the sound of my body. An example of this would be to do three tai chi movements, slowly and intensely, while speaking a poem or monologue. For example, I can use "To be or not to be" and allow the tai chi postures to shape the sound. This exercise, which freed me of my limited constraints of meaning and emotion, opened the door in my research to investigate my profound, true voice. While you do this, you must not be afraid of the sound or the images that your own voice brings. Training of my body teaches me to break my everyday physical structure, and training of my voice provokes me to break my everyday way of speaking. The structure that I rely upon to speak in life is distinct from my true voice. If there were an electrocardiogram for the voice, an "electrovoicegram," it would affirm that one's way of speaking reveals one's past, one's history, one's historical conflicts.

When I'm training, I invent ways to imitate other vocal structures. There is a relationship between imitating other voices and finding your own voice. This exercise is directed toward understanding my own structure, breaking it, and expanding it. One set of structures I have worked with is street calls. People in my country sing out the things they sell on the street. *"Me-l-l-l-l-l-o-ns! Me-l-l-l-l-l-o-ns!"* I observed how they placed their voices to shout in different ways and how they placed their bodies in order to accomplish it. Because of the distancing I must achieve to imitate another's voice, it brings me closer to discovering my own voice. In other words, the avenue of imitating voices does not engage me personally, and when I achieve that imitation, it gives me a greater trust to know my own. And always, the primary basis of the search is to respond vocally to my body's impulses. That relationship is enhanced by imitation.

Another field that was very useful in researching the voice was singing. With singing I rediscovered the value of breathing. What I did was to join the search for breathing with my body search, following the notion that voice, breathing, and body are a total element. I assimilated singing exercises in my training. It is very important to me to keep my voice as a solid thing that can traverse space and time. Then, voice can execute action. Of course, to sing is also a pleasure! It allows the entrance of musical structures as part of my research. I learn a song in the same way I learn a tai chi exercise. I enter the musical structure, I learn it, I explore it, and then I am free to leave it. I did a show based on the songs of Bertolt Brecht, and it was very hard for me to detach myself from those great, historic monuments of the theater, the performances of Lotte Lenya or Helene Weigel. In order to detach myself from them I listened to them repeatedly and drove myself totally into the way they sang. After that, I could separate myself from them and find my own way into that musical structure. I respected the rules that I placed on myself; I practiced them so much that they allowed me to go beyond. Once I find the answer behind the rules, I can begin to construct new rules. Then I am free to visit all the vocal houses.

Another form of research I engage in is the investigation of elements [scenic or property elements]. I can work with a stick, a chair, or with a pair of high-heeled shoes, but I always give myself concrete rules. Working with objects allows other images to present themselves to me. *[This process is closely related to the technique of "breaking down" an object to which John Turturro refers. Teresa Ralli approaches it as a physical exploration out of which imaginative and personal discoveries are made.]* I often do this when I am in the process of creating a new show or simply when I am feeling bored in a part of my training. After I play a lot with the object, I allow that object to enter my eyes and then my whole body. Images arise which I can then fulfill. From these can come the beginning of a character.

We are currently engaged in a new show. The theme we are exploring is waiting. We have a chair. We have explored the chair in many ways: acrobatically, feeling its weight and volume in space; working with its silence and its sounds. One day, Miguel gave us the task of finding twenty ways of being seated in a chair. The technical starting point was finding those twenty ways. I then began working with them in a continuous sequence, working at first for precision. Then I experimented with changes of rhythm and tempo. My images started to emerge, and what I was doing with the chairs began to have meaning. That began the development of possible dramatic material, which Miguel is processing. The point when our research begins creating scenic meaning is when it stops being training and it starts becoming dramatic.

In the first stage of my life as an actress, I constructed characters that would be defined fundamentally by a social profile. In our first show, called *Copper Fist,* we all performed miners and workers. The only moment that I performed a woman, I don't think I even noticed the difference. At that time of my life and the times in which I was living, there was no room for going deep into the individual as a character, either masculine or feminine. When my vision of life and theater became more complex, I started understanding that in order to speak about life in general, I had to spring from particular characters. I discovered the pleasure of composing the human profile of a character. That is also when I started working with my feminine aspect. It began when I decided to do the Brecht songs. Yuyachkani was doing a collective, big show, but as my son was only four months old, I could not work on their schedule. So, I decided to do a show with me alone onstage for the first time. In the process, I realized that a majority of the songs that I had chosen had the gaze of women. I feel women have a gaze, another angle from which they look at things. Perhaps it was the way that I was responding to the songs and processing them that led me to find their feminine gaze. It was a process from which I learned a lot, and I am still thinking about it.

I find that I don't have the need to reinforce the sexual aspect when I'm representing a female character. I am enjoying sensuality rather than sexuality onstage, and in my life as well. For many years I only wore pants because I had to be a strong woman, but recently I've discovered the pleasure of wearing a skirt in my life and onstage. When we began the new project, the one about waiting, something happened to me on the first day. I decided to put on a slip and I didn't know why. Soon, I gave all our female actors slips. It was an instinctive gesture. I realized that I was expressing my need to show a part of my private feelings, which is to show my own fragility. Being in the clothes that I have on at home when nobody's watching is making me work my body in a different quality. There are subtleties and a delicacy, a fragility of gesture I assume onstage. I think it is a reflection of where I am in my life. I am beginning to feel serene in my loneliness, without having to show a lot of strength because I am a divorced woman. I feel how my life and what I'm looking for onstage are feeding each other. I am starting to give material about my own loneliness onstage, which is something I wouldn't have talked about in any other show before. I have to achieve a moment in which that particular loneliness of mine can say something meaningful to the spectator. In order for that to happen, I, as a female, human being, have to feel free to speak about my own weaknesses.

What does it mean to be free to act? In spite of carrying around all these images and ideas inside, it is to have the feeling that I am a perfect white sheet of paper on which I cannot write, but can paint and draw what I wish and, then, return and recompose myself once again. That is the instance of freedom. I believe that for almost everything I feel free. I say almost everything because nothing is absolute. There is probably something that I'll encounter tomorrow.

Joe Mantello's performance in the demanding role of Louis in Angels in America *was superb. He came to this role still sorting out the enigmas of acting. Must the actor experience pain in order to convey pain? Does the actor have to be the character? Is it permissible to have moments on stage not motivated by genuine vulnerability? How does an actor find a separation between the theatrical event and himself that will allow him to survive the experience? The actor playing Louis must endure a great deal of suffering as both the actor and the character, not the least of which is caused by the audience's perception of the character as hateful. How does the actor struggle against his desire to be liked? How can he use the audience's feelings of disgust instead of being victimized by them?*

Joe Mantello has found answers to address these challenges that often diverge from what he was taught in graduate school. He's developed a process that enables him to be in the moment, but not to carry the burden of that moment into his life. This discovery harkens back to childhood: his acting is allowed to be play. And, after sorting through all of the conflicting lessons he learned in school, he has begun to work like himself.

In keeping with the theme of his interview, Joe Mantello struggles less with his process as the director of the acclaimed Love! Valour! Compassion! *and* Three Hotels, *an art in which he has no formal training, than he does with his acting. He finds trusting his directorial instincts a much simpler matter, even in the face of criticism. There are several reasons for this, but one most certainly is that he has no contradictory voices in his head to tell him how to go about it. As a director, Joe Mantello is free to go with his instincts. So far he hasn't come up against a problem that he lacks the intuitive techniques to solve.*

"FOR MANY YEARS I THOUGHT THAT ACTING HAD TO BE PAINFUL."

The whole notion of drama school is so strange to me. I think it's absolutely essential and it also completely fucked me up for five years. At North Carolina School of the Arts the training was really eclectic. We had a Russian clown teaching his techniques, we had teachers trained in Meisner, and all of these British people. There was a constant bombardment of techniques, each canceling the other out. I didn't know how to reconcile what I was taught with actual, practical experience. As a director I've seen actors who are so bound by theory and by a kind of classroom mentality that it blocks inspiration. So many American actors have been trained to do nothing until they feel it. Meanwhile, the rest of us could all die waiting until they do. It's like, "Watch this space. More to follow." It's the end of the run, and finally, they're reaching for the heavens!

I'm starting to be a big believer in simply doing what the text asks. If it says cry, just cry and see where that takes you. I don't always have that kind of instantaneous access to my emotions, so I've had to figure out another approach to get into it. Of course, if the gesture I begin with has real scope, then I better damn well fill it or I'm going to look like an asshole. And that's the one thing you can count on about actors: they don't want to look like assholes so they're going to find a way. For instance, in the first part of *Angels in America* there is a scene which opens with my character, Louis, on the floor of the men's room, sobbing. I look at that description and think, "Okay, maybe I can figure it out and ground it in a personal reality." In the meantime what I've forgotten is that I'm stage right and have to run to stage left, underneath the stage, where the dresser's waiting. I completely change my costume, hop onto the platform which slides out onto the stage, and then I sob. There's no time to go, "My mother, my father, my childhood!"—all of those great things you do in class where you have the luxury of time and preparation before you start a scene. There are times when that's just not practical. The lights are up and I have to be sobbing. What do I do? I fake it. That's what drama school didn't tell me. It's okay to fake it. I don't have to feel it. I, Joe Mantello, don't have to be devastated. In fact, it's probably better if I'm not because I could be so comfortable sobbing that I stop reaching out to the other actor. I wish someone had said that to me in acting school because it's absolutely true.

I'm embarrassed to tell you what I do to make myself sob. It's a combination of absolutely cheap tricks and work with gesture. When I finish dressing and I'm running out of the quick-change room, I splash water on my face so that it feels wet to me. I get onto the platform with maybe five seconds before the platform comes out, and I start to breathe in the way I breathe when I sob. Then I approximate the sound that I make when I cry that hard.

As long as I don't attach a judgment to what I'm doing, like this is fake or good or bad or real, I'm free to fill the gesture.

I have to tell you that there are also moments every night in this play where I cry real tears, especially in the scene when I come back into the hospital room to tell Prior that I want to come back to him. Stephen Spinella, who plays Prior, and I have been doing this play together for quite a long time, and I just look at him and am overwhelmed with feelings for him. For those moments onstage we, as actors, share the intimacy that those characters share. On days when we do both parts of *Angels in America* [Millennium Approaches *and* Perestroika] together, I think back to moments we experienced earlier that afternoon in the matinee, and it seems like we've been through so much. We've accumulated so much pain and heartbreak over those seven hours that I can readily release into it.

For many years I thought that acting had to be painful. However, it was only painful in the sense that, because I was trying to make it painful, it wasn't working. *That* was painful! But I've realized that I can actually enjoy what I'm doing. I can be very serious about it, very focused and entertaining, but it can actually be fun. I am just playing. It's a play. When I play and let it be a play, that's when things like surrendering to pretending to cry make sense to me. Because I'm playing. In the final moment of the scene in the beginning of act 2 of *Millennium*, Prior's on the floor of our bathroom, bleeding, and he passes out. I go sobbing to the heavens and the panels close, lights out, end of scene. Then I say to Stephen, "Get up, crybaby!" and we laugh, running down to the changing room. We change costume and come back onstage and we play. If I only lived the reality of this show night after night without allowing myself to play, I wouldn't be around right now. Actually, I've been finding that the thing that keeps me most alive is playing before we go on-stage. I run around in my underwear getting made up and visiting everyone and just having a great time. Then, when I go onto that stage, even if I'm doing something that's hard or devastating, I'm still playing and I can commit to it in that spirit. I've found a way to adapt, though I can't imagine it would work for everybody.

Now in my work I throw caution to the wind and see what happens. But the good thing about me is that even though I dive in and flail around, when I hit upon something that I think works, I know how to retrieve it. When Prior reveals the lesion to me at the beginning of the play, the script says Louis collapses, breaks down in tears. So how do I do that? We did it a couple of times and I had stayed with him, connecting with him, and it wasn't working. Then, we did it and it happened for me. I went back and analyzed it. I discovered that I had physically touched him, saying, "It's just a burst blood vessel," and he says, "No, it isn't." Then, I turned away from him and pushed the lesion away from me as he said, "Look at it." I was using everything I had to pretend that everything was fine, that it was going to be okay, and knowing, at the same time, that our lives were irrevocably altered.

The nature of Louis and Prior's relationship changed between the Los Angeles and New York productions, largely owing to George Wolfe's brilliant understanding of the characters and the play. He felt, and I agreed, that in the L.A. production, Prior was not culpable in the breakup of their relationship. He was saintly and Louis was an asshole—it's actually more complex,

JOE MANTELLO

but that's the gist of it. To address that problem, George had Prior do a gesture following his revelation of the lesion which says, "I'm keeping this for myself because I'm afraid you're going to leave. I'm not going to share information with you, and when I do, I'm going to overload you completely with physical and verbal images: bleeding, diarrhea, 'the wine-dark kiss of the angel of death.' " In the New York production, Prior's journey with the illness is a very personal one, and his part in the demise of the relationship is that he doesn't give Louis a chance to engage. I thought that was fascinating because in L.A., two pages into the relationship, it was clear that this was the end for these two people. Louis was going to leave Prior, and the audience just waited for that tragedy to play itself out. George asked me to make choices centering on "this is extremely difficult, this is overwhelming, but I love him and I'm going to stay." So, in New York, I made the positive, active choice to work the relationship out—until I couldn't do it anymore.

George talked about there being a third entity in bed with us. There was Louis and Prior and there was the disease, and we couldn't find a way to make that new, triangular relationship work. Then he put it into concrete terms which we could bring onstage. He said that every relationship has rules and asked us to define the rules that existed between Prior and Louis before the lesion. The rules were Prior takes care of Louis; Louis gets to act up like a child and Prior makes him feel better. Well, what happens to this relationship when the rules change? All of a sudden Prior says, "Now you take care of me." I found that playable. We have those two pages to establish the history of the relationship between these people who have lived together for four years. You will never see them like that ever again. Concentrating on that also freed me up to play my response to the revelation of the lesion. I didn't have to play that down the line I was going to leave him; I just had to play "this isn't true." Then at the end of the scene I can really play, "I'm going to come back and I'm going to make this work."

When I'm having trouble as an actor, it's likely that I'm trying to make the moment about too much. I'm embroidering it with physical details, character things. I'm in my little world playing Louis, but I've stopped playing the scene. Then I remember that the answer is probably to be as simple as possible. I'll give you an example. There's a scene I have with the nurse in *Millennium,* when Prior is asleep in a hospital bed. To this day, after almost two years, I'm still working on that scene. What happened was that I was playing devastation or exhaustion, I was crying, and I wasn't actually in the room with that woman. Even though it is in that scene that Louis leaves Prior, that event is not the actual bones of the scene. The scene exists between Louis and the nurse! It wasn't until we were in performance that I actually realized that. Ellen McLaughlin and I are still figuring out how to play the scene between us and how to take that stuff that I'm feeling and put it into our interaction.

So many people that Louis comes in contact with judge him: the rabbi, Belize, and the nurse. Louis is looking to be judged. Tony Kushner, the playwright, and I always saw Louis as wearing oversized boy clothes that he could disappear into when things got hard, when he was being judged. I actually sort of hide in my clothes in life, and it's been fascinating to explore its meaning. Louis is swimming in his clothes. They make him look like he just wouldn't grow up. If I have an image of what the character looks like early on, then I can start working within it. In rehearsal I always wore an overcoat or a scarf that I made sure was too big for me. I found that it informed the acting choices I made and it helped me to personalize things.

The hardest part of doing this play is to risk being unlikable. In *Millennium* the audience is able to suspend judgment on Louis. There are enough people who identify with his journey to concede that there are sympathetic and likable things about him. He's just unable to deal with what life has dealt him. But in *Perestroika* there is a point, every night, where judgment kicks in—and I feel it. Because I took it personally as an actor, it was devastating at first. Consequently, I backed away from some of the choices I had made in an effort to be more likable. I made him less difficult in the attempted reconciliation scene between Prior and Louis on the park bench. I backed off being absolutely as hard on him as he's being on me. But George said the most brilliant thing to me, and I remind myself of it on the nights when it gets hard. "You have to dare to do unspeakable things in that scene because then your journey back and your redemption are greater. You have to go down there and risk them not liking you in that scene and for several scenes to follow. You have to risk feeling awful when the audience applauds Prior when he says, 'Fuck you, you little shit bag.' " And nearly every night they do applaud. So, when judgment is passed on Louis by the audience, even though it's hard to take, I let their feelings of disgust up Louis's stakes even more. I make my case more forcefully. I have to believe I have a case; I've got all these rationales for Louis's actions, and I don't judge him. I remind myself every night that they don't hate Joe, I'm not a bad actor. These are the demands of the character and I have to fulfill them. Anything less than a full commitment is being unfair to the play.

Despite the emotional difficulty I face in taking that risk, it's easy to entrust myself to confident, good directors. If I feel like they're going to take care of me, as George has, I will completely surrender to them. Anne Bogart directed me in a play called *The Baltimore Waltz* by Paula Vogel, which we did at Circle Rep. I loved her so much and I believed that she believed in what she was saying. Even though she wanted to work in a way I never thought I would work, I went with her. She wasn't making anything up out of whole cloth, she wasn't doing it for effect. This was how she saw the play. She worked very physically, she was very precise, but the process had absolutely nothing to do with the way in which I was used to working. There was no breaking down scenes, no talking about the relationships of the characters. For instance, she did this fascinating exercise in which she said, "Come up with five tableaux that represent moments in the scene. They can be realistic or abstract." If the scene were based on you interviewing me, one tableau would be my pulling away from you in alarm, resisting your questions. The three actors immediately started asking a million questions, but she said, "Come up with five tableaux—whatever that means to you. I'm going to go out of the room for five minutes, and when I come back, you'll show them to me." And out she went! I didn't know the other two actors, and we were kind of giggling and uncomfortable. "Well, for this part of the scene one tableau might be you standing like this and me doing that. That's one. Now I'll do this and and you do this. That's two." She came back five minutes later and she said, "Show them to me." We did them. I said to myself, "What the fuck is going on?" Then she said, "Great. Get into tableau number one. Now, just start the scene." And we're doing the scene. She said, "Go to two." We all switched into two and continued doing the scene. "Go back to one. Now go to five." A strange theatrical event started emerging, like alchemy. It was really fascinating. Even though I didn't know what we were doing at first, I could surrender to her process and play because she's so bright and so decent and confident.

Having said all of this about acting I realize that my sense of structure is more conscious than I will probably even want to admit. We've been talking mostly about *Angels in America* because for the last two years that's what I've been acting in, but I've also been directing—sometimes concurrent with my performing. Somehow the director Joe is directing the actor Joe all the time, and they're having this conversation that I am not consciously aware of. If I were to analyze it, I might be able to say this is why I can direct one play and act in another during the same period of time. That director/actor conversation has been held in my head all of my life, so I don't even listen to it anymore; it feels like instinct. One informs the other so I don't see them as two separate entities. If I'm working with a good director, I shift out of that part of me that makes me want to direct—the part desirous of controlling the overall vision. Then, somewhere on the train ride to the other theater in which I'm directing, I have to assume responsibility for that vision, for communicating a world to other actors.

I feel like I'm entering an interesting phase of my life. I'm more confident and creative than I ever have been. I'm not really interested in making choices that will please people or that are "right." As a director I feel comfortable listening to my instincts. Even if I don't really know why I've made a particular choice or why I want the sofa to be red, I trust that somehow it will reveal itself to me. I wish I felt more that way about my work as an actor. If I think that I've achieved what I want to achieve as a director, I don't really care what anybody says—my mother, Frank Rich, anybody. As an actor I'm still so vulnerable to the slightest comment. When I started directing, I could hide behind the fact that I was really "just an actor." If it wasn't good, there was a reason why: I was "just an actor." Now I take myself more seriously. I still have a bit of a sense that I'm visiting the world of the real directors, but that illusion is getting harder and harder to support.

MATTHEW SUSSMAN

The ethic "the show must go on" has become a cliché by virtue of its accuracy. It drives the mechanics of theater to a degree that would surprise nontheater people. That it is built into the business side of show business is easily understood, but it also propels much of the creative process. The play is "ready" on opening night, "ready or not." The actors and director have a predetermined rehearsal period, and they gauge their development accordingly.

At the intersection between the business and creative sides of theater lies the role of the understudy. Principal actors can get sinus infections or break legs or die, and the understudy is the essential system backup. As such, the understudy goes virtually unnoticed until the emergency light flashes. Suddenly he is the single most important person in the theater.

In his interview, Matthew Sussman speaks about the "meta-acting" process of the understudy. How does a talented actor who has not benefited by participating in a rehearsal process, but has merely observed one, reach his performance? How can he make certain that it possesses the integrity of being grounded in an emotional reality and, at the same time, honors the performance text evolved by the regular company? Where does acting begin and imitation leave off? Freud said that civilization was "created under the pressure of the exigencies of life at the cost of satisfaction of the instincts." The same can be said about the role of the understudy. Is the understudy allotted the joy of *implementing and experiencing his creativity, which is a fundamental perquisite of acting?*

Matthew Sussman had never understudied before, and he had never appeared on Broadway. He found himself in what had to be the theatrical event of the decade, understudying Ron Leibman (Roy Cohn) and Joe Mantello (Louis) in the Broadway production of Angels in America. *He is a graduate of the acting program of the Yale School of Drama, has appeared and starred in regional theater productions, on television and in several films. He is also a screenwriter, having collaborated with Anna Cascio and David Thornton.*

His interview is one of the most enlightening in the book. His struggle to have an acting process implies how essential process is to performance.

"FOR THE UNDERSTUDY, TWO TEXTS EXIST: THE WRITTEN WORD AND THE PERFORMANCE TEXT THE ACTORS ARE DOING EACH NIGHT."

I was told at 6:45 P.M. that I'd go on that night as Roy Cohn in *Angels in America*. Ron Leibman had a sinus infection, and on top of that, he was having side effects from the antibiotics. He was drained and weak and his system was out of whack. The doctors decided he would have to take the rest of that week off. I went on for him for those five days. Then the producers said I was going to do the matinees until further notice.

As Joe Mantello's and Ron Leibman's understudy, I was already scheduled to stand in for a full week as Louis and a full week as Roy during their vacations. Who would play Roy in the matinees the week I was supposed to go on for Louis? That was a close call. Ultimately, Ron realized that it was going to hurt the show and was able to push himself to do those two matinees. So that he could have a couple of days off, I picked up his Saturday-night performance the week before and Monday-night performance the week after. So, I closed my week as Louis on Saturday, had Sunday off and went in as Roy on Monday. The real gymnastic feat would have been playing Roy in the afternoon with someone else coming in on an emergency basis for Louis, and then switching over to play Louis myself that night! Luckily, it didn't come to that.

Anyway, this summer I've gone on more than thirty times between these two roles, and it's certainly had a positive effect on my confidence to work under challenging circumstances. Specifically, when I started the job, I felt pressured both by how challenging the roles themselves were and by the excellence of the actors I was covering. It was rather overwhelming, and I wondered how I was going to achieve a credible level of performance without the benefit of the wonderful and lengthy rehearsal process these actors had. Many of the actors in the Broadway production had done the play before, so they were already well grounded in their characters and the arc of the play. Then they had the added and rather extraordinary benefit of working with George Wolfe in New York. How was I ever going to attain a performance level so that I could hold my own in this ensemble? I was concerned with everything from playing the throughline for each of these very different characters to finding the emotional truth moment to moment; things one normally gets through rehearsal. The actors' emotional investment is very, very high in *Angels in America*. It's not something you can just finesse. It was clear that it was going to have to be found for real. As I got started, the gap between where I sat watching the company rehearse and what I would have to achieve seemed like an impossible gulf to cross.

Ultimately I improvised the process. I approached it more or less as a patchwork, stitching together the elements. In all, I'd say it worked well enough that, for example, the recent week I went on as Louis, I was happy with where I got in my performance. It was a solid beginning. I never felt the work was fully developed or finished. How could it be? But it went well, George and the company were pleased, and I enjoyed the performances very much. Honestly, I never knew if I was ready to go on by the time the occasion arose, but I was ready, or as ready as you can be, I guess. Realizing that helped me have faith that I was working in the right way. Even as an understudy, without the benefit of a director, a real rehearsal process, and repeated performances, it's still possible to come up with something if you do the preparation and leap in boldly. That leaping part is particularly important I think. You can't feel your way around tentatively.

One of the understudy's main challenges is finding the balance between being in a predetermined framework and doing your own acting. Another is, how do I step out on a Broadway stage without a fully rehearsed character? One thing that's been invaluable in dealing with both these problems has been working extensively with my coach, Tim Phillips. With him, I've had the chance to work on the characters and the scenes in a slow, methodical way that's really helped me find my way. He appreciated the fact that I have to fit into an already crafted production so that our work together is connected to *this* show. A lot of my real preparation, my most meaningful rehearsal, has been done in Tim's studio.

Back at the theater I do give a lot of credit to a very good stage manager, who rehearsed the understudies. But let's be honest; the production is not the stage manager's vision nor does the stage manager usually have the kind of working vocabulary that an actor and director share. We had a wonderful company of understudies, but rehearsing once or twice a week with actors with whom you won't actually be playing can only net so much.

An essential part of the predetermined framework is the rhythm the actors have established in a scene. I'm a pretty good imitator of people's rhythms and not just as an actor. I find that sometimes I involuntarily change my rhythm according to whom I'm talking with. So anyway, absorbing the rhythm wasn't a problem. Making that rhythm specific for me so that I knew what that rhythm was about was the challenge. When George Wolfe came to see me perform, he would ask things like, "What is behind that relentless rhythm of Roy's? What drives him?" One of the essential elements of acting is physicalizing specific, internal aspects, but in this case I already had the physical model of the character first from watching Ron. I had to work backwards in a way. Roy Cohn is a very vivid character. The organ in this creature that is beyond normal proportions is his brain. I had this image of it as one of those oversized science-fiction alien craniums from an old 1950s movie. Everything happens there. His intelligence, the belief that he is smarter than everybody else, is his comfort, his tool, and his weapon. In the course of the play you see him at full brainpower and then watch him struggle as it weakens. With this character, this is not an intellectual concept. It's physical. Roy is constantly moving forward because his brain moves faster than the rest of the world. When he's saying or doing one thing, he's already started the next. George clearly pointed out to me the specifics of this in the first scene in the office. Roy has his hand over the receiver and he's telling Joe that the judge, whose wife he's talking to on the phone, is a geek, and before he's finished saying that he's already back talking to the wife and asking her what show she wants to see. Unlike a normal person, he deals with the next task almost without finishing the first. He's talking to you, listening to you, and absorbing what you say before you're finished. That's actable and it absolutely dictates a rhythm. When Roy pauses, it's for a very specific, clear reason. Otherwise, he essentially never stops. Later in the play when he's struggling with his illness, he has to stop and start. Previously, I would sometimes get notes from the stage manager in understudy rehearsals like, "Drive through, drive through." Yes, you do that, but you just work up a sweat unless you know why. I had some sense of the reason behind the drive, but once it became clear, it was fun to play rather than exhausting. But this happened only after I started performing. This understanding of the performance rhythms was one of the last things to fall into place.

I'll give you a good illustration of this. When we started our understudy rehearsals, we had all watched company rehearsals for weeks and seen many performances of the show. Then it was like, "Okay, guys, start acting *Angels.*" For the first couple of weeks of understudy rehearsals, there was a concerted individual effort on everyone's part to play the roles differently. It was partly impulsive but partly a conscious decision as well.

The stage manager said, "You know, you really have to pick that up there." And the actor's response was, "I know I do. I'll get to that, but right now I really need to get that other voice out of my head. Otherwise it'll just be an imitation." The rhythms and values of the scenes were all over the place, but it was an important part of our odd process. Eventually, what happened for me, in part because I had to start going onstage so often, was that once I began to get out from under the sense that the only way to say these lines was the way someone else did, I started to allow myself to embrace some of Ron's wonderful choices which work so well for the character and the show. The difference was I finally felt free to do so rather than feeling that I had to. The difference is subtle, but it's the difference between making something your own and copying someone else. I got the bonus of drawing on some of the great choices these terrific actors had made, and I finally felt I could use the choice because I had a sense of the character. It's not the same as creating a character from scratch, but it does make filling in more satisfying.

One of the realities of this particular job, one of the techniques of understudying, is to grab the things that work for you that the actor is doing. In fact a lot of the "direction" you get is what the other actor does and who the actor is. You absorb an essence of them and the things they do that work for you. Then, if you go on enough, you begin to say to yourself, "I can drop that. I don't need it. I've got something else." For instance, as Roy I tried to maintain some intimacy with Joe in the bar scene. I looked for more unbroken physical contact with him than Ron did. This worked better for me. It's a scene about being older, about fathers and sons. Ron does that scene great, but I can't bring the weight of age to it. I tried as much as I could to stay with Joe, to keep it close, keep the connection going. I look to see what effect I'm having on him. I look for signs that he's bonding to me. In so many of the scenes, Roy's in his own orbit, but in that scene it was important for me to feel like I was making real contact; it was a human-scale seduction. For me it was an effort to let Joe know that I could be there for him, that I could really listen to him and that I could share something of my background and personal life with him. I'm not sure that was the most successful scene for me or not, but I use it as an example because I felt I had a different approach to it than Ron.

On the other hand, certain vocal properties and physical gestures have become part of the text. For the understudy, two texts exist: the written word and the performance text the actors are doing each night. That performance text is like a transparency laid over the written text. There are comic or dramatic beats that have developed through the idiosyncrasies of the actor and his approach to the character, in collaboration with the other actors and the director. For instance, in the bar scene, Roy talks about being family, "la familia," and then, just at the top of what looks like a hearty embrace, Ron mimed shooting Joe in the head with his finger like a Mafia execution. That's a big laugh in the show. It's not in Tony Kushner's text, but the gesture, the laugh—the whole beat—has become part of the scene, and I adopted it with my own tiny bit of variation.

In understudying the role of Louis I did not have to transform myself as totally as I did for Roy. Roy Cohn is a great, highly theatrical role and I loved doing it. But it was a twenty-five-year age stretch and a very different temperament than my own. But Louis, challenging as it is on its own terms, in terms of who I am right now and who the character is, is a good match. I really could not ask for more. So, while I admire Joe Mantello's performance enormously and do craft a lot of the rhythms and timing along his model, in some ways he has had less influence on me in the sense that I could bring more of myself to the role. I was more able to leave myself alone and just be. When you feel right for a role, it really carries you along. Especially with writing as actable and rich as Tony Kushner's.

Still, in the understudy position as it is, there were scenes I felt intimidated by before having had a chance to play in front of an audience. I understood the men's-room scene, but it's technically tricky and very quick. I love Joe's work in that scene with his switches from moment to moment. First he's sobbing and then he turns very flirtatious. Joe is very loose and precise in the switches, and I wasn't sure how I'd make that work for me. But I had to and I did finally become physically comfortable with it. Louis allows himself to become more flamboyant, more effeminate around Joe than he allows himself to be around Prior. He allows himself to take on a different, more openly sexual role. I thought that was really a great behavioral thing that Joe had discovered about Louis, and I've tried to incorporate that.

People often want to know if the sexual preference issue is a problem for me. It really isn't. For one thing I always feel that unlike a lot of men my age, I'm very strongly and openly emotionally bonded to my close male friends. I'm drawn to a lot of the same things in men that I think women are. Finding an aspect in myself to relate to men isn't an alien experience. I do, however, lack a familiarity with the physical language of homosexuality. There's the big kiss at the end of *Millennium,* and I was never worried my world was going to fall apart when I did it for the first time. I just didn't know what it would feel like to have my mouth on another guy's mouth. As an understudy, even if you rehearse all your scenes, you never experience them in real performance time because you never do a true run-through. When I got to that scene in performance, it just felt like the release was the most natural, inevitable thing to happen. Now I am watching the rehearsals of *Perestroika* and I'm not in the moment of anything. I'm watching them do this new scene, hands all over each other, squeezing this and touching that and smelling each other, and I'm like, "Whoa!" One of the actresses pointed out to me that if I were understudying a role in which I had a really sexy relationship with a woman, then I wouldn't be starting from scratch in a four-week rehearsal process, working through the strange, theatrical intimacy until I felt comfortable with it. I'd be biting my nails if I had to jump into that relationship as an understudy worrying, "How am I going to look really comfortable with this woman?" Intimacy onstage is always a challenge, and you need time to work through it. Joe and David are doing that now. I'll have to deal with it later.

When you talk about why a character does something, you get into subjective interpretive territory. And it is certainly in this area that the understudy is especially limited as an actor. Increasingly, as I live with them more, I have a stronger sense of how I personally connect organically to these characters. I am no longer as beholden to the actors who created them. However, there is little room for my reasons why. I am not there to invent the role. Given the reality that the cast and director have created the performance text I mentioned, there is a double standard that the cast has for understudies as opposed to actors who come in as replacements. There is very little room on the part of the cast for the understudy to bring a different interpretation to a scene. Understudies are likely to get result-oriented notes like, "You have to do that part faster." Whereas, when a replacement comes in, he or she is given a wide latitude to create the role. The actors are more likely to respond to these changes with, "Great. That's interesting. That's exciting. Let's see what we can do with that." That difference is a really hard part of being in this position.

I don't think I would choose to understudy again unless it was economically necessary. It's an incredibly challenging, difficult job and an honorable one. I'm entirely proud to have done this job. But though you are absolutely critical to the life of the production, you can often feel like the unwanted guest at the party. I heard so many times, "You saved the day. You deserve a medal." But an understudy goes from today's hero to tomorrow's inconvenience. It is easy to be viewed as a manifestation of a problem. And it can be disheartening when you go back to not being part of the company after you've gone on often. That's really disorienting, and at times uncomfortable. Especially with a play as inspiring and rewarding to perform as this.

To have covered two extraordinary roles, to have been a part of *Angels in America*'s first Broadway production, to have performed on Broadway so many times this summer, to have been able to put on a gray wig and play a man twenty-five years older than myself in the professional theater, I say to myself, "Wow! I'll never forget this as long as I live." But you pay a big price as an understudy. You have to give up so much of yourself as an actor without getting a great deal back. "Saving the day" and "deserving a medal" is not what acting is about. The job, and joy, of acting is developing and experiencing a role to the fullest extent of your ability. Limiting that experience is painful. In an actor's education understudying is a great thing to do once. I'm glad to have done it, but I'd rather take the lessons I've learned and move on.

ZOE CALDWELL

Zoe Caldwell's acting process is one of excesses: excessive characterization, excessive emotion, excessive activities. In her interview she makes it quite clear that her method stems from fear of exposing herself. Out of the need to palliate this fear comes her unique artistic expression. With disarming frankness she admits to all the defenses that she uses and finally discards en route to her exposure of the character's need and, thereby, of her self. The excesses also hold a key to her ability to take interpretation to its limits and to risk all. She allows herself the grotesque, magnificent, grief-stricken, joyous, and hideous, as colors in her palette. Hers is not a comfortable process, nor are they comfortable performances. They are, however, brilliant and richly human.

Unlike most American actors, Zoe dismisses the idea of analysis of the role. She neither thinks of nor plays actions per se, nor does she decide upon the character's objective. She speaks, instead, of finding a character's "pattern," a seamstress's word that is unique to her. This character's "pattern" is like a Platonic ideal that she must first discern and then give mass and life.

The wellsprings of her performance techniques and philosophy are deep and richly varied. From radio to comedy turns at birthday parties as a child, to repertory theater, to Broadway; from Shakespeare to Whiting to Williams; to Tony Awards for her performances in The Prime of Miss Jean Brodie,

Slapstick Tragedy, *and* Medea; *she learned from other actors, the oldest tradition of theater training. This is, perhaps, why there is excess in her process. Without the support of a specific learned structure an actor must build her own process out of her experience and talent. Proceeding in this intuitive way must sometimes feel like working without a safety net. Zoe Caldwell devises her own net and then finds a way to dispense with it.*

"EVERY NIGHT I PRAY, 'PLEASE, GOD, LET ME JUST BE CATHERINE.' I DON'T PRAY, 'PLEASE, GOD, LET ME GO OUT THERE AND DO SOMETHING EXTRAORDINARY.' JUST LET ME BE CATHERINE. THEN I START THE JOURNEY."

I hadn't acted in seven and a half years before I did Terrence McNally's *A Perfect Ganesh*. I was offered a lot of plays, yes, but nothing I was attracted to; nothing that dealt with what I think theater's purpose is. An acquaintance of mine came backstage after a performance and told me of a horrendous conversation he had had with a family member during which he had felt emotions that made him feel deeply inhuman. But, he said, "Tonight, things were revealed on the stage that made me feel human again." That's what theater is supposed to do. A character that you've become involved with does something that you are not able to do in real life. You feel relieved and connected because you see that your feelings are not inhuman. It is our responsibility to take care of these issues of our humanity in the theater, and I don't think we are doing enough of that.

I had known Terrence McNally for a long time, though never well, but I did admire him. He always has said, "I'm going to write a part for you." Then he said quite categorically that he would write this play, but all he told me was that it was to be about two women from Connecticut who go to India on a vacation. That could be anything, but it sounded as though I'd get a lot of laughs, and because I'm usually the heavy, how wonderful it would be to play comedy! But he never sent me the play.

Then they rang from the Manhattan Theatre Club and said, "Will you come and read Terrence's new play?" I said, "Well, yes, but would you please send it to me so I can read it?" I'm not a very good reader, first, second, or even twentieth go-round. It takes me a long, long time. And they said, "Yes, yes. We'll get it to you." By happenstance, they didn't, and it only arrived on the morning of the reading. When I arrived at the theater, the only thing I knew about the play was that I was to read Catherine. I must say, all of the other actors read beautifully. Frannie Sternhagen read magnificently, and Dominic Cuskern was perfect! I read, stumbling along. "Duh ... cat ... sat ..." But the play made me weep and laugh. At the end of it I said, "I'll do it *if* you still want me." I would never get a part if I had to audition.

I'm sixty and I've been professional for fifty years, and I've only done one audition in my entire life. I was born with a fine-motor-skills disability and I couldn't do small things, like sewing on a button or writing, but my gross motor skills were good, so I could dance. I learned toe, tap, ballet, eurhythmics, all that stuff. When I was seven, my mother decided that maybe it would be a good idea if I learned what was then called elocution. In the suburb where we lived was a woman called Winifred Moverly Browne, who was really an extraordinary voice teacher. She taught politicians and businessmen how to speak, and it wasn't just elocution. She gave me a little audition, my first and last! Then she told Mum how much it would cost, and Mum said, "Well . . . ," she'd have to talk it over with my dad. The Depression had hit and we were very poor. Winifred Moverly Browne said, "Let me take her on spec while you discuss with Mr. Caldwell." And she trained me on scholarship from the age of seven to the age of eighteen. She was a sort of Jean Brodie, but very well adjusted, with a marvelous husband and no children. I suppose I was a kind of surrogate child, although she never laid anything on me. I guess she just wanted to pass on some knowledge. She took me to galleries and gave me books to read, all the stuff that my mum and dad would have done if they'd known about it, but they were busy just making ends meet. Winifred Moverly Browne opened another kind of learning, and she gave me my breathing and my voice. Seven till eighteen, two lessons a week, and vocal exercises to do every day—that's a lot of vocal work! It was all diaphragmatic; the power was all from there.

Finding my true voice in a role is something of a journey in and of itself. When I start rehearsal, for example in *A Perfect Ganesh,* I don't really have a voice at all. I don't want to expose anything because it will be so empty, so lacking in knowledge. Then I go through a period when I blow the character into areas that she shouldn't be, giving too much of everything. I have an enormously high energy level and I push—vocally, too.

When I get a little run on something, I do it to within an inch of its life. For instance, I would make my first entrance not trusting the fact that I have a whole journey to make and a play to make it in. I felt I had to make an impression immediately. I had all the luggage and my first "Oh, for a muse of fire" was enormous, and everything I did was far, far, far too much. This is what I always have to worry about. I need an editor badly. I think when actors reach a certain degree of success, they're cast for exactly what they can bring and then nothing more is asked of them. Or, if they overact, people are loathe to say so. I absolutely need someone to say, "No, no, no!" For years my husband, Robert Whitehead, the producer, who is my best editor, would say, "Zoe, cut it by half. You don't need to work so hard." But I never could understand what he was saying in a way that enabled me to apply it.

That changed when I did *A Long Day's Journey Into Night*. Jason Robards directed at first, then Jose Quintero could only give us two weeks. Robert kept saying, "Get Harold Clurman to direct." I knew Harold very well, but I'd never been directed by him. By the time he came and saw one performance, the play seemed seven hours long! It was pure indulgence beyond belief on everybody's part, and I was doing anything and everything to keep the audience awake. Harold said, "Zoe, let me tell you a story. There was a great actor in the Yiddish theater called Rudolf Schildkraut. He had a son called Joseph Schildkraut, who was just beginning his career in the Yiddish theater. Schildkraut elder went to see Schildkraut junior play his first role. Joseph came on the stage wearing a very large, very black, obviously false beard. Eventually it became too much for Schildkraut senior and he stood at the back of the theater and shouted, 'Beard! Beard! Where are you running with my son?' " Harold went on to say, "Zoe, I adore you and I think you are a very good actress, but too often when I see you in the theater, I want to stand and shout, 'Characterization! Characterization! Where are you running with my actress?'" And I understood.

He demanded that I do nothing. Now understand: I had literally explored every single detail of every possibility. I'd been more arthritic than anybody. I'd been more drug-addicted than anybody. I had gone to the limits, ridiculously! I was, however, amazed by the power of doing nothing, with everything stewing beneath. It was also terrifying because I was doing nothing in front of a paying audience. That has become my acting process. I've got to go the limits to be able to pull back and then sit in the self. I find that the closer I get to trusting and sitting in self, the more my true voice emerges. Only then can I begin to edit and explore. The thing that stops me from getting there quicker is feeling the responsibility to entertain.

I'm also a great believer in punctuation, and I follow it exactly. If you went through the script of *A Perfect Ganesh,* or any play, you would see that when there's an exclamation mark, that's an exclamation. If the line is very, very quick, with two commas, I will give it only two commas. I obey the punctuation of the text in the way a musician obeys the score. Ask a writer at rehearsal what he meant and you usually get a pretty silly answer. But his subconscious and his gift understood at the time of writing the play, and it is there, in the rhythm of the text. Actors, then, are the instrument through which the playwright can speak to the audience. I don't think any good actor analyzes the text for the structure of each scene. We are the channel, the vessel, and that can be a pretty holy thing, but we are not the creators. So, I obey the punctuation because that is what the writer heard.

In fact, I won a Tony by obeying Tennessee Williams. The play was *Gnädiges Fräulein,* one of two in *Slapstick Tragedy,* and it lasted only one week, but I won a Tony. I am usually the most pliant of actors, but I realized in rehearsal that the director was unable to help me. I said, "Listen, it's much better that I go and you get somebody who will do what you want because we're not doing what Tennessee wants." And he said, "Stay. I promise you I won't give you any direction." At the theater, there was a young man on a fellowship and I asked him to help me follow exactly what Tennessee asked in the text. If I did something that was not what Tennessee wrote, he was to haul me over the coals. Tennessee called for a pratfall. I learned from a circus man how to do proper pratfalls. I used the exact rhythm and punctuation Tennessee called for. We, Kate Reid and I, had to sit on the front of a little derelict house smoking Mary Janes on two rocking chairs. Sometimes we'd rock in unison, sometimes out of unison, sometimes wildly out of unison; sometimes we'd fall out of the chair, sometimes we'd stand on the chairs; but we never left the chairs—which was exactly what Tennessee had written. I literally did what Tennessee asked and I won a Tony.

I will give you another example. I teach Shakespeare at Florida Atlantic University. I'm the Eminent Scholar of the Theater Department. The students were doing Sam Shepard's *Lie of the Mind,* and they asked if I would give them a critique. One student who was studying Shakespeare with me in class was really kicking shit about having to be scrupulous about the punctuation, and as Sam Shepard wasn't Shakespeare, she felt free to be quite snarky. She was playing the brain-damaged girl so she turned her toe in and was acting up a storm in the brain-damaged department. This, of course, told us nothing, but made you think,

"Why is that girl acting so badly?" The next day, during the critique, I told her what I'd felt and she was not pleased. I said, "You were helping the playwright to within an inch of your life, and he doesn't need that much help. He just needs you to be a channel." She went away in a snit. The next day she came by and said, "I've been so foolish. I went over the text last night and realized that the text is one word, full stop; two words, full stop; one word, full stop; three words, full stop. If I only have the capacity to put forward one or two words before I finish a thought, I can just play the person and the audience will know she's brain damaged."

As to research, it varies from play to play. If I'm playing Medea, I do a little university course on ancient Greece and that's easy. Catherine, in *A Perfect Ganesh,* is from Connecticut, and I live in northern Westchester, which is close. I know these women rather well. I began watching the local ladies, taking careful note. I watched where the pain was in the woman who's drinking and smoking and seeming to have a terrific husband, terrific life, and wonderful clothes, but underneath . . . ? I knew Catherine had to seem to be easy on the surface, and that if anyone's got a problem, it's going to be Margaret. Catherine's going to be terrific to travel to India with and you're going to have a good time, because she's grown-up and sophisticated and easy and she wants to see everything! Of course, you very quickly find out that's not so. However, as an actress, I can't start with the outward, social covering and then go in. I have to act the pain overtly, or act the joy. Only then do I allow the normal social covering to be gradually built up until, eventually, a recognizable human being emerges.

The freedom to expose the character's need comes to me only after opening night. The same thing happened in *Medea* and *The Prime of Miss Jean Brodie.* On opening night I'm still overacting. Of course it is a defensive pose. When I'm going overboard, I'm protecting myself from anybody being able to see me. I hide, then gradually let pieces be seen. That's the thrilling, really profound time for me. Once I cut the pattern of the part, I can begin to really listen.

Part of cutting the pattern is the discipline to be physically, mentally, and vocally fit so I can meet the requirements of a role. If I am required to shout across the river eight times a week, as I am in *A Perfect Ganesh*, then I must do that and not lose my voice. Or, I wanted Catherine to look a certain way, and I was about twenty pounds overweight. Two weeks before rehearsals I simply went on a fast. If my creative mind demands a new behavior, then I will comply and do whatever must be done to become the character.

Every night I pray, "Please, God, let me just be Catherine." I don't pray, "Please, God, let me go out there and do something extraordinary." Just let me be Catherine. Then I start the journey. It requires a lot of trust and concentration to bring forth whatever is demanded of an instant. But my body and emotions are ready to do whatever it is Catherine's going to be doing. Achieving that concentration begins from the moment I wake up in the morning. I am preparing to go to play the part. My kids noticed that and they didn't like it. Now the boys are grown-up, but my husband always notices it, and he doesn't like it—but he understands because he's a theater man. You see, we've often done plays together, and then we're talking about the same problems, thinking about the same issues. But he's absolutely divorced from this play, and it is truly hard. I feel he needs me. But it is good to be flexing my acting muscles again.

I get to the theater three hours early, which is stupid, but I always do. I put on a bit of makeup and set my hair, trying to make it look as though Catherine has had her hair done the day before the flight. As the play goes on, I gradually let my hair, and everything else, fall apart. Then I spend a great deal of time laughing with the chaps in the dressing room and chatting with Frannie, whom I've come to love. We have a lot to say to one another, because we're actually preparing to go to India as Margaret and Catherine. I pack all my bags every day before every performance. Initially there were towels and sheets in my bags, but that wasn't good enough. So I chose clothes from my own wardrobe, and I perfume them and pack them in a certain way before every performance. That's supposed to be the property woman's job and she would have done it, but I have to do it in preparation for Catherine.

In *A Perfect Ganesh* I take grave risks when I shout across the river. It is not a pretty shout. I'm not afraid of showing ugliness on the stage. Some people hate that. When Catherine seems deadened by hatred, with no place lower to go, Ganesh then takes her down to the river on the next leg of her journey. He appears this time as a little boy, someone to whom she can relate. If he had wanted to make her happy, he could have simply played with her at the river, but he knows that she must go still deeper. He provokes, provokes, and provokes her. And just as she's open and having a lovely time, he quietly says the name of her dead son, "Walter." It's just extraordinary, that whole idea in the play, don't you think? Until you are prepared to go down, down, down, as Dory Previn says, "where the iguanas play," you can't possibly be well. Catherine has to go there. Medea had to go there. And in life, a lot of people have to go there. I know some people in the audience must feel, "Oh, Christ, that's too much!" But that's what some people have to do to be clean again.

Even Medea gets to be healed. When you give all of yourself to anybody, it's a terrible thing. People do it all the time. Medea had everything: position, the love of her father, potent powers, beauty and her virginity. And then that great, golden, glorious Greek hero came and she gave him everything, everything, everything, until there was no self. There are several accounts of a parent killing the children after the other parent has abandoned the family. They wipe out their own family because they feel that they themselves no longer exist. Jason has left Medea with nothing, so she regains self by obliterating all. Ha. Ha. Ha. It is a feat of theater! All I hoped for at the end of *Medea* was the audience's understanding of what she did. I didn't want her to look wondrously appealing. I wanted her to be so very foreign that people would think, "Oh, I don't want to spend the evening with this woman or know her problem," much less be sympathetic to her. The triumph of theater is when the audience recognizes, "I, too, have felt that and weep for her."

In this way the Greeks were very healthy, I think, and they used their theater marvelously well. I mean, they had mothers marrying sons and sons killing fathers and all that antisocial stuff we all want to do at some point in our lives. I believe if we had more real theater like that, and people had access to it—not just expense-account people, but everybody, not "Can you afford . . . ?"—but everybody in the theater, sharing it communally, not with a videotape, alone in your bedroom. Lonely people are scared people, and scared people do scary things. Human behavior *is* sometimes appalling, but experiencing it theatrically, communally, is the function of theater.

MARCIA GAY HARDEN

An actor who works toward merging her self with her character must trust her psyche for good and ill. On a fundamental level she must find her own feelings and impulses interesting. This is sometimes a difficult trick. Moreover, the issues that she struggles with in life are often the very ones that will contribute most to the development of interesting characters. An artist's work depends upon the clarity and confidence of her communication of "self" to "other."

Marcia Gay Harden is an actor for whom process is as vital an issue as performance. They are inextricably bound in her interview. She is blessed with an acute sense of observation, emotional availability, poetry, musicality, intelligence, impulse, and insight; the substance that makes for a great actor. Her struggle with every role is to trust these attributes, allow them to merge with the character and to "be." The key to doing that comes when she stops saying, "The character wouldn't . . . ," and instead lends her own behavior to the character's moment.

Her penchant is for complexity, yet she always strives for a deeper, simpler note. This paradox, in which the actor's essential gift, in this case a complex artistic response, equally poses performance problems and successes is not uncommon. Without a process that brings them into consonance, an actor's raw talent and psychological makeup can create and sabotage a great performance. In her interview,

Marcia Gay Harden discusses two roles: the character of Harper in Angels in America *and Verna, in the Coen brothers' Miller's Cross-ing. Harper, a complicated, almost operatic character, posed enor-mous artistic and technical challenges, but the greatest was in trusting herself enough to let her own behavior merge with the character's. In a very different rehearsal process, she analyzed Verna's impassive mask, then unearthed what lay behind it.*

The question that must be addressed by every actor is, How much of my self do I bring to the character? The answer she reaches has its concomitant acting process. Marcia Gay Harden is accruing the professional experience that will enable her to reach both a comfortable decision and a comfortable process.

"I FACE THE SAME STRUGGLE IN EVERY PLAY: THE STRUGGLE TO ALLOW MYSELF TO BE."

Speaking about the process of acting makes me feel shy and vulnerable. Writers in film and the-ater magazines make actors seem stupid for speaking with reverence about this thing we love. Earnestness is irritating on some level, and we're so cyni-cal in this day and age. I feel like protecting myself by being glib and saying, "Acting? Yeah, you fake it." But acting is beautiful. It's pure and it's also such a machine. Give an actor a note and it elicits thousands of different questions and responses. It's like one of those pachinko machines: a marble goes through this labyrinth of pro-cess, clink, clink, clink, and you win the prize! There's the place you know you can go, but there is also an element of chance, of mystery. I find that beautiful. Anyway, I'll try not to censor myself.

I desire to be able to act with greater simplicity; unfortunately, that's not my particular penchant. I tend to want to do more. One of my teachers, Ron Van Lieu, told me many times, "You are enough. Just you, Marcia." How many times do we think, "I want to be anything but me. I am not enough. The character is interesting but I'm not interesting onstage." I can remember a scene in *Month in the Country* in which I had to say, "I love you." Ron said, "Do it on your voice." I resisted and said, "I love you," using a breathy, "sensitive" voice. "That's not sensitive," Ron said. "That's boring. Now, get on your voice." I did, and suddenly I was sobbing and the scene worked. I'd made a connection to myself and to the other actor because I had allowed myself to be enough.

As soon as I'm on my voice, then I must pay attention to the sounds of the words and get on my breath. For instance, there is a moment in *Angels in America* when my character, Harper, says to Prior, "Deep inside of you, there's a part of you, the most inner part, entirely free of disease." That's a long sentence and the words have a lot of little clicks and sounds. I made several mistakes in saying the line: I ran on the words *part of you* so that they came out *pardofyou*, I never hit the *z*'s in *disease* but said "disseasse," and I inverted the words! Tony Kushner, the playwright, twice gave me the note that I was inverting, but I kept making the same mistake until finally he said, "It's much more beautiful if you do it the way it's written." Well, excuuuuse me, Mr. Kushner! So I went back and learned it properly. Then I thought about the sounds. For some reason I felt embarrassed to articulate them, so I explored them. The *d* of *deep* was such a strong thrust inward. Articulating those *t*'s was like striking a triangle! And the final *z* sound allowed the sound to travel out, filling the theater, and it put a period on the end of the sentence. I had been onstage performing that line with great feeling, but my feeling wasn't enough. The line was more beautiful than my feeling. Applying technique opened the door on that moment. I didn't have to do so much work. I didn't have to think, "Did they see my tear on that line?" It no longer mattered, because if I hit the triangle and put in the final period, the moment was a billion times more powerful than my puny tear alone.

I completely understood the music of Harper's tragedy. It's operatic with big sounds and gestures in an almost Greek tragic style. But the music of Harper's comedy was elusive at first. I have to give the director, George Wolfe, and Stephen Spinella, who played Prior, the credit for helping me hear the possibility of Harper's jazzlike comedic rhythm. I wouldn't want to misrepresent our genuine verbal ability, but we also spoke in musical rhythms, and I've never worked with people who understood and matched my need to do that. George would say, "Marcia, I want you go *ba ta ba-báá*. I'd say, "I know exactly what you mean, but I feel it should go *ba tá ba ba báá.*" He'd say, "Okay, try it, but make the *tá* stronger." He asked for a stripping down to single notes of music to express deeper thoughts. Sometimes I'll draw on paper, making squiggles to represent what I feel and hear as the emotional rhythm of a scene. I'm feeling angry so I make angry squiggles. When I'm finished, I have on paper a visual/emotional/rhythmic representation of my character's arc.

I face the same struggle in every play: the struggle to allow myself to be. To allow self to become character and character to merge with self. In *Angels* the fight was horrible! The night before opening, critics night, George Wolfe took my wig away. It was beautiful, long, reddish, thick, wavy hair that spoke "prairies" to me, and I thought it was right for Tony's image of Harper. It made me feel softer. Well, George just took it away. He was probably waiting for me to come to that revelation myself, but unfortunately, I can have extraordinarily bad taste, especially when it comes to anything I'm using to cover myself up. We were in the makeup room and George said, "You're a beautiful woman, Marcia, and I want that to be seen. The hair is hiding you. It's hiding your connections," and he literally wrenched the wig away from me. It was a scene! I was a sobbing mess and had a tantrum. I took a big gob of makeup and screeched, "Oh! Oh! I'm a beautiful woman, am I? Why don't I go onstage like this?" And I smeared the makeup on my face. "I won't even bother rubbing it in!" The makeup people and I all laugh about this scene in retrospect, but believe me, I sounded like a madwoman!

An actor's very personal shit, the stuff you take great pains to avoid, is exactly what is going to make something exciting happen to the character. George's gift as a director is that he knows that and he finds a way to bring you through it. He spoke to a part of me that I take extraordinary care to cover up. He said, "Come on out, it's going to be okay." I found Harper's vulnerability and rawness all through rehearsals, but I had created it like a groundhog does, in an amazing underground labyrinth. Finally, he said, "Come out of the hole." It felt horrible and scary. All the work had been done, but I required George's push to allow the human moment to be revealed, and Harper was there.

You let a character breathe the moment you say, "I am enough." I remember working on *Three Sisters* with Paul Walker. We will all miss him. We worked toward permitting ourselves to occupy the space. When many actors approach Chekhov, the women sit on the edge of their seats and everyone acquires an English accent. Paul wanted us big and full of life. We ate Russian food and particularized everything we looked at and touched. He wanted us to create big, broad Russian accents—nothing specific as long as it was broad—and gestures big enough to accompany them. Then we got rid of the accents and there we were, full people, occupying the entire stage and theater. Even so, at one point I had a foot hiked up on a chair, in a man's style, and I said, "Oh, God! Sorry. This is a period when women would never do that." Paul laughed, "Marsh, you think in all of Russia not one woman ever put her foot on a chair, ever? Besides, it said a million things about the character to me." That opened up a door on a kind of aggressive behavior that I personally have but that I wasn't permitting the character to have.

A release happens when you quit saying, "My character wouldn't." One day in rehearsal for *Angels,* Mary, the stage manager, came up to me and said, "Boy, your own sense of humor was coming through today." What had happened was that I allowed Harper to look with a smirk out of the corner of her eye at her stupid husband as opposed to glancing up at him in awe and fear. My reaction to something he said was like, "You Mormon-lying-idiot," and all of a sudden I rolled my eyes. I quit playing an idea of the character. I allowed myself to merge with the character, and Harper was there.

It's interesting to me how different the process of

film is from theater. Working in film, you're always moving right on to the next setup. It's not as intensely a personal experience as theater. In film, you're expected to come in having worked out emotional transitions and character. I'm particularly glad for my training when I work on a film because it enables me, on my own, to find the truth of a scene. Unlike theater, you must give over almost all other control to the director and producer to make the film they want to make. When I saw the final print of the movie *Miller's Crossing,* produced and directed by the Coen brothers, I was surprised that my character, Verna, was as flat and stoical as she was. I'd given them many takes that had greater scope, shape, and emotion and lighter music. But the Coens chose the low, base tones. However, in the context of the whole film I saw that I was an instrument in this director's symphony. I love the music they recorded. Of course, the Coen brothers' process is also very theatrical in that they want you to build a full, living character. If Johnny Polito's performance in *Miller's Crossing* had been any bigger, he would have levitated. It was gorgeous!

Another issue to factor in was that the Coens were being true to a style of filmmaking rather than to a historic time. Verna was a gangster moll and she was written in our image of that film icon: cool, smoky, husky voiced, cigarette dangling, suppressed. I had to be true to the text, but I wanted her to be real. There were millions of women in the twenties and thirties who talked just like we do now; they weren't all cool gangster molls. But my job was to be a gangster moll. Unlike Harper, Verna's emotional life was not immediately clear to me. So I came at it from the outside.

First I checked out lots of old Clara Bow, Greta

Garbo, Jean Harlow movies. I looked at period photographs of women. I reread Dashiell Hammett. I asked myself, how did Prohibition and the strain of the coming back to America after the war affect men's and women's behavior? In the 1920s and '30s women were becoming emancipated in whole new ways. Then I looked at the basic facts of the character. For instance, she played poker and she won. Poker. Poker face. What is that? A mask. So I first discovered Verna's outer mask, and only then could I begin to figure out what it covered. She had those high, plucked eyebrows of women of that era, and her hair had to be worn short. Her voice expressed a woman who didn't give much away, and that was important because everybody in this world is lying, really, or miscommunicating.

Then I could begin to go deeper. Was she direct or indirect? If she's indirect, how did she get what she wants? Why does she operate behind the scenes? What's in it for her? What's the grift? Well, Verna's first and foremost objective is to save her brother Bernie, played by John Turturro. Secondly, I chose to play that she really loved Tom, Gabriel Byrne's character, and wanted to be with him. Those were my answers. The rest provided the struggle. The superobjective of saving Bernie plays out in every single scene. In order to save her brother she couldn't alienate her powerful lover, Albert Finney's character, so her feelings for Tom couldn't be public. Saving Bernie came into play when she made love with Tom the first time. When Tom says, "You need to get out of town," Verna says, "What, and leave my brother to be killed?" In all of these scenes the objective stays consistent but the form of attack changes. In other words, I play a different action to achieve the objective. As I pursue my objective by playing my action, I have to check to see if I'm having an effect on the other character. Actors who don't check in are not alive in the situation; they're not listening and watching. It's like tennis; if you simply play your action, all you're doing is serving, serving, serving; and after about three consecutive serves, ain't nobody going to watch that game. Checking in doesn't have to be an enormous dramatic moment. Listening and reacting can happen in the flick of an eye.

Verna's most interesting moment is when her mask breaks and she reveals her little dream that she and Tom could go away somewhere and be together. This moll has this naive little dream of love and escape, wants desperately to save her brother's life, and in the course of the movie, finds she cannot commit murder to achieve these goals. That was the internal life which was covered by the impassive mannequin mask. The break in the mask reveals the human moment, the struggle to align herself against the opposing forces at play in her life. She's like a landscape of ice in Antarctica on a *National Geographic* show. You watch this ice for two hours, and the moment you remember is when the ice cracks, even if soon after, it returns exactly to its placid state. That moment of shift is drama.

As actors we're always at the drawing board. It's always the beginning. You're always learning the same things again and making the same mistakes. Acting is not a linear progression. I don't think you reach a point at which you don't even have to think about what you do because you just do it. I think you take the same steps over and over again. Certain steps do become condensed as you know a way of working. It no longer takes me a week to figure out my objectives or the beats; I see them, smell them, and feel them immediately. But I always have to say, "Play the scene, not the laugh; play the character's intention, not your idea of the intention; don't play what it "should" look like, play what you're doing; don't play the how, play the what; put your attention on your scene partner; listen, did you hear them say that?; let it resonate within your body; get on your voice; can't you be innocent in your own voice? It's always the same equations. With experience you do reach the point where you can sight-read the music. But how to play it?

FRANCES STERNHAGEN

Frances Sternhagen's interview is filled with observations and opinions about life, marriage, and people. There is a direct correlation between these observations and her acting process. She says, "I find it very easy to fill moments from within." One of the primary reasons that this is so is because her emotional life is always present. In her interview it manifests itself in the form of well-observed anecdotes. Her own history is her ready reference.

Hers is an intuitive process. Her performances in plays like The Heiress, On Golden Pond, Equus, The Sign in Sidney Brustein's Window, The Good Doctor, *and* The Pinter Plays, *all of which netted her Tony and Obie nominations and some awards as well, prove that there is little need to resort to a technique if the actor's vulnerability to the words, the situation, and the other actors is readily engaged. This is not to say that she doesn't have those techniques available to her. She simply doesn't need them too often. Of course, she also has unerring actor's instincts. Her point of entry is repeated readings of the play. She gets a sense of "what moments feel important." Then she repeats the lines aloud, over and over until she finds their truth. She places great faith in both the physical act of saying the words and the emotional information her body derives from gesture. While she occasionally has to resort to the technique of emotional substitution, she generally finds herself using her life in unconscious ways.*

For all of her easy access to herself, she is still going to have to stand up in a large theater and project that character and those words to the back of the house. She makes a terrific point about meeting the purely technical demands of theater and resolving that discomfort as quickly as possible.

Frances Sternhagen's interview reveals an actor whose inner life is so rich, available, and trustworthy that she can rely upon it to provide her with most of what she needs.

"I FIND IT VERY EASY TO FILL MOMENTS FROM WITHIN."

The first reading is often a very nice experience where you see how people fit into character and you get an idea of what they're going to do with the lines. I always do terrific first readings. I hope that I'm not one of those people who don't grow after a good first reading! I don't think I am. There was a time in the 1960s when directors had actors sitting around the table for two weeks before they got up on their feet. I don't like that because I know that when you first get up on your feet and start blocking, it's very uncomfortable. It's sooooooo comforting just sitting around that table and reading, being intimate and imagining you're terrific! Boy, you'd better get on your feet fairly quickly and get over that discomfort and start floundering and discovering what is going to inform a line best in action and find it out early! Floundering is a necessary process that you must get at fairly soon.

I remember being in the stage play of *The Sign in*

Sidney Brustein's Window, and Zohra Lampert, that darling person, played the lead, Iris. Zohra was one of those bewitching film actors. I first saw her in the movie *The Black Hand,* with Ernest Borgnine, I think. She played an Italian wife on the Lower East Side of New York, and her performance was so real, so wonderful, it was like watching someone who wasn't an actor. In *The Sign in Sidney Brustein's Window* she spent most of her rehearsal period talking very softly and being very intimate. She's a fragile person, and Hal Linden and Alan Schneider were both trying to bring her out and let her be comfortable in her process. When it came time to project, she couldn't, and as a result her performance just wasn't there. I've found that it takes a long time with each new role to get comfortable meeting the technical demands of acting onstage. I can give myself one day in which to do it very softly to find an emotion, but I better be able to project it out soon, because if I can't . . . ? I've got to go through that discomfort in every play.

It's a very different thing in a movie. You can be intimate. Of course, you also don't get a whole lot of rehearsal. Most movie directors, and this goes for the good ones, too, simply cast. You work on your own, and then, before you shoot a scene, they tell you little things that they have in mind that are sometimes absolutely contrary to what you've planned. You have to adjust—and very quickly. It may be a simple problem like not knowing what the business of the scene will be. For example, in *Misery,* I didn't know that I was going to be dealing with books and papers in a particular scene. In the time it took to light the scene, I had to figure out that on such and such a line I had to move this number of books so that it would all work out right. Richard Farnsworth is a darling guy, and he's very sexy in his own quiet way and so gorgeous with those blue eyes, white hair, and white mustache and everything. Our husband-and-wife film relationship was easy to establish because he's so nice. But he's not a very experienced actor; he started as a stuntman and he would blow his lines a lot more than you would expect. That was something of a relief to me because it gave me more time to plan my books and things.

However, sometimes the changes are not quite so simple. It's important to have your whole character development in your head for a movie, and not only because you shoot out of sequence. I remember on *Outland* I knew who my character was and I began playing her slowly and sarcastically. Right away the director, Peter Hyams, said, "No, it's got to be a lot faster." And I thought, "Ooooooooh! Okay!" While they were lighting, I scurried off by myself and ran the lines really fast so that they came out zing, zing, zing. I found that experience alarming, though it didn't really challenge my basic premise of character. She was sarcastic and bitter, and if he wanted it faster, I could be sarcastic and bitter, faster.

Sean Connery was lovely to work with in *Outland*. I don't think he goes far from himself as an actor, but his self is very direct, very uncomplicated; very male. One bit of male behavior which was maddening, but also made me laugh, happened during my close-ups. He would sing and hum—Cole Porter or something—like this, "Doo dee doo dum dum dum." I didn't say anything to him, but I thought it was just so male! Men are so damned confident that they don't think about other people because everybody has always thought about them! It wasn't mean at all; it was just totally male! If I had said, "Would you not do that now, I'm trying to do this scene," he would have apologized. I didn't though because I knew I could concentrate and it would make me look so sort of "Pulleease, I'm doing my lines." I thought I would rather have him be a friend, a buddy, and not think about it.

A lot of actors have difficulty concentrating with all the noise on movie sets. I remember in *Fedora,* Marthe Keller used to get mad because Billy Wilder was telling jokes, keeping his crew happy. I would just go off and concentrate and let Billy tell his jokes. I was amazed that Billy Wilder wasn't aware that the actors had to have quiet. But he's such an unusual man anyway, and he's terribly funny. He's an old-fashioned director. I asked him at the beginning, "Can we find a time to talk about my character?" And he just said, "You do what you were doing in *Equus.* You will be marvelous." He wasn't going to tell me anything and so I just made my own preparations.

I start working on a script by reading and rereading the part aloud. Quite a lot. I think about it and about what moments feel important. If I don't have to, I don't usually start memorizing until I've got the blocking. I just like to mull it over. I had a teacher at Vassar who was quite neurotic and strange. She did the unheard of: she taught by giving line readings. She would keep saying, "I'm not giving you a line reading. I'm trying to get you to understand truth in the line." She primarily dealt with the classics, and her young women students tended to get very lyrical and meaningless. So that, when she would yell this line at you, she was trying to tell you what the line meant. I very often have to do this to myself. I've found that the more I say it out loud, the more the truth of the line comes to me. It's just that simple. I have no image of the action when I'm repeating, I'm just letting it sink into me, seeing what emotions or thoughts occur while saying the words. Sometimes I will really understand an emotion by myself, and sometimes I will have a superficial understanding that I know will begin to increase as I work with other actors.

My husband, Tom Carlin, used to laugh at me because he didn't approach text in that way. He was a character actor, as I am, and I never actually knew what he did. Tom's process was mysterious. I will never forget the time we were in a simple play by Alice Cannon called *Great Day in the Morning*. Jose Quintero directed it and the cast was wonderful. Tom was playing a character called Tricky Hennesee, an Irish ne'er-do-well, a real scrapper. He apparently read it wonderfully because Jose cast him instantly. I was playing Colleen Dewhurst's sister. While we were rehearsing, Jose came to me quietly and said, "I don't know what to do about Tom. Nothing is happening. I don't see anything." Being the wife, I thought, "Oh, dear, talk to Tom, not me." We took the play to Detroit before coming to New York, and Tom and I shared a dressing room, which is always a mistake. The day we got our costumes for the first time, Tom put his on, and in the dressing room he started moving around and became the Tricky Hennesee that Jose had been looking for. Onstage that night he was absolutely transformed. He was obnoxious and funny. Jose came to me afterwards and asked, "Where was that all this time?" And I said, "Waiting in the costume box." Tom was extraordinary. He never approached working on a character the same way twice.

One of the reasons I married my husband was because when the man I had been going out with for four years, a very attractive, nice guy, asked me to marry him, I asked him, "What happens to my acting when we get married?" I was brought up in a time when women shouldn't be angry and should take care of the children and the house and this and that. He said, "Well, you give it up, I suppose." Well, that settled that. So, when Tom proposed, I asked him the same thing and he said, "What do mean what happens to your acting? You keep doing it. You're good at it." I said, "Oh, thank you!" and I married him.

Most of the time I think I do emotional substitution unconsciously. I let the emotion come through the physical act of saying it. Then, if I hit a snag and it doesn't feel true, I have to look for comparable things in my life that will inform the moment. This was best illustrated to me when I played the mother in *Equus*. There was a moment in the first or second scene when the psychiatrist interviews the mother and father about their son, Alan. He asks how Alan had been brought up and what they had taught him. And my character talked about—because he had killed these horses—how she had told him about her family and her grandfather's horsemanship. Then the psychiatrist asked, "Have you ever talked to him about sex?" And she talks very rationally, and very—what's the word?—not puritanically, but with that schoolteacherish explanation that makes it all sound very simple and comfortable and practical and loving. Her husband was sitting on the bench while she was doing all the talking, and she gives a bland explanation like, "It was between a man and a woman who loved each other very much." My next line had to be a cry, "Alan!" out of nowhere. And not just "Alan!" but "Aaaalllaaan!" Help! What am I going to do? How do I get there? I remember going to the stage manager and saying, "Bob, I don't know what I'm going to do with this moment." He said, "Well, you'll come up with something." In another couple of days I went over to him and said, "I still don't know what I am doing, but it has something to do with sex." He said, "Sounds good to me."

At the point in the scene before the cry, I would look over at Michael Higgins, who played my husband, and he would nod negatively, almost imperceptibly. That nod meant "Don't" or "You don't know what you're talking about." I can't say exactly what it was, but it started to be about all those years of being married to Tom and having six children and the times we grew up in. There were times, as with all of the women I know, when I didn't want sex. My husband did, I didn't. Before marriage the woman is perhaps the most sexually aggressive, whereas it was almost characteristic of marriage that when she's had children and there's all this business of "Who's going to get the kids in the morning?" and "You really want sex now, in the middle of the afternoon, when the kids aren't in bed?" that the sexual drives seem to reverse. There were times I can remember when my husband said negative things like, "You don't seem to want sex anymore." And it was like, "Oh! Come on!" Well, when Mike nodded at me during that scene, I was able to infuse all of those things from my marriage into that one word, "Alan." It was so wonderfully spontaneous. Mike came from my era and he was also Catholic, and that imperceptible little nod was so full. And you know, we never talked about it.

I remember another time that was similar in the Pinter plays that I did off-Broadway in 1964 or '65. Harold Pinter came for the first ten days of rehearsal and wasn't a whole lot of help. I remember when Hank Forsythe asked him, "What does this character mean when he says . . . ?" Harold said, "I don't know, I just wrote it." After seeing the plays, someone came backstage and said, "I don't know what he's talking about, but he has his subconscious very close to the surface." And that was Harold. In *A Slight Ache* I was playing the middle-aged wife of a rather typical, noncommunicative suburban English couple with no children. The husband has been very supercilious to her throughout breakfast, and they have that wonderful scene that has been done forever in acting classes about the wasp in the marmalade jar. At the back gate there is an old match-seller whom the husband is very disturbed by. He calls the match-seller in, sits him down, and starts talking at him, revealing things about himself. Of course, throughout the entire play the match-seller doesn't say a word to anybody. Finally the husband yells for his wife to come in and she says, "Well?" He says:

"I can't get anything out of him."

"Well, I'll try."

"You won't either."

"Never mind, I'll try."

The husband leaves and she starts talking at the match-seller and she reveals that she finds him very interesting. She compares him to, perhaps, an affair she once had years ago. She starts flirting with him, and at one point she says, "You look rather warm. Would you like me to mop your brow with my chiffon?" And she gets closer to him and she kneels down and says, "You're a sturdy old thing, aren't you?" She puts her arms around him. . . .

Well, it was either the dress rehearsal or first preview and I burst into tears at that point. The next line was, "I'm going to keep you. I'm going to give you little toys to play with." I suddenly realized that she so desperately wanted children and that her husband would have none of them. She was so lonely. Alan Schneider came to see it and asked, "Where did you get that moment?" And I said, "I don't know! I don't know!" Sometimes you don't know what it will take to be free. But it was in the script: "she puts her arms around him." The feel of his body made me burst into tears.

I find it very easy to fill moments from within and, if you have a good play, to keep refreshing them. Some moments come from finding what feelings arise as I do a gesture onstage. A lot of good moments in acting come when I allow myself to just brood about it, think about it in the subway, in the car, around the house. Some come when I am simply going over the lines to myself. I think that my subconscious stews about what these things mean to me. I really believe that acting, for me, is a very mystical and sort of religious experience. I find things out through acting that I don't find in any other way. I find them more in plays than in movies, where not as much is demanded of you and you don't have enough time to work on things. But in plays with a three- or four-week rehearsal period, you have time to work things through. Especially if it's a good play, and there's not much point in doing a play that's not good.

JOE SENECA

Few actors have a working method derived from a single source. Most of the interviews in this book show a slow building of process acquired through experience and from many teachers. Joe Seneca is the exception. After a long stretch of career in "show biz" as a musician, singer, entertainer, and songwriter, Joe Seneca turned to acting. He found immediate success in such plays as The Death of Bessie Smith and Ma Rainey's Black Bottom and has appeared in and starred in films such as School Daze, Crossroads, The Verdict, and Mississippi Masala. He went to the Strasberg Institute to acquire "the jargon" of actors and walked away with a readily applied system. He employs Strasberg's classic object exercises and sensory recall with ease. The way in which he finds the intersection between himself and his character is refreshingly clear.

Why did he find the process effortless when others struggle to make these techniques accessible? I offer my own theory. Joe Seneca came to Strasberg's techniques as an adult. He had a life that was filled with experiences, emotions, and the humility of knowing his strengths and weaknesses, whereas young actors have more limited experience and often a great deal of undiscovered inner territory. They have to learn both the technique and themselves. Joe Seneca was already familiar with half the equation.

When two characters confront each other, two good actors open themselves up to

*the possibility of strong feelings arising between them. In those in-
stances, feelings such as hatred or sexual attraction are possible
consequences for the actors, not just the characters. It takes
courage to seize these feelings and use them in the moment. Of special interest in this interview is the process by which Joe Seneca explored his character's relationship to another character by "going
with the flow" of the actors' personal reactions to one another. It
made theatrical sparks fly in* Ma Rainey's Black Bottom *and created two memorable performances: Joe Seneca as Cutler and
Charles Dutton as Levee.*

"I LIKED THE STRASBERG METHOD."

I guess I've always been in the arts and show business.
A school buddy, Eddie Parton, and I started a group
called the Three Riffs. We did nightclubs, supper
clubs, vaudeville, radio, TV, stuff like that. It was never
just doo-wop; there were bits, acting and impressions, integrated into the material. After that I continued on as a
songwriter. Then I worked at the Children's Television
Workshop during the first years of *Sesame Street*. I stayed
there for three years getting hung up in research, and I
wanted to get fired so I could get unemployment. In the
meantime Dan Wilcox, who later became one of the producers of *M*A*S*H*, was the head writer there and we
were pretty good friends. After hearing me read, he said,
"Joe, you should go back into performing." When I finally got let go from the Workshop, Dan's sister, Nina
Wilcox, was doing a play at the Manhattan Theatre Club,
The Death of Bessie Smith. I auditioned and got the role,
and from then on, things started to roll in acting.

There is a relationship between entertaining and acting and that is the fact of you against them. The one You and the big Them. The one You has to please the big Them, or the big Them is going to get the one You. And then the critics, well, they will really sock it to you if you're not delivering. The fact that I was used to performing in front of large audiences made the transition to acting easier. It was never a big thing to be onstage before a group of people. That in itself is a hurdle most young actors have to overcome.

Even though I may have had the talent to perform, the next issue to deal with was to learn the jargon of acting. I wanted to be sure that if I were hired to act in a play, I could talk and understand theater language. So I went to Strasberg Institute to study there. I liked the Strasberg Method. I guess you've heard about it so many times—they teach you to act from the inside out. The thought determines everything: the walk, the look. The whole deal with Strasberg is to make everything in the script relate to you so that even though you're saying someone else's words, you're attaching your own personal experiences to those words. If you can't find a related experience, you use one that matches the emotional place you have to arrive at in the script. So when you're laughing or crying onstage, you're laughing or crying at the deepest experiences you can call up to color your acting. Another of Strasberg's techniques that helps me is finding a personal object to attach to the experience I've called up. For instance, if I wanted to remember this interview, I might conjure up this lamp or this cup and really feel them to bring back this moment. It doesn't always work, but that's the idea.

I assess what the script and the character call for in rehearsals. I didn't live that man's life, so to animate him

I fill up his body with things I've done that are close to what he's done. Before a performance or a shot, I call on all the objects to see if they're working. If I need a laugh object, I touch that and I laugh. I make sure I touch each one and can go easily from one to the other. If one wears out, I get another one. But generally, if there's something really sad in your life, it's going to remain sad no matter how long you live, so if you touch on that thing, it's going to bring on that sadness. These emotions and senses we have in life are straight on. They're happy. They're medium. They're bad. You have those feelings and personal objects in your arsenal. You always have to improvise and make adjustments because no role is ever a cut-and-dry match to your life, but these things help you climb into the character's experience.

Before I perform I do a complete relaxation exercise and then prepare myself by going over my objects and experiences. After that, it goes into my subconscious and I'm programmed. Then I go on and live what I'm doing, associating the character with myself, and try to bring it off! I can't be thinking, "I'm going to grab my object," unless I'm really in trouble! The process works something like this: I did a *Golden Girls* episode where I was an Alzheimer's patient whom Estelle Getty meets on a park bench. In each scene there were two realities going. I had a throughline in response to Estelle's character in real time, but I also had emotional reactions that were unjustified by the situation and off I'd go. In order to trigger this extension of my character, I'd touch the button or that personal object that brings me to anger and trigger it at a time when it shouldn't be triggered. That technique worked well for this character.

Another technique I use is borrowing physical gestures from people I know. It's not imitation, it's trying to convey the essence of a person. For instance, in *The Vernon Johns Story* I played the deacon who both hired and then fired Vernon Johns. Finally, under pressure, my character allied himself with the faction of the church that had money and education and wanted to maintain their positions in the community. I saw this deacon as pompous, a man who wanted to *be somebody*. Now, I knew a man, a dear friend of mine, who used to smack his lips. I thought about this dear man and looked at him lovingly, and even though he wasn't pompous, I borrowed that lip smacking, and it made me feel like I thought I *really was somebody*. That helped me fill the body of that character.

So, I prepare myself in these ways; but when I'm heading out on the stage, like in *Ma Rainey's Black Bottom*, I forget all that and I'm just there in that recording studio and I begin to live as my character. I'm Cutler from curtain up to when I get home or whenever the character gets off of me. *Ma Rainey* was a case where my personal experience dovetailed beautifully with the theater experience. I know what it's like to come into a recording studio so I didn't have to call on anything—it was all there. I could put in my specific experiences and behavior and it made it even richer because it was for real. I had to learn to play trombone, and so that helped almost immediately. Getting my chops and learning the positions of that trombone made me feel like that specific musician, Cutler. The better I got at playing the trombone, the more I felt like the bandleader. And then that lead-in to the songs, "A-one. A-two. You know what to do," came out of my mouth one day and everybody cracked up. I kept it up and then August Wilson added it to the text.

At the same time I was working on the trombone, I started thinking, "Who is Cutler? How does Cutler feel? What are his habits? What does he drink? How does he feel about women? How does he feel about the guys in the band? Does Cutler really feel that way or is he just saying that?" From there, I begin to think in the terms Cutler might think. When I've done that, I have developed a train of thought that is planted in my mind. Every once in a while it comes up for me to use onstage.

A certain part of Cutler is Joe Seneca. Not all the way, but I share some of his feelings. The play takes place during a terrible time for the black man, the Jim Crow South. All back doors, short of money, everything bad. As the leader of the band Cutler has to go along with things, but he doesn't like it. I don't like it now and I wouldn't have liked it then. Cutler has a certain dignity, and although he can't personally do much to change things, recording these songs and protecting Ma Rainey's material were his chances to get out. He's a responsible guy doing a job. So am I.

The character Levee, played by Roc [Charles Dutton], is a legitimate pain in Cutler's butt. The reason Roc and I made fire onstage was because Roc was really into Roc and I was into me, and we both believed in what we did. I thought about Roc in some of the same ways Cutler thought about Levee. We just went with that flow. He's a very egotistical guy; everything revolves around Roc. Ditto for Levee. I knew how to drive Roc crazy, and I used that for our characters. In the last act, I told the story about Reverend Gates really slow. Leonard Jackson, who played Slow Drag, and I would milk that story for all it's worth. Roc didn't want to hear that slow story, and all Levee wanted was to cut his songs. Relating some of my experiences while we're doing nothing in the band room helped me blow off some steam. But Roc didn't want to hear anything unless it was about him. Neither did Levee. Me and Cutler, Roc and Levee; all in one. I give

Roc a lot of credit. He's a real go-getter and he brought that into his role. That desire to achieve has helped him develop a terrific acting career. At the same time, because of his drive, we could really get into it onstage.

As Cutler, the bandleader, and as Joe, the actor, I came down hard on him, and he wasn't used to that! Roc had been in jail, and the other actors sort of backed off from him. I never did, and Cutler wouldn't back off from Levee. During a performance he made me so sick that I reacted and made him really mad. He got so bad that I got scared and I broke my blocking. There was no way I was going to go near this guy who might cut me! I'm telling you, we weren't kidding. We were really into it. Afterwards I went up to his dressing room and said, "Look, Roc, if I offended you, let me know." He said, "No, no, no, Joe," as if nothing had really happened. But later that day he bought me a bottle of wine and said, "Man, everything's cool." He knew that I was right. It had been hot out there on the stage. But your job as an actor is to react to what is brought to you.

The longest time I ever had to hold on to a character was for the three and a half months it took us to film *Crossroads*. I played Willy Brown, a harmonica-playing bluesman who is incarcerated in an old-folks home. I con this young guitarist, played by Ralph Macchio, into smuggling me out and taking me to the crossroads where I had sold my soul to the devil long ago in exchange for a missing song of Robert Johnson's. I conjured the character from the many bluesmen I had known in my life. I used their accents for an essence of the character, and I put them in his skin. Before a shot you could hear me screaming my lungs out standing in the middle of that road in Mississippi, doing my exercises and relaxation. Then, I'd touch my buttons and get me in the mood of a bluesman.

BLACK EYED SUSAN

The seeds of Black Eyed Susan's acting process were sown with Charles Ludlam's Ridiculous Theatrical Company. A group of actors all "living full tilt," they embraced the insanity of life and investigated it in a sane, if ridiculous, manner.

My first visit to the Ridiculous Theatrical Company had Black Eyed Susan appearing, as she often did, as the love interest to Ludlam's unwilling Hamlet, in Stage Blood. Here were a group of people doing what Black Eyed Susan calls "playing the primary colors." In contrast to the dark, mirthless psychological exploration and war protest that was the basis of the New York theater scene at the time, The Ridiculous Theatrical Company's commitment to playing the obvious elevated them to the extraordinary. Ludlam was an inspired and outrageous lunatic onstage, and Black Eyed Susan counterbalanced him with her serious silliness.

Her interview is a guided tour of how an actor learns not to be trapped by her own identity. Black Eyed Susan's early training was in Stanislavsky's psychophysical method, but she found this preparation insufficient to meet the demands of Ludlam's broad, satiric strokes, in which the characters posed challenges far beyond her personal proclivities. Confusion often arises between young actors and their teachers precisely at the point where personalization will not meet the demands of the character, and imagination must be engaged. "Indication" is the curse levied at *young actors if they fail to personalize everything. Too often Stanislavsky's method is reduced to a small handful of inviolable, badly interpreted rules that effectively kill off the notion of play and imagination. In her interview, Black Eyed Susan talks of specific roles that challenged those rules and the ways in which she circumvented the difficulties to make a big leap into character, and beyond her limitations.*

"USUALLY I START WITH SOMETHING IN MIND AND THEN I HAVE TO CANCEL IT BECAUSE I'VE LIMITED MYSELF TOO MUCH. THE BEST THING IS TO TRY A THOUSAND DIFFERENT THINGS, TO FIND THAT FREEDOM IN MYSELF."

When I was a young person, I suddenly realized that I was not who I thought I was. I was no longer merely a product of my upbringing. I was much bigger than I had thought I'd be. I was living full tilt, along with everyone else in the world. I saw that I was quite mad; not just angry, but much too crazy. The operating reality was that life did not make sense, so why not explore that madness in a constructive way?

I didn't know exactly how I was going to proceed with that exploration. Then I ran into Charles Ludlam again. I first met Charles at Hofstra College. Several years later he asked if I would like to work on a play of his that the company he was working with, the Ridiculous Theatrical Company, was about to do. Then there were a bunch of us ... and we each thought the others were crazy. There was a great freedom and camaraderie. Nobody made judgments. And Charles was such an idealist and had great ideas about theater! This was exactly what I had wanted.

First of all—and this had never occurred to me—he wanted to make the audience laugh. I was emotionally geared toward drama, but Charles said, "You can always do drama later. Try comedy first." He would come to my apartment and do Norma Desmond when he was doing *Screen Play*. It was improvised and he was a master at improvisation and very, very witty. I was simply taken by this person who could transform himself. And I said, "You know what I like about you is that you act the obvious." And he cracked up laughing. He went for the way it should be, the primary color.

At first I did feel somewhat timid about the size of the choices Charles wanted me to make. Except, I agreed with him. I had an idea in my head how to play a character. But how to transform that into the reality? I never liked the reality. He said, "You have to get over that. The idea only lives in a certain stratosphere. Physicalize it. Transform it into the human dimension. That's what it means to be a creator." He wanted a theater of scope. He thought that kitchen-sink drama, which was prevalent around us, had people who thought small, and small is what they achieved. He said, "Go for something big." He encouraged me to nakedly play my character's need. The size of the need demanded choices that were akin to the size of tragedy where the character dares to want something enormous. Of course, this led to comedy.

When I first knew Charles, I was introverted and very, very quiet. But when somebody is constantly throwing the word *courage* at you, it finally comes to mean something, and I suddenly got the courage to try things. In *Caprice* and *Exquisite Torture* he cast me as women who were rich and powerful. They posed enormous challenges to me personally and artistically. When we started rehearsing, he said, "No, you have to be much, much more forward. These women aren't like you. They're not withdrawn in any way. They're not paranoid. They're not afraid of the world. They're not intimidated." I was using myself in the ways I had been taught as an actor, but I didn't know how to make that enormous leap.

Caprice is about two opposing fashion houses. Charles played one fashion designer, Caprice, and his opposite is a designer named Clifford Adamant. Zuni Feinschmecker, the character I played, is caught between them. She was like Pat Buckley, who just wants to be in the latest things. Add her fashion sense to her assertiveness and wealth, and she just wasn't me! I found my way into the character by developing her voice. I don't remember the exact source for it, but I probably heard it in a movie. It was a high soprano, almost like I was singing opera. "Oooh, Caprice, how aaare you, daaarling? Oh, it's soooo nice to seeee you." It helped me transcend my own inhibitions.

Feinschmecker means "good taste," and the name Zuni already tells you that she's a little bit out there. I saw a very beautiful photograph of a Zuni Indian wearing shell jewelry whose expression I used because she looked fierce. For months we went to fashion shows and we'd see these ultratall, skinny models wearing clothes. Now, the women buying those clothes don't look like the women modeling them, but they felt like fashion models, so they walked like fashion models, taking on the aura of the clothes. I borrowed that walk.

Caprice dresses Zuni in terribly silly things like a

baby-doll outfit—it was totally ludicrous. But not only was Zuni satisfying her desire for new fashion, she was also trying to satisfy her husband's limitless appetite for costume-fantasy sex. He wanted her dressed as a baby doll, which was fine with her because she thought the outfit was gorgeous and Caprice designed it and she's nuts about Caprice. But somebody calls Zuni on the phone and says, "I saw your husband. He's taken up with a Girl Scout." Her husband is a pervert. He's taken up with a child! Zuni experiences a lot of pain. As an actor I had to find the way that Zuni felt pain that was distinct from my own experience. In life my pain lasts a long time; I almost question my very existence. But Zuni didn't do that. She was hurt and outraged, so she had a fit! "I have heard enough. I will not dress as a Girl Scout. Never, never, never!" Personally, I would say, "How have I failed him? How did I not know this about him?" But Zuni says, "I wasn't responsible for that and I'm not having any part of it." When I put that voice, the model's walk, and the fierce expression in the photograph together with Zuni's words, I was able to achieve the level of extroverted confidence I needed. Then Zuni could go into action!

In the early days, Charles used to say that I filtered too much of my acting process through my intellect. I thought and thought about what the character wanted, but it didn't become physicalized. I saw his point. I also watched myself too much as an actor. I knew that I had to change those things or I would never be happy. So, instead of thinking about what my character wanted, I tried to make her need completely innate. I began to let it spring from a feeling of terrible hunger, as if I were so hungry that I couldn't go on and my head throbbed and I couldn't keep working. I had to eat but there was no food around, so what was I going to do? That is the character's journey. Bringing it down to such a biological need helped me to grapple with it on a much less intellectualized level.

Rule number one in playing comedy is you have to make that character very real, deadly serious. That's what we worked for during rehearsals. Rule number two is give up some control. Often in life you do things very seriously and other people laugh, and you wonder, offended, "What are they laughing at?" What they're laughing at is probably the way your face and body absurdly expressed that seriousness. When you're playing comedy, you can't dictate your appearance in every single moment. You have to sacrifice a certain personal seriousness and gain an intrinsic levity. For example, in order to listen to my brother's justified harangue at the utterly selfish, lying, abusive woman I played in *Love's Tangled Web*—I mean, she's so selfish that she feigns being completely crippled and makes people carry her around so they won't see her slight limp—I used as my model John Brachmeier's saluki. When you model yourself after a dog, you're well on the way to sacrificing that personal seriousness I just mentioned! I loved that dog. She was smart and I know that she knew she was very, very beautiful. If John yelled at her when she did something wrong, she'd look around the room as if she were thinking, "Well, he's certainly not speaking to me in that tone. To whom could he be referring?" That's the gesture I used. The saluki gave me the levity, the freedom, to play the scene. Of course, there are times when other people's personal seriousness is at stake! I played the last empress of China in *Eunuchs of the Forbidden City*. Originally, Charles was going to play it, but he thought I'd be better. He played the dying emperor and he said, "Lie down next to me and do something intimate." So I stuck my tongue right into his armpit. And Charles said, "Yeah, that's exactly what I mean. But don't do *that*."

When I'm playing a role, I can't pass a judgment on the character because I wouldn't be able to be truthful. For instance, I did a play directed by Julian Webber at SoHo Rep last year. It was a Joyce Carol Oates one-act, called *Tonal Cluster*. It was based on an actual murder that took place on Long Island. The son of a middle-class couple killed their neighbors' daughter. The convention of the play is that the boy's parents are being interviewed by a television talk show host. The host asks incredibly embarrassing questions and eventually puts them on trial. These parents are in total denial about their son, which evidently was true. Julian kept saying, "This woman doesn't know as much as you know. Try to play a woman who allows herself to think about only ten things. She's narrowed herself down that much." That was very, very hard for me. I had to look at each line carefully so as not to give away any of myself. To play her I couldn't bring my current self to her.

So I based her on myself as a teenager as well as several Long Island housewives I knew back then. They were actually bright women, but their niceness and sweetness were phenomenal. When I lived on Long Island, I had no worldly experience. I thought back to those days and how I regarded the world. I wasn't on to people. I didn't know people were highly motivated and after something. It was sort of like living in a cocoon. So, I thought of myself in a closed space, and my mind became smaller. Then I had to think hard about the motivation of each line. Was I avoiding? Did I plainly not understand?

In order to answer the questions as honestly as I could, I had to find the way to not understand what the talk show host was getting at. If I experienced a fleeting inkling that I was being asked a loaded question, I made the decision that I didn't know how to answer it. I repeated things as a way of not knowing how to answer questions. As a matter of fact, when the character finally expresses herself, people laugh at her as if she's holding something back. But she wasn't; it was denial and avoidance.

Julian was really helpful, but of course he's English and they're so thorough! I love a good director. Even if they're not particularly good with actors, if they can communicate their vision, I'll go with it. I most often take the style of the play from the director. Lee Breuer had a big vision in *Lear*. I played Albany, Goneril's wife. In Breuer's adaptation of *King Lear* he reversed the gender of all the roles. Because I learned to make a fool of myself in rehearsal with Charles, I always feel the freedom to try many, many different ways to get what that character wants. Lee wanted Albany to be a slight Southern gal who made a bad marriage. That marriage was probably good for three weeks and then turned rotten 'cause my husband, Goneril, runs around, drinks too much, and is flaunting an affair right in my face. Lee said, "Play her as a drunk. Try that. A woman who just takes to the bottle, and who then suddenly finds that she has to take action because it's not only her life that's being ruined by her husband's nefarious, devious activities, but Lear's as well." Suddenly one night I thought, "With this Southern accent, I'm just going to do Blanche" [Dubois, from Williams's A Streetcar Named Desire]. I used the powerlessness of knowing something is not right but not knowing what to do about it. I framed that in the poetry of

Tennessee Williams's women and culture. They're on the fringe, not directly related to life. They're living a bit outside because they're living on the edge.

I didn't come back onstage until practically the end of the play, but I come out roaring drunk. My horrible, sadistic husband has just come screeching up to the house with his hussy. So, when Kent tells me that they're going to kill Lear, suddenly Albany comes to life. She says to herself, "Okay. It's much bigger than just me. Goneril's lost to me anyway. Why am I doing this to myself? Drinking isn't going to bring him back." I took the bottle and threw it right in the garbage can. I had to right the situation. That last part is very true to the story in Shakespeare's *Lear;* however, there Albany is always a righteous, decent person, which I found terribly boring. I'd much rather play a person with a great change. A big revelation is always preferable!

VINIE BURROWS

Vinie Burrows reads the entire text of the play she is performing before every performance— not just while she is in rehearsal and collecting information, but before every performance. What does that say about her acting process? It bespeaks a serious and intelligent approach. She is assiduously respectful of the material. She uses this reading to deepen her connection to the ideas and to the character, and sets aside time each day to build the bridge between her daily life and her work life. It also refreshes her contact with choices she's made in exploring one of her primary rehearsal techniques: scoring the material. She works like a conductor or musician, sensing the tempi of the sections and making choices about how they might be rendered. This technique allows her to open to the inner music of the text. With the score securely set in her mind before each performance, she is then free to improvise on its themes.

Vinie Burrows has had a challenging life as an actor. As a youth she appeared in many Broadway plays including Wisteria Trees with Helen Hayes, the revival of Green Pastures with Ossie Davis, and Alan Schneider's production of The Skin of Our Teeth. She worked with Thornton Wilder on three plays and appeared in the American premier of Genet's The Blacks. Despite her work in these notable productions she grew disappointed with the quality and quantity of roles offered to African-American actors. Out of her anger and frustration, she produced and directed her first one-woman play.

With children to raise and enormous creativity that demanded expression, she became an actor/manager. She's given five thousand performances of her seven one-woman shows in the United States, Asia, Europe, and the Caribbean. For both her artistic successes and for her political work for women and against apartheid, she has been honored with awards by Actors' Equity, NOW, and the Working Theater, to name only a few. Our interview had to be rescheduled because she was called to an emergency session at the United Nations, as chairperson of the Sub-Committee on Southern Africa of the NGO Committee on Human Rights. The obvious integrity and dignity of her self-created life and artistic work notwithstanding, Vinie Burrows still suffers each rejection and hurt at the hands of the commercial theater world.

I interviewed Vinie Burrows while she was playing the role of Obatala, one of the Yoruba orishas, god of sixteen paths, in Pepe Carril's play Shango de Ima. As an actor and a person, Vinie Burrows has undertaken the diligent perfection of as many paths. Both her life and her work have a singular dignity and a sense of striving for "the strongest and simplest choice." She says, "I also have a soul." She does not expand on this idea, nor on most of the ideas in the interview. Take her words at full value. Imagine working purposefully to engage the depth of your own being as Vinie Burrows does.

**"THE ARTIST IS ALWAYS
SELECTING, ALWAYS REFINING,
ALWAYS SEARCHING FOR THE
CLEANEST, STRONGEST, SIMPLEST
CHOICE. THAT'S WHAT THE
WHOLE SEARCH IS ABOUT."**

I am remembering my early years when I was the pro-
tégé of a wonderful woman named Doris Sorell, who
came out of the American Negro Theater. I credit her
with my basic technique. Whenever I act, I go back to
prime things that I learned from her. She trained as an
opera singer before coming to theater, and scoring your
part was an important part of her instruction. Take a
symphony, for example. You can look at it as a complete
piece. It will also have andante, adagio, allegro, and con
brio movements. You can look at a script in the same
way. What is the overall color? Then, what are the vari-
eties of colors and dynamics that make up its parts? If this
scene is con brio, you use your voice and body to express
that. You find the pitch, color, and rhythm of the beginning, middle, and end. You have to locate the climax in
order to know how to begin and then find the colors of its
parts. Then you begin to know where the piece is going
thematically and emotionally as well.

Once I've scored the whole, if something is not
working, I can use technique, variety in pitch, rhythm,
color, to change the dynamic. These are the notes of the
piece, la, la, la, la, la; but there are many worlds I can create with these same notes. So, if I artificially alter the
rhythm, something within me will happen, and I make a
new discovery. As an experienced actor I now find I have

all the time in the world to make a change, even in the midst of a performance. I can stop in the middle of a section, make an adjustment, and continue. I remember Helen Hayes once got an acting note from Josh Logan. She must have thought it wasn't right and decided, "Want that note? Okay. I'll give you that note!" So she took that note and she did *everything* in that color. He was livid. "How dare you, madam!" There was a big blowout. But imagine having the technique to be able to do that! She was an extraordinary craftsperson.

The real question that is answered by technique is, how do you sustain an excellent performance night after night? I've seen some wonderful performances by amateurs in the theater, touched by inspiration, which they could never repeat. When I was a very young, very pure actor, I just acted! There was that childlike, wonderful freedom, that welling up. Part of my journey as an actor is getting back to that first freedom. It takes a lifetime to get back to that simplicity. Then, when you have the welling up *and* the experience *and* the technique, you have something really special.

You also need intelligence unless you're going to be Trilby to a Svengali. Short of that, you have to know what the words mean. You have to know what the writer's saying with your part and with the entire piece. That's not necessarily easy. Normally, I work on my own in one-woman shows, in the age-old tradition of an actor/manager. In that case, I generally have only myself to rely upon to unearth the meaning of a text. But currently I am playing Obatala in *Shango de Ima,* a Yoruba mystery play by Pepe Carril at the Nuyorican Poets Cafe. She is the Mother of Earth and of Man; the Lawgiver; Father-Mother; King and Queen. She gives birth to Shango de

Ima, King of Lightning and Fire. It is a very complex play and it involves working with several other actors. The cast as a whole is only now beginning to understand the play as we run it in performance. People who act off-off-Broadway work all day and then rehearse four hours at night, so that is part of the problem. But so many of their discoveries could have taken place sooner had they exercised their intelligence and applied it to the meaning of the words, to the script.

Beyond technique, it is inspiration that is the most vital element of the acting process. After your research, scoring of the piece, and the demands of learning the lines, there comes a time of quiet waiting for the idea which clarifies a scene, a character, or perhaps the totality of an entire piece. That inspiration, or insight, may come suddenly, but when it comes, you know that the gestation period is over and the actual labor begins. As an example, I was perhaps two weeks into rehearsals for *Medea,* in anguish because I was still searching for guidance, for inspiration. I went from Santa Clara to San Francisco for a Sunday-morning service at Glide Memorial Church in the Tenderloin district. It was packed with a motley group. The singing was great and spirited. When the sermon began, the presiding minister said, "Life begins on the other side of despair." That was the "Aha!" moment for my creation of Medea. Everything fell into place and I rode that impulse with ferocity. My work as a creative artist became focused and grounded in that implacable reality. My joy was overwhelming. Of course, working with great material makes the waiting easier and may even quicken its coming.

While I am waiting, I meditate, I think about the play and I always research and read. For *Shango de Ima*

I'm also reading about the life of the Afro-Cuban because Pepe Carril, the playwright, comes out of that tradition. I am reading in depth about the orishas, the gods who represent the aspects of existence. I have rediscovered C. L. R. James, whose monumental book on Haiti has been extremely useful in deepening my understanding of some of the play's issues. That deepening may not show up in the performance in obvious ways; I may have simply found greater clarity in my relationship to another character. But it is there. And I always prepare for each performance by reading the play.

The acting process is endless; the drive to simplify, to clarify, to find the strongest line that makes the performance part of the universe is eternal. In my lifetime I have experienced less than two dozen performances which felt like part of the rhythm of the universe. I remember one incident. I was in costume in a rather primitive dressing room of some school, waiting to go on. There was a theater magazine, and I opened it up and discovered that Thornton Wilder had died. I had been out of the country and I hadn't heard. I worked with Thornton on several plays, *Skin of Our Teeth*, *The Happy Journey*, and *The Long Christmas Dinner*. He was a dear, dear, brilliant man and very kind and generous to me as a young performer. I was stricken by the news of his death. I decided that what I would do was to go onstage and tell Thornton, through my performance, how I had grown and developed as an artist. I wanted him to be proud of that. The people who saw that saw one of the greatest performances they'll ever see in their lives. I went on knowing that he was there in that audience with those spectators. My consciousness was heightened. I eliminated all extraneous elements. There was no busyness, there was no fussiness. It was direct and clean and simple and strong.

My characters came right out of the earth and I was there with each one.

Nothing we have discussed so far regarding process and technique has been affected by racial issues. However, I would not have gone on the solo career path had it not been for the racism of the commercial theater. Commercial theater afforded me no outlet for my talents. I did not "remove myself from commercial theater." While I was waiting for those opportunities to come, I produced my first commercial solo production, *Walk Together Children*, in 1968. Take a look at the twelve New York newspaper and magazine reviews I got which said I was marvelous! I said to myself, "Oh, the time of opportunity is here!" Appearances on the *Today* show, *The Merv Griffin Show*. "Oh, it's here!" And then, nothing. Nothing. I received a call from an agent at William Morris who said, "You can do better for yourself than we can ever do for you."

Then someone called to say they were casting a commercial and needed an actress to play a Pygmy. Was I interested? I was so hurt. I was so hurt. I wasn't going to lie down in front of a truck, but I could use my anger and rage and frustration at a system which couldn't use me to develop my own career in earnest. I had two children to raise and support. I looked at my assets and started creating, producing, booking, and in many cases, directing my one-woman shows. I toured theaters and schools all over the world. I wrote letters and press releases and answered the phone and I financed my family's life. So that was the impetus. And, while rage is not a part of it now, I am still wary of the system, because even when it does use someone, so often it uses them up.

I persevered, and in the process I not only made a living, I deepened my capacities as a performing artist. I've had experiences which would not have come if I had been whisked off to Hollywood to last for two years. Even though theater is the venue in which I work, I am also a cultural worker. I am the chairperson at the United Nations for the NGO *[Non-Governmental Organization]* Committee on Southern Africa. I was one of a four-person delegation sent by the U.N. to investigate the condition of women and children who are victims of apartheid. I'm the international secretary for Women for Racial and Economic Equality. You don't go to Hollywood as a commodity and get that sense of yourself as a person. And see, no one can take that away from me.

I consider myself an artist. I didn't always. I worked in the theater and referred to myself as an actor. Then, one day I was talking and characterized myself as an artist. I don't use the word lightly. I also have a soul. I don't care how you define soul. I have one. My soul has become more and more a part of me and I recognize that it is always there.

I start with characters that are interesting to me, who say something to me. I choose them out of my limited experience. I don't presume to determine what the audience should walk away understanding. I reveal to them, and they take from that what they wish. My job is to reveal these people as clearly, as simply, as authentically as I can: the women, the men, or Obatala, the god. It's a tremendous responsibility, which sometimes overwhelms me. And then I get a wonderful letter from someone who has seen my work and it makes me feel as if I'm going on the right path. You know, Obatala has sixteen paths—she is mother, father, humility, love, vengeance, simplicity, king, queen, wisdom, serenity, destiny, nothingness . . . and she travels them all. I am on my continuing search as well. To show all the paths.

ROSA LUISA MARQUEZ

Performance site, play, and chance are some of the motivating theatrical pretexts in Rosa Luisa Marquez's work. She is a professor at the University of Puerto Rico, an actor/director and a major proponent of social and political theater. Greatly influenced by the scope and agenda of the Bread and Puppet Theater and by the Forum Theater of Boal, Marquez has staged huge, colorful theatrical events and smaller sociological theater interventions in Puerto Rico and around the world.

Rosa Luisa said to me, "In your work you look for answers. I know there are no answers, so I just ask questions and play." The certainty of that statement was quite provocative and impelled me to reexamine the reasons why I make theater. Although those reasons still reflect who I am and what I'm interested in, her statement opened a door on a broader range of techniques that celebrate theatricality itself.

She rejoices in all of the elements of theater. The director steps out from the darkness of the auditorium and appears onstage as a performer, clearly controlling the action. She has put a unique spin on Brecht's ideas by virtue of the vividness and vitality of her vision. Together with her longtime collaborator, artist Toño Martorell, they create a visual theater in which the design elements, the actors, the site, the idea, and the audience play equally dominant parts in creating the event.

The actors and the audience play with

each other and with the "rules" under investigation. This calls for highly developed improvisational expertise. In her book, Brincos y Saltos ("Leaps and Bounds"), she integrated the techniques of all the theaters that fascinated her over the course of twenty years to describe in detail a collection of theater games that her company uses. In this interview Rosa Luisa Marquez discusses parades, theatrical events that collide and interact with other artistic installations, and Forum Theater. And for all her seriousness of intent she has sheer fun in the process.

"I AM TO SHARE WITH YOU VERY LITTLE TIME AND VERY LITTLE SPACE SO I ASK MYSELF, 'WHAT CAN I INVENT WITH YOU SO THAT THIS SPACE AND TIME CAN BE MORE PLEASURABLE?' "

At home in Puerto Rico, Toño Martorell, my collaborator, and I create theater performances everywhere, even at funerals! Our first explorations of site-specific theater came from parades on the streets in San Juan. We had been marching politically on the streets for many years and were fed up with those very boring marches where we just repeated slogans. A parade has to fill an enormous space so its images and gestures must be large. Theatrics cannot be intimate on the street. One performer alone is not enough: you have to have twenty. That goes along with Caribbean aesthetics. The sunlight of the Caribbean is different from the sunlight here in New England. Colors are very bright and people fill their houses with objects and wear clothing in these vivid colors. The colors and sounds and smells of the streets, the kinetics, the movement of people, all were elements we needed to use if we wanted to create a theatrically appealing parade. The topic of the Gulf War was the provocation for one of the parades, but the street was very telling in shaping its structure.

So we called together the people who wanted to say something about the war. These people were professionals in other fields, and while they were committed to this work of art, it was not their main area of expertise. What are their skills? What are their limitations? We went to the performance space to play. It is a space that is overwhelmed by lush greenery. What relationships can be established among all of these forms? Coincidentally, Toño, who is a painter, writer, and performance artist, had a current exhibit of design elements. We asked ourselves, "How can we talk about war with these elements and with these people in this space? When we started working, we discovered connections we hadn't anticipated. Those things that arise during play trigger a subconscious interpretation of what we are doing.

The site for the theatrical event is not the central organizing element of theater, but it is very important. For instance, this room we are in can become a pretext to create a theater piece. [Pretext *is used here in the sense of a theatrical strategy to be explored. The ostensible theatrical purpose is to play with the room. The issues that will arise will do so in the playing. There is also a play on words: the room can be seen as the pre-text, or the theatrical element that exists before the words.*] How do I play with everything in the room? How does everything in the room play with me? These are questions I could answer in a performance. I'm seated on a sofa, my sight line

ROSA LUISA MARQUEZ

is towards the opposite wall of the room. That wall has two cutouts: one reveals an elevated door with a platform in front of it, and the other is simply an eighteen-inch square framed by molding. So, a conversation can take place between an actor's body that's in front of the elevated door and another actor's face that's in the square cutout, or a torso in the cutout and an arm in front of the door, or a body on the platform and a backside in the cutout. The space is bathed by a particular kind of New England light, and I can work with what that temperate, American light evokes in me. The room is giving me information to work with, and what I do is I organize that information. Eventually that organization will produce meaning. It's like poetry. You juxtapose things that are not usually combined.

The actors create the piece as they improvise and play in the particular space. It was the actors who put their arms or behinds in the cutouts and conducted a conversation. Their playing offers options to the director. The director becomes the script sequencer, but the performance text all comes out of the notion of an actors' play. The actors have proposed actions from different points of view, and then I, as director, select. In a way it is what is done in traditional, psychological theater. Those actors show the director behavior, and she says, "No, not that, perhaps . . . try this other way." Yet, I think there are considerable differences. In traditional theater one has to fill a void, that empty theater space, in order to produce meaning. For me, every space is a theatrical or an artistic space because it's filled with sensory stimuli. I would rather get creative provocation from a space than fill a void. I use words as just another element like movement, like site. It is fiction that I'm creating onstage.

There is very little separation between my work as an actor, director, and writer. It is very hard for me to separate myself from the work of art, so I am always finding ways in which to integrate myself into the process! I have working methods that came about while looking at the work of others; for instance, Kantor, the Polish director. He directed puppets and people, and there were times when you didn't know which was the puppet and who was the person. He remained onstage, directing during the performance. If he thought the play should have a different rhythm, he stopped the play and "rewound" the action. Or, in a Bread and Puppet Theater performance, if your ladder falls, there's no problem. Peter Schumann, the director, stops the show and goes in and fixes it. And Augusto Boal developed his whole system of work, Forum Theater, so that he could be "The Joker" and direct the audience, bringing them into the performance. In the process of trying to explain to myself what Kantor and Schumann and Boal do, I've become an artist of that sort. I cannot separate the creative process from the performance process. I find ways in which to be onstage. Some of these arise from the urgency of the moment and I am pressed by "the show must go on," but I'm also pressed by "I want to be in the show." So, I end up performing 80 percent of the time!

Here is an example. In 1986, I developed a piece with Toño Martorell based on a series of his paintings of the Puerto Rican family. Toño would find a photograph, then draw or paint it, and then he would alter it. He took a wedding portrait of a bride and groom from the newspaper and did a drawing of it. He tore up the drawing and put one of the figures facing down and one facing up. He took a group photograph from a high school album and

ROSA LUISA MARQUEZ

drew on it and then cut out one of the faces. He did the kinds of things we do to photographs, like tearing out someone you can't stand or carefully cutting out someone's head to put in a locket. Another was a photograph typical of those sent from New York when the migration from Puerto Rico began, taken on the roof of a building with a view of the city in the background. Toño drew it and illuminated it with color. Each one of the fifty photographs was treated differently. Then we created a theater piece on the same theme, the Puerto Rican family.

The group that I was directing at that time created their own images of Puerto Rican family life in collective sculptures. Many of them coincided with the drawings, though the actors had not yet seen them. Then we made transitions between each of the images. What evolved was a Catholic wedding sequence, with costumes and everything, from the moment the bride is facing the mirror, putting on her veil, to the moment of the family portrait in front of the altar. At that point, we enacted an event from Toño's mother's life. On her wedding night her husband roughly tore her gown off. All of our costumes were constructed out of paper, with the help of the audience before the performance. We had the groom/actor turning to the bride/actress and tearing off her dress. We did the play with the exhibit surrounding it, and there was a confrontation between the actors' work and Toño's.

I'd always been interested in the relationship of the conductor to the orchestra and how that relationship could be reproduced onstage. So, I placed myself onstage as an orchestra conductor and conducted the actors' rhythms. I also created sounds with musicians who were on the sides of the performance. They were to either look at me or sense me so I could cue them to get the precise rhythm of the play. So, that's one way in which I suit myself both as a director and as an actress. I had a performance presence onstage, and at the same time I was directing from stage. In traditional theater the director removes herself from the performance on opening night but still gives notes so that the play comes closer to her vision. Okay. If in reality we are designing this event as directors, why can't we be there and be observed as we direct? I feel that this is another layer of theatricality and reality. Maybe it was a formal investigation of that layer, but at the same time I feel better if I'm there.

I like the artificiality of the stage. I like the stage to have its own set of rules. Onstage I can approach different rhythms that I would not approach in real life, different forms, different connections and chronologies that I can not get to in real life. To what end? To be able to see all the connections; to enjoy theater as one would an abstract painting or music which is not necessarily intellectual; to open and provoke connections and options that will allow me to transform "This is that" into "This might be that . . . but it also might be *this.*"

Forum Theater is a good example of work which provokes transformation and new options. We did a very realistic piece on prejudice at home. The setting was the home of a family that was supposed to be unprejudiced. The Son's high school teacher, who is black, visits the family to complain about the kid's behavior and warns them that he may not make it to college. After the Teacher leaves, the Son says, "Dirty nigger." The Father is outraged and says, "How dare you say that . . . we are all equal . . . Catholics and Christians," etc. Then the Daughter brings home her new mulatto boyfriend, and the Fa-

219

ROSA LUISA MARQUEZ

ther says, "He can be your friend but not your husband." The girl hesitates, but finally complies. She returns the boyfriend's love token saying, "I cannot continue this relationship."

Then I, as the Joker *[or go-between between the actors and the audience]* ask the audience, "Do you agree with this ending?" And most of them say, "No." "Okay, we'll restart the play, and whoever has an alternative to the problem should say, 'Stop,' and go on the stage and replace the oppressed character." Talk about realism! People are always willing to discuss options, but in this type of theater they have to act them out. They cannot say, "If I were in her place, I would do this." No, they have to stand up and assume the character's place. Participants come onstage emotionally charged. What they witnessed onstage made them indignant. This form of theater is very close to reality. In fact, it is an exciting moment of hyperreality.

Actors in Forum Theater have to be very good improvisers and must follow the line of their character. They cannot shift character just because an audience participant proposes something nice. To broaden and train actors within the mind-set of these characters, we bring many people into our rehearsals to comment on situations and behavior. Then, after each performance, we discuss options that arose or what was done out of character, so that next time we can react accordingly. There is no way that you can foresee every possibility. I remember one day a male student substituted the Daughter and he was ready to beat the Father up. And I, as the Joker, said, "This is theater. These are my actors. They have to continue performing. You cannot beat them up. You have to remember you're onstage." So part of my role as the Joker is to keep the experience theatrical. I must be pleasant, I cannot alienate the audience, because if I do, Forum Theater will not work.

The objective is to have as many alternatives as possible. For us, Forum Theater is a research experience. Whenever options are offered onstage, it's important for the audience to know that options have repercussions. When I stop the action because they have found a solution, I say, "Okay, we have seen this person offering this solution. Just remember that if you chose this particular solution, you are responsible for its effects. If you decide to leave with your boyfriend, what will you have to face in society? Is it possible, given this context, to run away with your boyfriend when you're eighteen? Are there other options? I just pose those questions. We do not play out those effects.

Except, once! I went to a women's halfway house, an institution one step between jail and freedom. They were dealing with a subject that was very sensitive: one of the women wanted to get a weekend pass. However, her son was a drug addict and it would put her at risk to be with him because she was in drug rehabilitation. So the Mother wanted to convince the Son to stop taking drugs. We had a captive audience! And nuns were supervising! The nuns went onstage and offered Christ as the only solution, and the Son kept saying, "I tried Christ. He doesn't satisfy me."

The women tried playing the Mother, offering a lot of different solutions, and it was difficult to watch because it was so close to their reality. Whenever the Mother would say to the Son, "Stop doing drugs," he would say, "What kind of example have you set for me?" and this was being said in front of the real mother and her community. It was difficult. Finally, one woman said, "Okay, I'm not playing the Mother. I'll play the Son's Aunt, because I know this guy's aunt in real life." And I said, "Okay, do that." So she went onstage and she said to the Son, "We have done drugs together. I am rehabilitating myself. You don't want to rehabilitate yourself. You're a first offender. I'm going to report you to the authorities because first offenders might get three years in a rehabilitation center and I'd rather you go to a rehabilitation center than to die or go to jail, okay?"

Talk about a confrontation between the limits of reality and fiction! So I said to the women:

"Do you agree with this?"

"Yes."

"What next?"

"A judge and a courthouse."

These women knew a lot more about law than I did because they had gone through many trials. So the women became the Jury, the Judge, and the Lawyer. And the collective solution was to place the Son in a rehabilitation center. The Jury approved, and that was the end of the piece. I told the woman whose story we dramatized that this option was not prescriptive, that this was another way of discussing reality. She could have discussed this with her friends and they could have given options, but through theater we found another way of communicating. Theater was not the only way, just one way—an alternative to private conversations where these options had not been discussed.

So here is a type of theater that can research a problem. It is game-playing, but it is not so removed from psychological theater. People in Forum Theater place themselves into situations where the subconscious plays an important role. I find people resisting less and willing to give more of themselves than if they had to explain what's going on through *logos,* the spoken word.

I like to construct—life is a construction, too. Each decision you make is a chance to experiment with a new structure in the game of life. The word *construction* is related to play. It's related to inventing rules. It's related to time and space. I am to share with you very little time and very little space so I ask myself, "What can I invent with you so that this space and time can be more pleasurable?" As an undergraduate, I was very impressed by the absurdists who said that somebody played a trick on us and just left us on earth to play, in order to kill time. We find ways in which to get ourselves into routine activities every day, and we entertain ourselves while waiting. Many actors and directors try to explain life onstage. I don't feel that life is explainable. I think theater is a game and I can create my own logic. Maybe it is a wish to become God!

LILY TOMLIN

Lily Tomlin is one of the first women who used communications technology to give voice not only to her talent, but to her point of view. She distinguished herself as a member of the ensemble in Laugh-In by taking her characters beyond the sketch hook so that they were capable of sustaining a life, not just a one-liner. In these early characters she began the evolution of a feminist and socially conscious commentary that found expression in award-winning one-woman shows like The Search for Signs of Intelligent Life in the Universe.

Whether the material is her own, written for her by longtime partner Jane Wagner, or someone else's, the imperative in her work is balanced equally between the idea being expressed and the performance. Physicalization in action, her powerful visual sense, and her intuitive emotional connection to the material and themes are Lily Tomlin's inroads to communicating the essential idea behind the character's story. While she uses no formal acting techniques, she does employ activities in a highly creative manner. A cutting edge aspect of her work is her instantaneous inhabiting of multiple characters who speak to each other. To do this required an exploration of ways in which to "seize" a character in a split second so that she—or he—is immediately clear to the audience and to herself. She speaks in detail about the extreme physicality of her very first monologues and her realization that in order *to keep creating these extraordinary people she would have to simplify and refine her approach.*

Lily Tomlin is one of those artists who define themselves: there simply is no one else like her. By the end of her interview the joy, physicality, imagination, drive, and above all, the sense of responsibility that comprise Lily Tomlin's working method are clearly perceptible.

"THE THRILL WAS, AND IS, TO EMBODY THE IDEA THAT THE MATERIAL REPRESENTS."

When I was in college as a premed student, I was in my first play. And it was in my second play that I created my first monologue. I had a friend who was very imperious. Her personality alternated between Snow White's stepmother and Susie Sorority. Like once, in zoology class, I was mindlessly digging up my lab table with a compass point, and she turned to me and said, "I just abhor mindless vandalism." Anyway, one day she said, "I'm going over to the theater to read for *The Madwoman of Chaillot.* You should come along. There are a *lot* of *small* parts." I went, but I had no concept of what it was to read for a part. In fact, I didn't read because I was too nervous, but I filled out a form in case they needed someone for a walk-on. Sure enough, I got a call the next day.

Three of us were supposed to be the mistresses and wives of the capitalist men in the play. In the first act, we were extras in the background of the café, but in the second act, we were to go down into the Madwoman's cellar and disappear forever. I led the three of us down this whole, magnificent, winding, circular staircase. Every time we did it in rehearsal, I would improvise a new, silly, flamboyant entrance, and all of the drama majors used to run out to watch it. They'd comment on the intensity of my concentration, but I was unaware of that. I was experiencing myself onstage as just being and believing the reality. I remember feeling illuminated, as if I had an aura, and I thought to myself, "Oh, God, would it be great if I could make a living doing this!"

The drama majors thought I could act so they gave me six parts in a variety show in which they were doing parodies of *Gunsmoke* and the Academy Awards. I had no respect for the material, it was sophomoric. I thought, "Gee, I do better stuff than this in conversations." However, when I got up to do it, I couldn't. I was dry. I was nervous. I didn't know what *it* was. Actually, for many years I couldn't work someone else's material easily because I could see so many ways to do it, I didn't know where to begin. So anyway, what happened was that in the following days they gave away all my parts, one by one, without saying anything to me, until I was left with only one bit in the Academy Award takeoff.

Well, there was this woman who was the star of the show. Her real name was Sarah Lee but she called herself Sydney. She was very glamorous. She was like five ten. Her blond hair literally hung over one eye. She wore French-cut, electric-blue tights to rehearsal and high heels—she was a vision!—and she had never spoken a word to me, though later we became friends. By this point in the rehearsals I was so insecure that I had taken on nerdlike qualities. I was off to the side sort of practicing, mumbling to myself, desperate about going out to do this last bit, which I was sure I was going to lose. Sydney was leaning on the piano on her elbows with her legs stretched out, and she swung toward me and asked, "What did you say?" I was galvanized. I couldn't speak. Then she said, "If you can't be direct, why be?" Well, that was the final humiliation! I was stripped of everything. When I went out to the Academy Awards sketch, I had nothing left to lose so I started improvising, and I was quite funny. I pretended I was reading cue cards incorrectly and said "acadeeemy" instead of *academy*. I'm sure it was lame, but it was better than what they were doing. After I got a little acceptance, I relaxed.

Then, a terrible tragedy happened. Sydney's boyfriend got killed in a car accident so she was unable to perform for a few days. The kid who was the producer was going around saying, "We need one more bit. The show is too short." And I said, "I have a bit I think would be good." I really didn't know what it was going to be, but I had a general idea because I'd been ad-libbing it in conversation. Grosse Pointe had just been exposed as being secretly segregated. This was around 1962. People were covertly given demerits if they were black or Jewish or even for being swarthy. The scandal that had recently blown the whole secret wide open was that a Jewish doctor who invented something important, like a mechanical heart, was denied the right to buy property. I took this kid Joe aside and said, "We'll do a bit. You'll interview me like I'm a Grosse Pointe matron and you'll ask me all about this scandal."

Now, even though we lived in Detroit and didn't even own an automobile, I knew everything there was to know about the Ford family and Grosse Pointe. See, my mother's maiden name is Ford, and all through my childhood she vicariously lived through the Fords, reading the society page every day. Charlotte Ford was just my age and was just about to have her debut, and so I was very conscious of the Ford family's doings. In the bit, I was a Grosse Pointe matron named Mrs. Oddly Earbore III, and I talked about my social activities, my charity work, and my daughter's debut party as the interviewer attempted to ask me about the scandal. I was totally in control up until the last moment. I said, "I see by my clock that I have an important engagement and so I'll be bidding you a very tasteful ta-ta," and I would get out of the chair, spreading my legs in a most ungainly, unladylike way. The whole scene was so focused and regional that, of course, it was the hit of the show.

I went on all the local TV shows as Mrs. Oddly Earbore III. I arrived at the studios dressed in fox furs, a hat, and a suit. I insisted on going there as that woman, not as myself, and everyone at the studios related to me as if I were Mrs. Oddly Earbore III. I remember going on Ed McKenzie's night show on one of the big Detroit stations, WJBK or WXYZ. Ed knew that I was playing a character because he had seen our show, but the technical director and cameraman didn't. They knew that they were to pull the camera back at the end of the interview so they would get a full shot of me as I stood. However, when I spread my legs, I heard the cameraman say, "Oh, God, we've got to do it all over again." That was what I thought was the richest, the most interesting, and the most fun: to be that person or at least to make you think I was that person. Then we're all going on the same trip. That's the fun of it.

I must have been good at creating my own characters, responding to my own impulses, and working on my own. I know I got a great deal of enjoyment out of it. I remember working on one of my earliest monologues, Lucille, this woman addicted to eating rubber objects, talking about how she's now a normal, everyday, socially acceptable alcoholic. If I changed one inflection, one nuance, or even switched the order of a few words, it was as if I had an epiphany. I'd say to myself, "Oh, God, *that's* how that's supposed to be!" When my poor friends came over, I'd do the monologue for them as if I were going to show them something brand-new. They must have gone through hell! I was tireless and so impassioned. My obsession to do it was unbelievable. I just loved this work so much. Going to the Improv, having a new monologue to work on, being so excited and thinking it was so great, so interesting. I was mad for it.

Part of that tirelessness was pushing myself because I didn't know how I was doing it. My first characters were all great physical parodies. Lucille Debier, the rubber eater, was clearly loaded. Lupe the World's Oldest Beauty Expert was physically, broadly etched. All my characters were crisp and defined but extreme, because that's how I thought you could differentiate between them. After I'd done my first four characters I thought, "How will I ever think of anything else to do? How many ways can I change my voice and my face?" And, of course, what I learned is that I have to do less and less.

I probably learned this gradually. If you really look at my work carefully, some of my early work is gruesome. How I ever got famous, I could never say! I can show you Edith Ann on *Laugh-In* and it's so terrifyingly bad. And then, just four years later on my first special, she's quite real and suddenly engaging. You can project yourself onto her. Now, in my one-woman shows I have to create a dozen characters who can be readily differentiated by the audience so no one is confused. Each one has to have a voice and a body and everything else. What I work toward is to create a character and make it my own in some way so I can seize it and live it in any moment.

What I've always loved about what I do is not just the performing of it, see, it's the idea, the concept, the material. I have very good selectivity. I've always known when something was fresh or interesting. The thrill was, and is, to embody the idea that the material represents. Lupe the World's Oldest Beauty Expert was a great character, but the monologue was wonderful, too. During the course of it she would rejuvenate her face, and then she'd sneeze and it would all fall down again. I was very proud of it as a monologue. On the other hand, someone recently sent me a script, and after I read it I thought to myself, "Why would anybody think that it is worth the effort to rehearse and mount this material?" People are stuck in some old psychological place in which they think this mediocre, corny stuff is revelatory. To me it's nothing but old psychic material that the species needs to be liberated from. I know it must be important for some people, but I can't bring myself to do it. I'd rather do Lupe and say, "Perhaps you've read my ground breaking work on the aging process? I discovered that time is a continuum; which, simply put, means it cannot be stopped."

I guess this brings up the projects in which I work on someone else's material. That was really difficult in the beginning, especially if I approached acting as something different from what I just did intuitively. The first time I went to an acting class in New York when I was around twenty, I tried to integrate the intellectual concepts into something internal and emotional, but they didn't make sense to me. I remember doing a scene from *Bus Stop*. In an effort to integrate all these bizarre exercises and put them through my body, who knows what came out? It must have seemed very grotesque, because I could see that the class was baffled and it was humiliating. Then I did the scene again and went on my instincts and impulses, and it made more sense.

I don't really do Stanislavsky, certainly not consciously or formally. Although I always thought a good autobiography for an actor would be called *Sense Memories I Have Known*. I know what sense memory is and how to call it up, but whatever process I have, I derived from osmosis. I just do what I have to do, or what comes up or what works. Often my body tells me to do something, and when I do it, it feels right. I don't even know that I can really learn technique because I'm either too intuitive or too visual. There are so many actors I respect and am astonished by who utilize techniques that I hesitate to say anything negative on the subject. But, for instance, when actors break down scripts, I'm dumbfounded. I get very confused by approaching acting intellectually. I've tried to work with a teacher who was very intellectual, but finally, for me, the work has to be feeling oriented. I trust myself enough now that I think if I were cast in any part that had substance, I would be true enough or honest enough that I would never be off the mark.

You know, I don't use Stanislavsky's approach, but I do use activities and a lot of background material. I always see the character. I imagine her behaving in the moment, and then I get ideas for business or behavior. For instance, on the film I just finished with Danny Aykroyd and Jack Lemmon, I am the daughter of a man accused of being a Nazi war criminal, a big SS officer. Danny plays a university professor who kills my father, unbeknownst to me, and winds up marrying me. As far as background for the character, I was going to have her have a South American accent, because she was raised in Ecuador. So I developed a nice South American accent with a slight German overtone if I needed it. The director had something else in mind, a Swiss/German accent. Well, I rationalized that I was raised in a German community, rather protected, isolated, maybe even went to a convent school.

The tone of the movie is comedic, but the circumstances call for something darker as well, and the activities have to suit the material. I don't know if this will be in the movie once it's edited, but in one scene we're crossing to Germany in an ocean liner and we have this very comedic wedding night. After we have sex, he rolls off of me and we have this little dialogue in which I tell him with guileless sincerity that I have never liked having sex, but with him I thought it would be different . . . but it wasn't. When I thought about the scene beforehand, I visualized taking a Kleenex, see, putting it between my legs, and running to the bathroom at the end of the conversation. We shot it that way, but actually, I visualized an earlier part to the activity. When I say, "I don't like having sex," I wanted to be blowing my nose very naturally. It would foreshadow the Kleenex between the legs, but I also thought that cleaning my nose while saying "I thought with you it would be different" would be a very funny activity for the moment. I don't mean ha-ha funny, but funny. However, because of the camera placement and the nature of the shot, I had to be close to Danny and I never got to try that. But it didn't stop me from using the tissue between my legs, later.

Choosing the right activity can determine so much in telling the story. I remember in *The Late Show,* I had to come into the dark bar from the bright sunshine to tell Art Carney about selling some grass really cheap to get money to buy information. I wanted to convey the fact that it was hot out and that I was bothered. Bill Macy played the bartender, and my character thought he was a lowlife. I wanted to do two things, which I ad-libbed. I came into the bar and I said, "Let me have a Coke." I watched as he went to put ice in the glass, and I stopped him from using his hands with, "And use a scoop," because I had contempt for him. Then, I drank this big, tall glass of soda down without stopping, looked him in the eye, and said, "This is Pepsi." I really believe that selectivity is an important part of being an actor.

You have a lot of opportunities to play on film because you do a take and you've planned all these physical activities and then new little ideas come. When I did *9 to 5,* ten, twelve, fourteen years ago, I was still at a place where other people's material daunted me. In order to feel prepared, I wanted to choose a lot of things to describe who the character was. I went to Colin Higgins, the director, and I said, "Oh, Violet's got to have a bunch of children to show why she stays in this job. And her mother should live with them, too." So he let me have two—I actually wanted triplets—but he gave me two little girls in Bluebird costumes. You only see them outside the garage. Oh, and a teenage boy. And you see Violet's mother with a neck brace on, because I wanted the responsibility for her injury occurring while I was driving. So, this family life brought up the potential for all sorts of physical stuff, like bringing all my kids' drawings to work and putting them up over my desk or taking all the paper out of the wastebaskets to bring home for the kids to

LILY TOMLIN

draw on. I came prepared to do all that, and of course I hardly got to do any of it. Every day I brought in activities to use in whatever scene we were shooting. Like, there were a couple of entrances that I had to make into the big secretarial pool of which I was the boss. I wanted to be very nurturing so I cooked up what to bring to this person or to put on that person's desk. Then, added to the activities, Jane Wagner would give me great lines. When Hart gets promoted over me, my line was "I've never seen anybody leapfrog so fast to the top, in my life," and Jane gave me the line "And I've got the bad back to prove it." Colin let me use that, but I must have driven him crazy.

KATHLEEN TURNER

Kathleen Turner is not simply an actor: she is a movie star. In her interview she reveals some of the reasons why this is so. While many actors interviewed in The Actor Speaks make the transition between stage and film, they first speak of their performance and later refer to the exigencies of film technique. Not so with Kathleen Turner. Her expertise with regard to the technical demands of filmmaking is evident. Many of her acting concerns are technical: what is the width of the lens, the camera position, the nature of the shot? How else can she know which part of her body is actually in the frame, acting? She has attained technical mastery and has developed an acting process specific to film.

Kathleen Turner chooses to play strong-minded, strong-willed women, capable of taking care of business when necessary. It was not surprising to find her acting process reflective of her performances. Acknowledging empathy as a requirement of acting, she rejects the notion of finding commonalities with her character. She thinks what her character thinks, and this cerebral method is a hallmark of her performances.

She is in the enviable position of being able to star in films and then to appear in leading roles in plays like Cat on a Hot Tin Roof and Indiscretions. She discusses some of the difficulties in making the transition from an acting process for film to one for the stage. She also talks about the joy she experiences in be-

ing able to fully physicalize a theatrical performance. But above all, her interview directs our attention to the many demands placed on the actor in making films. She asserts that in order to be free to act she must have all of these technical issues under control.

"IF YOU CAN HIT YOUR MARK, BRING EVERY GESTURE WITHIN FRAME, AND GIVE YOUR VOICE EMPHASIS WHERE THE SHOT NEEDS IT—IF YOU CAN DO ALL THAT WITHOUT THOUGHT, THEN YOU GET TO ACT."

When I did *Body Heat,* I knew absolutely nothing about film. Luckily for me, it was Larry Kasdan's directorial debut, too. He followed the cinematographer around doggedly asking, "Why? Why? Why? Why? Why? Why? Why?" I was one step behind Larry, listening. I got the chance to learn as he did. If he had been experienced and had just told me to do something, I never would have known why half the time. I also learned what to ask the cinematographer and director before shooting a scene.

Film is very demanding of technique. At some points it's a matter of millimeters, of focus length or sound. Sometimes you're body-miked but you're acting in a big open space, so you have to make decisions about whether to pitch your voice to override ambient sound or for intimacy. If you can conquer all the techniques so that you don't even have to think about them—if you can hit your mark, bring every gesture within frame, and give your voice emphasis where the shot needs it—if you can do all that without thought, then you get to act.

Many wonderful actors aren't skilled in film technique and I find myself compensating for them. For instance, they're pulling themselves off-camera, and if I shift downstage, I can pull them back on. In *Prizzi's Honor* there's a scene where the ancient Mafia don, played by Bill Hickey, won't let go of my character's hand. Bill wanted my hand grasped right under his chin, but he kept drifting out of frame. I said, "Let me control it and I'll make it look like I'm pulling away from you, but I'll keep it in frame." He said, "How will you know? You can't see the camera." I said, "Well, I can feel it in the air." And he said, "Oh, you're such a witch!"

You learn to do it from experience and an understanding of what filmmaking is all about. A lot of actors never ask the lens size or have any idea what that signifies, which to me is just absurd. How can they be doing their job if they don't know this stuff? If it's a 75-mm lens, then there's this much space. The camera's going to see from here to here and from here to here, so you have to stay within these parameters. Of course, there are actors who are technically adept and it is great to work with them. Jack Nicholson is the best! On *Prizzi's Honor,* John Huston used to say to Jack and me, "Just call me when you've got it. We'll come in and shoot." Jack is so technically competent that all I had to do was act. That's freedom! But you don't get to have that freedom unless all the technical demands of film are met.

I worked on a film written by my friend Michael Lessac. To my mind he had to direct it, but he was a first-time director. At one point they were lighting a tight close-up shot. I left, and when I came back on set, there was another camera. I asked, "Michael, what's that other camera for?" And he said, "I thought we could just grab the medium shot while we were doing the close-up." I said, "Well, you don't understand. If it's a tight close-up, all of my reactions are here in my face. Nothing else moves so there's nothing to shoot." He asked, "So, you act differently for different kinds of shots?" I said, "Let's go to my trailer, Michael, and talk this one out."

In this day and age, acting is not just a matter of art, it's a matter of time and money. When I'm doing a major film, you can figure the costs at, say, $80,000 an hour. If you don't feel like it yet or you haven't quite gotten there, you're wasting a lot of money and a lot of people's time. That doesn't meet the qualifications of acting nowadays. It's the most dependent job imaginable. You don't get to do anything until everybody else has done their job and lets you walk in front of the camera. You're so dependent on everyone else that it's self-destructive not to be ready to give everything you can.

With Kasdan, in *Body Heat* and *Accidental Tourist,* the whole cast rehearsed for four weeks, like a play. There's almost no one who does that except Larry. Everybody ended up working free for two weeks because no studio wants to pay for four weeks of rehearsal. We had developed a clear arc and image of the piece so it was especially easy for us to shoot out of sequence. But, even without an extended rehearsal period, shooting out of sequence is not a problem. You think the whole thing through and determine the arc of your character. You learn how to do that, how to place it for yourself. Where are the character's changes? Where are the realizations? Where are the high moments of emotions in the film? Then you make sure that you get to that level when you need to. For instance, on *War of the Roses* we shot out of sequence with no rehearsal. Michael had just finished *Black Rain* and desperately needed the days off to rest before he started filming again. I had to think about my character, how her power grows, how her individuality grows. I had to make her a fairly strong persona in the very beginning but willing to sublimate her judgment to his. The scene in which she said, "I made thirty dollars. I sold a pound of pâté to our friends," and he says, "You're selling liver . . . to our friends?" was her realization that he didn't care about her interests. That is when she began emotionally detaching herself from him. The next illuminating turning point came later when she realizes that they've shared one common goal, his success, and as a result she has no life of her own. What makes it all the more frightening is that she has no friend to talk about it with. Keeping these developments clear in your mind enables you to go into each scene and tell that specific part of the story.

I would say I'm a cerebral actor. I'll only qualify that by saying I average about five stitches a film, so I'm a physical actor as well. I do most of my own stunts because I love it, it works better for the character, and because it scares the producers, too! I think what my character should think. I definitely think in terms of objectives. What does my character have to get in this scene and what do I want to convey? I absolutely do not look for the similarities between my character and myself. It's none of my business whether we seem to have areas in common or not. I don't feel like she is me at all. I can watch one of my films and laugh, "Oh, shit, that girl's so funny!" Obviously, there are elements of my stubbornness or my clumsiness or my sense of humor that I use to be her. You use what you've got. But acting is not about my real life. It's not about real time. I'm not living the moment. I don't think I filter something through myself. I perform. Acting, to me, is a selection of communicating signs. I know what I want to communicate to people. I choose the gestures and the tone of voice, and I'm given the words with which to convey it. My job is to illuminate the intention of the writer. I rather believe that all the information I have to have is in the script. Of course, you can work up the whole back story—all that stuff—but that doesn't change the given action you have to commit on that page of dialogue. I have the circumstances, I have the words, and I think about the intention if it's not entirely clear. That's all the information I need. I don't do any research per se. I use what's on the page and my imagination.

I'm not interested in characters who don't try and change something, who don't try and affect their circumstances. There are so many times in film that women are used as objects, not as people. Essentially, if you took the woman out of most scripts, you would simply have a man without a wife or a girlfriend, but it wouldn't change the inherent action, it wouldn't change the man's character. So maybe it's a kind of reflex woman's thing that I won't play someone who is treated as an addendum. And then, showing the character thinking is important to me as a woman. Therefore, manipulative women are interesting to play. They affect the action; in fact, they are the action. To some extent the characters I'm attracted to must be intelligent. They've got to be people with desires and intention, not just "the girlfriend" or "the victim."

The joy of film is that your choices can be so specific. The camera can record the exact word or hand movement or eye movement you intend. A 150-mm lens can make your eyes eighty feet wide. The moment you choose to blink or when you choose to inhale or exhale is what you're saying in the scene. Let's say the shot is of three of the fingers of your hand, and one is tense. It can be that specific in film. It's just fantastic. You choose exactly where you're going to show what you want to show because it's that tight. It's so glorious. When you act onstage you don't get to do all these beautiful, specific, tiny little things that film enables you to do. On the other hand, I love being onstage because there's no one between me and the audience. Nobody's going to step in and interpret me or edit me.

Onstage I use my whole body all the time: "What's my left foot doing? And my right elbow is just so happy!" It's just great! Even when I put everything I've got into my eyes, I never feel as alive as when I'm using my whole body onstage. I swear, there are nights when I can look out there and say, "That guy, tenth row, fourth over, is not listening to me. *Zap!* Okay, now he is." I swear, it's like you can read minds. It's amazing. You're just so alive and you have time to think of everything. If you've ever been in a car accident, you know that the ten seconds between your realization that you're in for trouble and the moment of final impact seem to last forever. You can make extraordinary decisions to minimize the hit: should I steer to the right; should I accelerate or hit the brakes? That's what good stage acting is: stretch, stretch, stretching time. You have time to think about what your hand is doing. You have time to think, "I want to hit that note on this word." You have time to make every single decision. Then, of course, after doing that for three hours, you want to throw up. Stage is more exhausting than anything, but fabulously alive.

Toward the end of the second week of rehearsing

KATHLEEN TURNER

Cat on a Hot Tin Roof, I was getting worried about my performance, and I thought the director and the other people were, too. I didn't seem to be breaking through to the character. I was totally committed to Maggie and I thought I had a really good understanding of her, but she just wasn't fully there. Howard Davies, the director, kept saying, "In this section you've gotten much lower and I've got to have you much higher." I'd start to build toward the high point and I'd hear this little voice inside my head going, "Big enough. Big enough." In film, if you get that emotional, it looks distorted. You cannot do things too large, not emotionally or physically, because it looks ridiculous. I don't care how real it is, how true it is, how much of a tragedy you truly honest to God feel, it doesn't matter. If it gets too big, it looks absurd. So I had this little editor in my head saying, "Okay, gettin' there, gettin' there . . . big enough!" Suddenly I realized I'd been adjusting myself to film size. And I said, "Howard, let's go back to the top of act one. I have something to show you." I'd forgotten the freedom of the stage.

Maggie is one of those roles where the actress first picks up the script and says to herself, "Oh, look! I talk for forty-nine and a half minutes!" Then you get up on-stage and realize, "God! I talk for forty-nine and a half minutes!" So, concentration and stamina were critical. They are important assets an actor can have for any role. You need stamina to rehearse, and then you must possess three hours of performance energy, which—let us not underestimate—is almost like adrenaline poisoning. You must be physically very, very strong. I'd say that concentration is my greatest asset as an actor. You must be able to concentrate so that the truth you've created is inviolable.

FRANCES McDORMAND

The throughline of Frances McDormand's interview is her vivid sense of turning her self-perceived flaws into strengths. She connects her personal growth to the moments when she was able to use what she once saw as a flaw to liberate a character. The felicitous result is that as she liberated the character, the character liberated her. She traces the link between her personal and artistic growth to a progression of women she played.

Producers and directors often classify actors; you won't get the role if you don't represent the type they're looking for. This failure of imagination on the part of the professionals with hiring power reflects the shallowness of their understanding and their lack of respect for acting. Acting is an art of creating images. As Frances McDormand says, "I'm an actor. I can make you believe I am almost anything using artifice and imagination onstage or on film. I've got from the bottom of my feet to the top of my head to do it." Having first come to grips with her limitations and turning them into assets, Frances McDormand then refused to be restricted any further than she would by simply being a woman. She set out to subvert the preconceptions of others and, in the process, defined herself as an actor.

In Blood Simple, Raising Arizona, Three Sisters, Mississippi Burning, *and as* Stella in A Streetcar Named Desire, *for which she won a Tony, Frances McDormand continues to create characters who teach her about herself and her acting as she frees them from the page. She is a realist, a feminist, and a responsible actor. She sees it as her obligation to keep her emotional life present, her analytical skills honed, and to take charge of her process so that she will have longevity as an artist.*

"IF THERE'S LONGEVITY INVOLVED, IF YOU SEE YOURSELF BEING AN ACTOR UNTIL THE DAY YOU DIE AND LIVING A HEALTHY LIFE, THEN THAT IS THE MOMENT WHEN YOU TRULY TAKE RESPONSIBILITY FOR YOUR TECHNIQUE."

It's impossible to extract my personal growth as a member of the cosmic community from my process as an actor. I can point to a lot of different things that happened in my personal life, as well as professional life, that fed into that change.

When I emerged from that incubation period of college and graduate school, years when I was allowed to think of myself as an artiste, I was hit with the reality of marketing, demographics, categorization, and everything that goes along with the business of being an actor. I was categorized as a Southern woman, bordering on poor white trash, who had maybe not even graduated from high school and whom men found appealing and vulnerable—with vulnerable being the key. Those were the only things they could write about me on their three-by-five index cards, when I knew I had a whole list of other qualities in here! For my first four or five professional years as an actor, I put so much energy into the defense of who I was that I developed no other ways of presenting myself. My own defenses weren't broken down until I reached the point when I knew, "All right. They're always going to categorize me. Accent. Not pretty enough. Too big. Too short. Too tall. Too skinny."

That acknowledgment enabled me to take a psychological scar and turn it around, using it to my advantage. It happened first with Stella in *A Streetcar Named Desire*. I began to put that vulnerable, bordering-on-white-trash woman to rest with that role. From that point on, I started creating my next four or five distinct and different images.

When I reread *Streetcar* for the audition for the Circle in the Square production, I knew, for the first time, that everything I had done as a person and as an actor had added up. I had everything I needed to play the role. I heard the language and knew what it sounded like. I knew how to use my background rather than allow it to use me. I heard the voice and I knew the body. I could use to my advantage what others had thought of as my deterrents from advancing as an actress. It was the easiest process I ever had.

The director had envisioned Stella as being a really plump, large, and very slow woman as a contrast to Blythe Danner's white-birch-standing-alone Blanche. At the time I was at the lower end of my weight, but I had sometimes been and always felt like I was a large person. The director was looking at me and saying, "I don't think you're right for my image of the role. You're too thin." That was the first time I had ever heard anybody say, "You're too thin"! My mind was screaming, "No, no, no. You don't understand! Not up here in my head I'm not!" Up until that point I had used my body as something to hide from. This time I could use it as a way to come forward physically and think of it as voluptuousness rather than unsightliness. I knew that Stanley would desire and marry his image of the mother of his children. I knew, for the first time, that I could use my body gracefully to create an image. Stella is the character who taught me grace as an actor. I didn't have to go onstage and try to make anyone believe—no, I didn't have to make *myself* believe, because I did believe. I could make the audience believe anything because I believed it so fully.

In the first readings of *Streetcar* I started looking for the basic structure of the play, the basic formation of the scenes. One of my problems as a younger actor was that I didn't know who the character was from beginning to end of play; in other words, where the dramatic arc of the character lay. I'd be going moment by moment and wouldn't find a strong character throughline. Now I try to find out technically, in a literary and structural way, how the character serves the entire play. What is her relationship to the work as a whole and to each of the other characters? What I think Tennessee Williams did with *Streetcar* is base it on an operatic theatricality. Blanche and Stanley are two divas for whom he's written arias. Blanche enters the room and sings an aria. Then Stanley enters and competes. Stanley opens with an aria and then Blanche enters and competes. Who is Stella? Stella is their audience. Without Stella there is no theatrical performance, no competition. They'd be battling and performing to an empty theater.

Williams has written the play for two characters who come in with everything they've got as actors. The actors playing Blanche and Stanley can be as technically calculated as competing in their theatrical styles! That's why I think the combination of Marlon Brando and Vivien Leigh in the movie, or Jessica Tandy onstage, worked so beautifully. Both women were technically trained, brilliant stage actresses. Brando comes in with this entirely new idea of an acting process. They square off and go to battle as equally matched opponents.

Stella watches the battle and goes thumbs-up, thumbs-down. You can't cast Stella with a sweet, docile actor who can be easily taken advantage of. She's got to be equally matched. Her whole purpose in the play is to be the observer, which takes just as much of an actor. If Stanley and Blanche have been equally matched, then the decision Stella makes is the decision the audience makes. Tennessee Williams says, "Make a decision who has won." The audience gets the information on which to base that decision from Stella.

A discovery I made as a woman doing that play is about the power that a woman gains in a relationship with a man by becoming the protector of his vulnerability. Especially in that situation: 1950s, second-generation Polish man. Stella is the only one in his world that he comes to in his most vulnerable state. He cries on her breast. The power that gives a woman! And also the responsibility that woman has to accept. She cannot reveal that dichotomy in her man, she cannot abuse it or even allow him to see that she sees his weakness. The beautiful, intricate complexity of it! It is not a belittlement of her role as a woman in the relationship, but an empowerment to accept a man's vulnerability, to be the protector of it and allow him to go forward in the world.

Williams's first description of Stella is that she's

narcotized. The sexual relationship with Stanley has narcotized her into an inability to make decisions or be objective about anything in her world. Blanche enters that world and snaps her out of it, and Stella no longer has the freedom to remain a love slave. She has to start making decisions. She cannot remain unable to think. To achieve that I slowed down my pace. I am very . . . I have a very . . . I speed! I have no patience. Stella was all about slowing down. Getting from point A to B and filling up all the air between those points instead of just jumping to B. When you jump, nobody sees you in between. Here, everything was purposeful. Half of the play she's pregnant, so working with that redistribution of weight really helped. My center dropped to my crotch. That's what Stella is; she's the future, the birth of the next possibility.

Slowing down was fabulous! I took up a lot of space being slow and knew that was the corrective to the director's fear that I was too thin. In life I had moved fast as a distraction: "Don't look at me." A moving target, no matter how big, can't be hit readily. With Stella I started staying still and completed it with Masha, in *Three Sisters*. Masha demands the full frontal position onstage and I found a great deal of power from being still in that position. Masha was the first woman I ever played onstage who didn't bounce at all. There was no petulance in the performance. Stella began the journey to playing a full woman. Masha was the destination. Now Masha has started a new destination.

I had played Irina six years before. Watching Mary Stuart Masterson play her fulfilled half of what I needed to play Masha. It was like watching myself, and also my younger sister, struggle with what I had already been through. It worked on so many different levels for me, personally and also as the character. I watched the actress struggling with her process, and I, as Fran and Masha, had a visceral reaction. I watched the character of Irina go through what she endures in the play, and I, as Masha and Fran, had a visceral reaction. I kept having physical memories of what I went through when I played Irina, "when I was that age."

David Strathairn and I invented a term, *shadow acting*. A shadow actor says, "Don't look at me. Look at the other actors." Everything I did as a shadow actor was about supporting the work of the other characters. Because your energy is being put into shaping someone else's performance, you fail to find out as much as you could about your own. "Let me help you. Let me give you anything you need, anything you want," and I exhausted all my energy in that direction. As a result, when it came to the full realization of my character, I didn't have enough information. With Stella I took this shadow-acting problem and used it appropriately. Stella is about putting out until the last moment of the play when she says, "I'm taking back."

On the other hand, with Masha I learned to not give anything. The only thing she gives in the play is to Vershinin, and that's a major dramatic moment for her. Ah, yes, there's one more time she gives. She empowers her husband in the end by giving him dignity. For the rest, it was all about, "Look at me. Look at me. I'm dressed in black. You've got to look at me!" It was a major step for me because I wasn't staying in the shadows. I was sticking my face in everyone's face. Now I am combining taking and giving more, but first I had to learn to step out of the shadows. Each of these women, Stella then Masha, led to the next.

One of the climactic moments for the character in

Eric Overmyer's play *The Deep Rapture,* that I just finished, has her breaking into hysterical laughter. She's built a lie to such grandiose proportions that she's walking a thin line as to whether it's going to work. When it does work, she breaks into hysterical laughter and tears and has this wonderful, little monologue. It was one of the hardest things I've ever done. Emotionally and technically it was the exact same sadistic thing that Chekhov does to the actor playing Masha in the first act. After sitting on the couch for twenty minutes saying nothing, Masha gets up to leave, bursts into tears, and then laughs through her tears. In *The Deep Rapture* the hysterical laughter really worked when the tears came out of sheer terror for my life. Then I could sustain the hysterical laughter for the entire monologue. This was exactly what Chekhov intended.

The moments come when you are ready to grapple with the facts of who you really are. The second movie that I did with Joel [Coen] was called *Raising Arizona.* Because of working on *Blood Simple* and subsequently getting to know Joel and Ethan Coen well, they cast me in the kind of character no one else was giving me the chance to do. I had never even gotten a theater audition for really broad comedy. I created a character with huge breasts and big hair with the help of the costume person.

When I wore the pair of prosthetic breasts that I used for the role in *Raising Arizona,* I became a large-breasted, big-hipped woman in the classic film sense. After that film, every script submitted to me called for a large-breasted woman. Big, beautiful breasts. I'd go into these auditions equipped only with what God gave me. The reactions were classic!

"You're a little younger than we thought."

"You're a little blonder than we thought."

What they were really saying was, "You're flat-chested! What happened?"

So, I started taking the prosthetic breasts into the auditions where I knew that the image of woman they wanted was large breasted. I would take out my little boxes and I would say, "I know what you're looking for, you're looking for a large-breasted woman. If there is not nudity involved, I have my breasts." They became my tools for creating the entire spectrum of "woman" for the people in the film industry.

The true vindication of what I was trying to do with these tools, my breasts in my boxes, happened on a film called *Chattahoochee*. The director's image of my character was Marilyn Monroe. The character whose wife I played had a nightmare dream sequence in which he's having sex with his wife. In her fervor, trying to excite him, she starts to accidentally smother him to death with her breasts. The shot was planned so that the man was lying in bed with his wife's breasts descending into the frame. Well, clearly I couldn't do that scene. I went into the audition and said, "I can't smother him with my large breasts. I don't have them. I'd have to have a body double." Then I pulled out my boxes and said, "I have these. I can create this character for you. All you've got to do is get breasts." He hired me. I created the woman. When this nightmare sequence of disembodied breasts happens, it truly is disembodied breasts that do the scene.

I was concerned about the well-being of the body double because she was being hired to be breasts. I felt I was using her. I said, "When you hire this woman, I want to be involved in every step of it. It's really important to me that she never feels like she's been hired just for her breasts." So this young woman comes to the set, and the director started explaining what she was expected to do. He was handling the conversation wonderfully. The whole time I checked in with her, "Are you okay with this? You understand what you're going to be doing? How do you feel?" She turned to me finally and said, "Well, you basically need my breasts, right? I think I have really good breasts. I actually had some work done on them to make them a little perkier." This nineteen-year-old woman had absolutely no problem being breasts. She was using her attributes in the exact same way I was. We were using them to create the image.

I'm an actor. I can make you believe I am almost anything using artifice and imagination onstage or on film. I've got from the bottom of my feet to the top of my head to do it. I'm already limited enough in the film business by being a woman. I'm not going to let them limit me more than that. I won't go into an audition wearing the prosthetic breasts. I'm trying to present myself as an actress who can *play* a large-breasted woman! I went into one meeting for a character who was a stripper with large breasts. The head of the studio was there, and I described the roles I'd done with my prosthetic breasts, and I showed him a picture of myself with them. I said, "But it won't work for this situation because they're not real and she has to strip." Basically I was saying, "I'm not the right person for this job, but it's very nice to meet you." Then I told the body-double anecdote and the woman executive in the room began laughing. We were laughing, laughing, laughing, but the whole time the male head of the studio wasn't laughing; he was just sitting there listening. And a beat later he said, "Have you considered breast implants? This is something that could be worked into the budget of the film." The woman and I just stared at him incredulously.

After becoming dissatisfied with the benefits I

reaped as an actor in television and film, I found a new commitment to doing theater, at least two or three plays a year. There I found my ethical community. In the process of doing more theater, I've rediscovered that I have an acting process. So now when an actor says to me, "I don't know how I do it. I just do it," I say, "Sorry, yes, you do." I'm only aware of that evasion in other actors because I've had to take responsibility for my way of working. Although you begin to base your sense of process around a common language, like beats, technique is still completely individual for each actor because it relates to our unique emotional self-preservation. If there's longevity involved, if you see yourself being an actor until the day you die and living a healthy life, then that is the moment when you truly take responsibility for your technique.

When most people suffer a great loss or hurt, they develop scar tissue that enables them to go on. The thickness of the scar tissue depends on the person's needs. It is as thick as is necessary to enable her to do what is required of her in the world. But as an actor I am constantly picking at the scab, and so the scar tissue never quite develops because I'm always going, "Wait a minute: pick, pick, pick." I do not intentionally recall when and how I got that wound and who gave it to me. I think that's bullshit. I allow my emotional life and the pain and joy of my past to be a present fact of my life and not something that I merely relive in memory. But because the scar tissue never forms entirely, the past never fully becomes memory, it remains an active part of my present. Not that I keep everything so present. Some wounds just naturally have to be submerged. But even they will rise to the surface when I both need them as an actor and am ready to handle them as a person.

That was such a big part of what happened with

Stella. The pain that I needed to find with Stella could only come to the surface because I had been able to place it somewhere and I could finally look at it. Then, technically and artistically, I could use it as an actor. I didn't have to try and trigger it. In the climactic emotional moment when Stella makes her decision between the past and the future, I didn't look at Blythe when the doctor took her out. The physical warmth of her body as it passed me, leaving me, and the shadow of the leaves on the floor were enough to connect me to whatever personal pain I'd experienced in thirty-two years of living. I can't tell you why they connected me to an emotional truth, but I knew that is exactly what Tennessee Williams intended Stella to feel. It is my opinion that if you work on good, well-written scripts, your evocative emotional life will develop.

I just finished working with Ellen McElduff, an actress who worked with Mabou Mines for about five years. She had a distinct rehearsal style. She learned her lines very slowly. During the rehearsal process she never made an extraneous effort to perform. She connected to the other people she was working with in the scene. She had very long monologues, very long lists, intricate wordplay. If she couldn't remember a line or a word, she would never bump over it and go on. She'd always stop and say, "Wait a minute. Okay," find it, and go on. Gradually, her characterization emerged. My process is in direct contrast to hers, actually backwards. I start performing big choices, always using my full voice from the very first reading at the table. As rehearsal progresses, I fine-tune, coming closer to myself. I use big, bold strokes of characterization to protect me while I'm doing all the shading. I'm getting closer, not to finding Fran in the character, but finding the aspects of myself I can expose for the character. It's the scar-tissue idea. While I'm picking at the scab, I keep a Band-Aid up in front by performing. I wouldn't mind trying to work in a different way, but I'm not sure I can.

I hardly spend any time with the script outside of rehearsal. Most of my work is done in the rehearsal room. However, in my brain there is a hole that is created, a compartment that is filled with nothing else but acting. When I'm not working, I try to simulate the creative process and fill that hole with other things, like cooking and reading. But it's never fulfilled as it is by acting. When I'm working on a role, everything has duality: Fran and the character. I do something and then that compartment in my brain says, "If the character were doing it, she'd do it another way."

Much of the believability of the theatrical event depends on the interplay between the actors. In *Moon for the Misbegotten,* for example, when Josie enters, the audience should go, "Oh! Too big. Unsightly!" In order for the audience to sustain that belief for three hours, the other actors had to help support the illusion. When I hit my brother, he falls down. When I put my hand on Jamie Tyrone's shoulder to push him down on the step, he goes down on the step. When I go towards my father, he steps back. They create the reality as much as I do. However, because of my relationship with Joel *[Coen].* I know so much about the process of creating a complete vision that I cannot rely solely on the other actors. Actors are very low in the creative process in film. You get jobbed in, and all of a sudden you're shown where your character lives or how your character dresses and what your character's taste in music is. It can be diametrically opposed to your month of preparation for the role. So, I can't just stay the actor. It's hard to admit because it sounds so trite, but I've become almost obsessive about collaborating with the costume, set, and lighting designers. Part of my process is shopping for my costumes and finding props essential to my character's daily life. In my real daily life I create my home, a world which people enter. When working on a character, I create my world onstage or on film and the audience enters that. Once that character is in my head and I start filling the compartment—this can happen after the first readings or even before an audition—I start walking down the street and thinking, "She'd wear those shoes."

Joel gave me some of the best advice I've ever had. He said, "The only control you will ever have as an actor is to say no. No matter how powerful you become, no matter how much money they pay you, no matter how many development deals you've got going, no matter how many playwrights are writing plays for you, the only real control an actor has is no. Using that advice, I've gotten to a point where I am considered a good actor now. But the marketing community can only say, "Really good actor. Excellent actor." Implied still is, "But what do we do with her?" I'm still hard for them to figure out. As far as I'm concerned, it's a lot better than being "excellent, vulnerable Southern woman with no education." I end up with directors who are concerned with the development of a script and want interpreters, not just personalities. So, I'm going to work with Robert Altman next on *Short Cuts,* and in the fall I'll be working with Jane Alexander and Madeline Kahn on *The Sisters Rosensweig.* I've fulfilled my personal goal as an actor rather than somebody else's idea of success. I've entered a very narrow marketing world, but one in which I can do what I want, which is to create a lot of different people.

DIANNE WIEST

Dianne Wiest renders characters who freely express their ambivalence while pursuing often conflicting desires. I find that human truth more richly conveyed in her work than in any other actor's. Understated poetry of expression, an empathic response to other actors, a wellspring of feeling, and an idiosyncratic impulsiveness comprise her unique performance style.

She has developed an acting process around her strengths and weaknesses. The fact that her self-perceived weaknesses contribute to her performances is interesting to observe. She attributes the complexity I saw in a character as either a reflection of her personal lack of ambition or her distraction in the moment. Nevertheless, this conspires to enrich her talent, not detract from it. When an actor confidently uses all her parts, she lends her character attributes founded in a human reality.

Her lack of training is, in part, responsible for the singularity of her vision. No other voices inform her process; what we hear is purely her own. While her acting process has some bold elements like working with imagery, props, and costumes, there is an essential delicacy in much of her method. She sees herself as making "choices of the moment," as opposed to pursuing sweeping desires.

I've always marveled at Alice's composure as she follows her impulse and falls down the rabbit hole. Here she is, a child, and instead of panicking, she's relatively self-

possessed in thought. It has taken Dianne Wiest twenty years to get
to the point where she too can follow her acting impulse and then
float down the rabbit hole in wonder and with confidence. Follow-
ing a strong impulse is the basis of her acting process.

"THE CHOICES I'M MAKING ARE CHOICES ONLY OF THE MOMENT."

A cting is like jumping off a diving board and not knowing where I'm going to land. I'm always surprised by what happens on the way down, wondering what's going to happen next. In the early years of my career I could jump off the board, but I couldn't swim. It took me so long to learn how to act, and it was very frustrating. My life would have been much easier had I gone to college. If I hadn't gotten a thing out of it about acting, at least it would have given me self-confidence and a point of departure. It's very hard to learn anything on your own, especially to learn how to act. It took me forever.

I was hired to play ingenues even before I knew anything. My first real job was in the Children's Company at the Long Wharf Theatre. For a season I did a new children's play every month. In a circus play I played a character named Winnie. She was a comic, overweight tightrope walker, and very, very funny. For the first time I dove and found myself swimming. I was able to repeat my performance, which had been impossible for me before. The audience's laughter allowed me an outlandishness, a wildness. I lost my self-consciousness, or some of it.

The following year at the Long Wharf I played my first tragic heroine in Gorky's *Country People,* which Arvin Brown directed. I was doing fine for half the run. I think what initially propelled my performance was that I felt so deeply for the character. Then came the second half. I dried up. I had no idea how to repeat my performance. Because I had so little technique, I had no resources to help me.

I moved around to different regional theaters and then ended up staying at Arena for four years. The company was wonderful and we were all good friends. Magnificent roles were simply handed to me, one after another, but I had no approach. It was hit or miss. The young actors I see today would rather die before doing what I did. One of the actors at Arena said to me, "The risks you take!" I took risks because I didn't know what else to do. I exploited anything in my life so that I could have a moment onstage. It didn't have anything to do with the work. It was bad acting.

I did learn the value of props and costumes at Arena. They help free me and I can usually find new ways to use them. But I regret not applying myself to all the things I could have learned there. When I finally left, it was because I realized that I was not serious enough about my work. I moved to New York and the way I approached acting changed. In a sense, I just grew up. The strategy I'd used when I was younger was exhausting. Everything conspired to make me self-conscious, which is the last thing you want to be. I began paying attention to the larger world and not merely to myself and how I could relate everything to my acting. I drew a big line around certain aspects of my life because I didn't want them to be used up in an acting context, or any context for that matter. I found some measure of confidence and I lost some self-consciousness as an actor. Somehow, during these twenty years, to my own surprise, everything I had learned so haphazardly all piled up and became a technique. Now I feel quite powerful in my lack of training—most of the time.

All right. So what is my technique? Now you've got me! Maybe as a result of my ambivalence about my acting, or the moment, or thinking I shouldn't be doing it this way, or not caring one way or the other, I might bring complexities to a character that don't belong there or, at least, weren't written. Part of my technique is that I risk not knowing what I'm doing or where I'm going when I'm acting. Sometimes that's interesting and sometimes it's not. Sometimes the risks are meaningful and sometimes they're not. There are times when I watch my film performances, I feel my intention as an actor is not necessarily what I'm conveying. It can be very unsettling, which, I guess, is often funny. On a movie I did with Woody Allen, he gave me the direction "Be more fragile." I did what, to me, was more fragile, after which he said, "You did the exact opposite of what I asked, but it was fine. But that's not all. You have no idea of what I'm talking about, do you?" And I said, "No, I don't. I did fragile. What are you talking about?" Sometimes I guess part of my technique is failing at trying to fulfill a direction.

In rehearsal I find it easy to work with images and make leaps from them. *The Summer House* opens with my character doing a five page monologue on a tiny balcony. I had many images of what this monologue could be, but I couldn't make up my mind. I remember jotting down on the first page, "She's in a little prison cell." Then I thought, "It could be an isolation ward in a hospital and everybody has a contagious disease but her." The director, JoAnne Akalaitis, gave me the idea that I never stop looking at myself in the mirror, and that led me in a whole other direction. Then the image of a dictator on a balcony came up. Following through on any of those images opens all kinds of doors. The far more difficult task is repeating it the next day. It's much easier for me to change the image and say, "Okay, now I'm Eva Perón," and avoid anything that I might have learned the day before. So I go and take another risk. Well, so what? It took me until the end of the run to feel secure enough to take a leap now and then and go back to what I did in rehearsal. And this is well into my career. But I had taken a two-year leave from theater and my lesson was, you have to keep at theater. If you go away for two years, don't assume it will all remain at your fingertips.

I find working with images extremely powerful when I'm alone onstage. When I'm acting with another person, I forget about the images entirely. Catherine, the voice teacher for *The Summer House*, said to me, "You're a very reactive actor. You'll lead if you have to, but you're more comfortable reacting." And that's true. I know I have to do my work, but much of my work depends on the other actors. For instance, next month I'm going to play a small film role, a psychiatrist. Now, I should be memorizing my lines. I should be making choices, and maybe I am. I sort of read it through and I'm content to just mush it around in the back of my mind. Sometimes I think about it up front. Sometimes I think, "Oh, brother! I ought to learn the lines because it's long and it's going to be shot all in one take." But basically, I just mush it some more and I'm content.

Some of the stuff that's mushing around back there

concerns whether she should be patterned on a number of women psychiatrists and psychologists that I know. They are very interesting women. I'm thinking about whether they have a common link that I could bring to this character. They all have this incredible curiosity about what makes other people tick. When I think about it, it's almost a little unseemly to look so closely into people. It's a little rude, but you have an office, a forty-five-minute hour, you're paid, so all your unseemliness is normalized by these formalities.

Then, I'm thinking about what propels me at the moment of the scene. I think the scene's about doing something against her better judgment. She thinks of herself as an honorable doctor and she should say to these two men, "I'm sorry, I can't help you," and close the door. What would make this very honorable woman decide to do something that she's not comfortable doing? Well, it's going to depend on the two actors I'm working with. She's probably touched by these two men, or vulnerable to their needs or charmed by them. What the actors do, what they bring to their roles, will determine how I play mine.

Some actors have an almost architectural plan for the character. I've always envied this. I not only don't have a grand overall plan, I don't have a pencil. The choices I'm making are choices only of the moment. My mind seems to be only capable of working in little jots. That's probably one of the things that makes me funny; although it's not funny to me, it's serious. I work this way: I don't know what's going on in my fellow actor's mind; I'm listening to him; I'm thinking; and I come up with a choice. I start to do it. Maybe I think, "No," and begin to go with a different acting choice. I often don't know why I'm making a choice.

I'll try to think seriously about a scene and describe the way I would work to you. All right, let's take the scene in *Little Man Tate* where I make the little boy a macrobiotic shake for breakfast and he throws up on the floor and on my legs. I'd say to myself, "Did I lose my pair of stockings? Have I lost my shoes, too?" Then I wonder if I have to take a whole bath now. Could I just wash off my leg? The issue I'm dealing with is how to cope with the vomit. I'm not thinking about the possibility of failing to achieve my objective or any of those things. My character was such an uptight woman. She hadn't had babies puking on her. So the vomit's potent enough. That's my acting. That's my grand plan. That's what I do, I guess.

ELIZABETH WILSON

Almost twenty years ago I stage-managed a two-character play at the Public. The actors were Elizabeth Wilson and Kenneth McMillan. Kenny's process in the first two rehearsals was clear to me. He listened and reacted, trying out strong actions. But what exactly was Elizabeth Wilson doing? She sat primly on the edge of her chair, her spine rigidly erect. She faced slightly away from Kenny, her neck craned in a peculiar position. She listened more intently than any other actor I had ever seen, often with her eyes closed. She took a long time in responding, but "things" had happened during that time. Her responses offered a world of information against which to react, but they weren't necessarily blasts of clear action. They were often complex, enigmatic, and textured. I have thought about Elizabeth Wilson's acting process many times over the past two decades. I came to understand that she was allowing herself as much time as she required to play her reactions through her body. She doesn't like to be rushed or find out too much too soon. After interviewing her, however, I learned a great deal more.

Elizabeth Wilson's goal as an actor is "to disappear into the character." She goes into the first rehearsal only with an idea of the spine of the play. What she is finding in those lengthy pauses is a sense of her character's mind, which she derives from the interplay between the actors, and how that woman serves the spine. Having assessed that, she assigns *herself a physical task. For instance, in her discussion of two characters, she made decisions about the way to use her eyes. She makes decisions about how a character listens. The way a person listens and physically looks at the world is a unique entry into character. Through physicalization Elizabeth Wilson begins the process of disappearing.*

As a young actor Elizabeth Wilson's goal was to "be in some dreamworld." She found that in the minds of her characters. There came a point, however, when she realized that her desire would lead her into playing clichés. Inspired by people like Harold Clurman and Sanford Meisner, she learned to reveal something deep about herself that made the character live. She could no longer disappear from her self by hiding in a character. Instead, she learned to lend her self to the character in the character's process of becoming.

"SO, IT WAS INEVITABLE THAT I ACT."

I think acting saved my sanity. I started acting when I was little because I was very unhappy and I could escape into another character. In a way, I'm an unnatural actor because it's not easy for me. But once I've found my way, and the character has become part of me, I am so relieved. It's very odd. I think it's psychiatric. If I'm not working on a character, I'm kind of sad. Well, I'm pretty much okay most of the time, I feel whole as just me, but I'm at my happiest when there is that other person in there. So, it was inevitable that I act.

As it happened, I was lucky enough to have parents who put me in contact with theater people in Grand

Rapids. Then I came to New York and got a scholarship, and one thing led to another. But it was as if I didn't have a choice. I'm not suggesting that I would have ended up in the loony bin otherwise, but I think I would have been—I don't know what I would have been. I always wanted to get away from my roots. I feel great guilt about that. I love my parents and all of that, but I just wanted to get as far away as possible. I wanted to be in some dream-world, some dream place. I found that in another person's mind, so that's the way I work that is most fun and satisfying.

Sanford Meisner, as everyone in the theater knows, is one of the great acting teachers, if it is possible to teach acting, which we could debate from now until the turn of the century. He has been ill and recently had major surgery. The fellow who takes care of him said that after the surgery he went deep inside of himself for three or four days, into a kind of Zen mode, concentrating on getting better. People would visit him and he would hear their voices, lift a hand, and smile, but he remained deep in this trance of determination. When he realized through this intense concentration on his body that, yes, he was going to live, he came back to the world alive and refreshed. He had succeeded in honing in on himself. I think that is a good example of what you do with a role if you're lucky. You disappear into another person without going so far that you totally lose touch. If you lose touch, then you're certifiable. But there is a way of disappearing.

Each event that you work on creates a different situation in playing a character. Let's talk about plays for a moment. Dear, dear theater. One of the last plays I did in New York was *Ah, Wilderness!* which Arvin Brown directed. It was beautifully cast with Colleen Dewhurst,

Jason Robards, George Hearn, and Raphael Sbarge, who played the boy. I was Aunt Lily. When you have a play as perfect as *Ah, Wilderness!* or *Morning's at Seven* or, to a degree, *You Can't Take It With You*—I'm thinking of some of the plays I've done in the last ten years—you start with the text. What I do is read the play over and over again. If it's good material, it's well worth becoming really familiar with—almost as familiar as the writer was when he or she conceived it. Then the character springs along with the action.

I try never to speak the lines of the play before the first rehearsal. I don't want to get set in any way until I've met the other actors, the director—all the creative parts. I have an idea of the spine of the play, but I know that the great joy is the collaboration. If I'm firmly set in any way, I'm not going to reap the benefits of meeting these other talents and the thoughts that they bring. Then, if you're lucky, you've got a director who is a leader capable of guiding all these parts, letting it grow, letting it sag, letting it grow—until it's reached fruition. I've always said that the rehearsals are like giving birth. Collectively, you establish this baby and help it grow, and you never, never know what's going to come out. You can't know—and you shouldn't.

The play has a theme, a spine, an action; and out of that spine comes your character, and its connection with all of the other characters. Once I have this knowledge, there is an inevitability about how Elizabeth Wilson, at this time in my life, in this place, is going to do this part. As I read *Ah, Wilderness!* over and over, I realized that in the first act Lily never opens her mouth. She's in love and devoted to Sid, who is the drunk, and she's wounded by what is happening to him. She cares about the family, but she sits for the whole first act and never opens her damned mouth. Then, the third act is like an explosion! She can't stand the way the family is talking about Sid, and she bursts like an atomic bomb. I always felt as if I were just exploding. Pieces were coming out of me, attacking the family in defense of Sid. I'm getting all red now just talking about it. Then she rushes off. That's why the part is so memorable and incredibly difficult. Lily is passive, but she's an active-passive. She listens to everybody and takes everything in. That's her niche, her role in this large family. The mother and the father have a lot to say. Uncle Sid gabs and gabs. But Lily's contributions are pithy but minor. Listening was the hardest thing, but most rewarding. She didn't necessarily have to look, but she heard everything. That was a good exercise.

So, with that in mind, my concentration was on being steelily still. She was so quiet and so observant. And she was a gentle, sweet, happy woman. I never felt that Aunt Lily was a neurotic woman, I think people would say, "Oh, Aunt Lily, the old maid." Not at all. Aunt Lily was a happy, happy lady because she loved this man and he adored her. He just happened to be a terrible drunk, and he could never sit still for anybody or anything. She sat in a very relaxed fashion. She was at home. She was a comfortable person. She walked in a very relaxed way. She was content with her body. So I derived the line of that character, the physicalization and the voice from the text.

Contrast that with Aaronetta, in *Morning's at Seven*. She was an unhappy lady! Aaronetta was living in a house in 1917 with her lover and her lover's wife. Now think about that! And she was a baby. She just never grew up. She was a brat and a real troublemaker. Of course, she didn't know how else to survive. She wasn't mature enough to know what love was; she just had an unrealistic image of romance. She was an unhappy, really neurotic lady. I knew an unhappy woman like that in my family. So all my energies were directed at being a baby brat. Because it's such a brilliant play, all this bratty stuff was funny. I played a lot of the role looking down. I didn't want to look at people so I looked at the floor and the ground and the grass a lot. I was mad all the time.

I played her in New York for over a year and I was so tired. She was just a mess. Finally, I had to leave that play because I was having a back spasm, which Aaronetta gave me. There was a moment after a matinee when I was really in physical trouble and I realized that I wasn't going to have to play her for a while, and I started to cry, "Oh, Christ, I don't have to be Aaronetta!" I just lay there in my little cubbyhole at the Lyceum and I wept with relief. "Get her out of me!" I hadn't realized fully until that moment that she was making me sick.

The role of Penny in *You Can't Take It With You* comes to mind as one in which the text didn't give me the line for the character. It came later. Penny and I have a lot in common, I suppose, and that's where the trouble was. I can be as flighty as anybody, and she's everywhere, all the time. She's happy, she's into a lot of business, a pseudowriter, and she loves her husband. This was a beautiful production, and darling, great, Ellis Rabb directed. I was playing with Jason, Colleen, Maureen Anderman, and Jimmy Coco and George Rose; both of them gone. It was a glorious production and a big success—and I had a hell of a time finding Penny. I thought I was going to get fired. We played for a month in New Jersey, but it wasn't until just before we went to Washington, to the

Kennedy Center, that I finally got my act together. I realized that my problem was that Penny was so close to me that I was trying to find something deeper. But it didn't exist. It's Kaufman and Hart, a piece of frosted cake, and it's just a lovely time. Even the serious parts are not much to worry about. And, oh my God, it's so fast! Once I rid myself of any kind of burden, once I stopped worrying about anything, I found a kind of joy in just being there, and joy in the pace. That sounds really superficial, but that damned play goes so fast and that's what was required. I also found a lightness, a way of moving in my clothes. Anne Kaufman, George S. Kaufman's adopted daughter, who can be a tough lady, came backstage at the Kennedy Center. She said to me, "Well, I guess the clothes make the man." It set me back, but she was right. The clothes did make a huge difference with Penny.

I'm in the middle of something right now which is, maybe, the hardest thing I've ever had to do. You know why? Because it's a real woman: Dorothy Van Doren, Mark Van Doren's wife. Bob Redford is an extraordinary director, an extraordinarily brilliant guy, and he's treating the film, *Quiz Show,* almost like a documentary. He's been working on this project for three years. He'd been looking for a long time to find somebody to play Dorothy Van Doren. Somebody said that he was looking through actors' photographs and finally he saw my picture and said, "That's her."

They presented me with a documentary film of the quiz show, and stories from *Life* and from *Time.* I got all this input before I even knew what I was going to do, which scared the shit out of me. The first few days, I'll be honest with you, I was out to lunch. I was up the creek because of all this input. Everyone had ideas about how

Dorothy sounded. The script supervisor came up to me and said, "Well, you certainly look the part." She didn't say it in a mean way, but she went on to say, "I hope you can play the character, because that's the way they're working on this." I've never had to deal with this much talk and so many things to look at and so much stuff and, of course, no rehearsal time. I'm not at all sure that I'm going to be successful. I'm still floundering, but as I get into it more and more, I'm finding a way.

I think what is finally going to happen is I'm not going to *be* this character. I'm going to *seem to be* her. There's something about Dorothy Van Doren that I certainly understand, but it's not deep in my bones or deep in my anything. It's been treated in the wrong way and I haven't—I'm scared. I'm running scared with her. It's almost as if there's no way for me to be Dorothy Van Doren. Nevertheless, they seem to feel it's all right, but I'm not content. I've been acting for a long time, and sometimes, like now in the middle of *Quiz Show,* I feel as if I have no technique at all. It's not that much of a part, but I'm in a fair amount of pain about it.

It occurs to me that maybe that's the character. This woman is not a happy lady. This woman is dour. She's dry. She's not content. She loves her husband but she's not— She's in her head, a true literary, cerebral type. Gee, maybe I've got the character and don't know it! She's just looking around, restless. Brilliant barbs, one after another. Mean! Oh, she says a lot of mean stuff. Maybe that's it. I don't know. Maybe I've got it and don't know.

There are actors who like to talk with directors, but in my case, most of the smart directors have known that Elizabeth doesn't like to be talked to very much. I like to know that the director is there, but I'm a pretty independent person and I need to do my own work on my own. Mainly, I get into trouble when someone talks to me too much and has too many ideas at the wrong time. I'm not saying that I can't take direction, because I do, but there's a time and place for it. I think I have to be pretty secure in where I'm going and who I am in this event, before the director is even useful for me. I have been incredibly fortunate to work with directors like Mike Nichols, Arvin Brown, and Garland Wright! They are great directors. But I'll be damned if I know what they ever said. That sounds very silly, but it isn't silly at all. If a play's properly cast, a director guides.

I can remember when we did *Uncle Vanya*. I was very well cast for Sonya, although I was too old to play the part. Early on in rehearsals Mike Nichols said, "You know, I think Sonya is a secret dancer." I got quite angry at him. I dragged him up the steps of Circle in the Square and I said, "Now look. You're saying too much to me too soon. I don't want to hear that from you now." And he looked quite crestfallen and said, "All right. All right." Well, I knew exactly what he meant, and maybe he thought I was being too leaden, but I wasn't ready to hear that. Later in my performance there was an element of that secret dancer. But at that point in rehearsal, I think I was assimilating. I was listening to the other actors and I didn't want to be distracted. I just wanted to hear it myself. Of course, I've worked with Mike many times since that episode!

The cruelest, most tragic, most nerve-breaking thing of all is working with a director who damages that line, hurts the growth, and ruins that trust. I once had a terrible experience—I'm not going to name names of terrible experiences because it doesn't matter. But I'll be honest with you, I've had a terrible time with British directors. Anyway, we were rehearsing this not very good play by a very talented writer. It was one of the first readings and we're sitting there, and this particular British director said, "You're not going to pause between words that much? What are you pausing so much for?" I wasn't even aware I was. I was just trying to feel through it. Well, it threw me, and from then on I couldn't seem to do anything. I tried to get out of the play but they wouldn't let me leave, and it was just a mess! I guess I'm too sensitive.

In the first twenty years of my acting I don't think I knew what I was doing. People were getting an essence of me and casting me as the neurotic or the spinster, like the schoolteacher in *Picnic*. If I'd not studied with Sandy Meisner or been to Harold Clurman's classes or worked with Bobby Lewis, or all the Group Theatre people who were my gods, and that's no joke, I would have been a very different actress. Then I got my act together and was able to play from myself more, so that what I was showing was deeper. It wasn't a cliché.

The first difference happened in a Hugh Wheeler play called *Big Fish, Little Fish*. I felt that this woman—I think her name was Rosemary—had such a great need to belong that I experienced it physically. When I came off at the end of the first act, I wanted to throw up. I was exposing myself for the first time in wanting so desperately to be somebody in the group and be successful and have them love me, even though nothing I did worked. There was something about the theme of talented people who, for some reason, can't seem to get it together that got to me. The second turning point was a play by David Rabe called *Sticks and Bones*. That woman, that mother, drove

ELIZABETH WILSON

me crazy because she was in denial. She couldn't deal with her son who returned from Vietnam blind. She was so out to lunch that it was horribly hard to play. God almighty, but that changed my life, too, because I was exposing parts of myself that drove people crazy. I got booed. She walked around the symbolic Vietnamese girl being burned right in front of her, but she remained in total denial. And, for some reason, I understood that very much. In both of these performances I went deeper than I had ever gone before. I allowed myself to expose the character's need by truthfully sharing something of myself with them.

Learning to listen and be in the moment were great gifts Sandy gave to me. I can remember in class—oh, I'm embarrassed to tell this story! Sandy had been my teacher for two years at that point, and he knew what he was doing. He was trying to teach me to be in the moment, and I guess I had a long way to go and sometimes I still do. He slapped me very hard and he said, "Now *that's* how you feel in the moment. That's right now." It was a painful thing, but it was an important lesson. It took that slap on the face from Sandy to bring me down to my guts, to the marrow, to caring.

Acting has been very therapeutic for me, no question about that. I've learned a great deal about myself from those experiences. I've also grown a lot as an actor. I seem to be able to expose myself more, the older I get, and I'm not afraid. I feel I'm very lucky to still be growing.

STEPHEN SPINELLA

Stephen Spinella has won two Tony Awards in the past two years for his performance as Prior in Angels in America. *This is a remarkable achievement. He has played Prior in successive productions, culminating on Broadway. The notable current in his interview is his description of the way he crafts the role so that it is always developing. He likens acting to Zen teachings; perfection is a process to which he humbly submits himself. The "sublime moment" between the actor and the audience can only happen with dedication and a paradoxical sense of both controlling and letting go.*

He separates his process into two areas, his rehearsal and performance processes. Despite having played Prior for such a long time, he allows himself to begin fresh with each rehearsal period. With a kind of selected artist's amnesia he surprises himself by rediscovering central acting issues, like the character's body, with each production. Had he taken on the body from the first rehearsal, he may have cut off a number of interesting new realizations and choices. His performance process is devoted to crafting the moments with greater depth and simplicity.

Stephen Spinella looks for aspects of himself to animate his performance. He takes us through the process of personalizing Grimes in Caryl Churchill's Serious Money, *a character distinctly different from him in behavior and experience. Spinella talks of making the "big leap" and the "small leap," in other* words, working close to himself or far from himself. But even the big leap involves an intricate series of operations in which he looks within for selected aspects of himself that correspond to Grimes.

He cites certain theater games learned from Omar Shapli and Paul Walker as giving him the necessary foundation of expertise and acceptance that has served him well. Whatever is happening on the stage in the moment is the universe he is in. His acceptance and assumption that he is an expert in that universe diffuses fear and keeps the live action truly live. He speaks of a technique he learned from Olympia Dukakis in which the actor slows down the reality of a scene so that he can feel his reactions, wed them to activity, and then play his action. This technique became the foundation of his process for several years.

Stephen Spinella has a complex process involving both internal and external dynamics. It provides a confident structure from which he can command his final need: the absolute control of the moment.

"ALL OF THESE THINGS, CHARACTER, PERSONALIZATION, SHAPING THE MOMENTS OF SCENES, ARE LIKE THE LESSONS IN *ZEN AND THE ART OF ARCHERY*. YOU SPEND YOUR LIFE FIGURING ACTING OUT BECAUSE IT'S ALWAYS CHANGING. YOU CAN NEVER DO IT THE SAME WAY TWICE."

When I'm in the rehearsal room and I'm doing run-throughs, I get to a point where I really feel like I can start acting. I've developed a relationship with the other character, I pretty much know what I'm doing all the way through, I've made decisions about the character's body, and I know the parameters within which the other actors and I are responding. I'm free and I can play. Then we move into the theater and we have sets and lights and costumes. At that point I find that what I really need is control. I need to be able to dominate the space in order to carve out each performance. I need to be able to say, "This is my moment. This is my sound. Nobody else can have this moment except me and my other actor." That's what I mean by control. In order for me to work, I have to have the undivided attention of everything and everyone: the audience, the backstage crew, the people who run the lights, all of them. And that's a tricky game.

I did my first film, *And the Band Played On*, and there were thirty people crunched into every corner of a small room. I was feeling nervous about having all that crew and camera equipment there. In the scene, Matthew Modine was sitting, Saul Rubinek was standing, and I was lying in a hospital bed. I had seen Saul in *Unforgiven*. I had seen Matthew in how many movies? And here I was and I had to do this scene in which I was very, very sick with AIDS. I had KS lesions everywhere. I was the only person who had lines in that scene, the other actors ad-libbed responses. I had complete control of that room. I was the king of that room. Because I had that level of control, I was able to share things with Matthew and Saul and I always knew where the camera was. Everyone was there for us, so it was a piece of cake. Well, it wasn't a piece of cake, it was a hard scene. But the point that I'm trying to make is, if I secure that control, then I can believe that with my skills focused in even a simple gesture, everyone will give me their complete attention.

Two Saturdays ago, at the end of the first act of a matinee of *Millennium Approaches [the first half of* Angels in America, *in the Broadway production],* a man in the audience had a minor heart attack and they called the paramedics to take him to the hospital. Luckily, it was during intermission and so we could just wait offstage. Then we had to do the first scene of the second act where my character, Prior, shits blood and Louis calls the ambulance. I was observing the crisis as it happened in the audience, and I noticed the difference between the real catastrophe and the theatrical one. Here was a real person having a real heart attack, with real paramedics, and the entire audience was just sitting around, casually talking to each other. Then Joe Mantello and I went out there and we faked a medical emergency. I faked that I couldn't breathe. I faked that I was shitting blood. I faked that I didn't want him to call the ambulance. And the audience didn't make a sound. They didn't move. They didn't cough. We acquired their absolute attention. The theatrical event requires the overwhelming focus of the audience. The actors, who have acquired that attention through control of the space and the moment, have power, and if the muse is with them, that power makes them soar.

I am absolutely, completely conscious of the audience. I feel what they are doing. I'm completely conscious of my other actor. I'm completely conscious of what's going on in my body. It's the height of reality. I actually feel as though I'm suspended above myself, or inside myself or in back of myself and my body. Everything is moving and doing exactly what it should be doing. And I'm saying to myself, "Now do this," making little, tiny artistic choices. "Go a little farther on that—go . . . go . . . really get them now! Really make this hurt!" I'm still playing my action, but at the same time, all choices are possible because I'm in absolute control. Ron Van Lieu, one of my teachers at NYU, always used to say to me, "I love acting because it's the only time in my life that I know exactly what I'm doing."

I always think of theater games and my games teachers, Omar Shapli and Paul Walker. There's this wonderful game called Expertise. In Expertise you are the world's greatest authority on whatever. The possession of expertise leads to another important idea: whatever I do is always, always right because I am the world's greatest expert. So, with a character, say Prior, if I start going in a different direction, then I suddenly know exactly where I am since I am the world's greatest expert, and of course, I'm right here where I should be. There is another game called Transformations, in which you and the other actors are in one universe and then it transforms. No matter how weird that universe is, you're all in it together. As

Paul Walker would say, "You're worshiping Buddha, you're going to the bathroom, and you're working with the computer. This just happens to be a universe where the bathrooms are all equipped with Buddhas and computers." We're all here in the same room and that's absolutely correct. We should be here. We are experts.

Because I played that game so many times, when I'm onstage and something changes, then it's supposed to change. My brain suddenly fills in all the information I need, which is a wonderful feeling. Then, "Oooh, I know where I'm going!" and I discover a whole new life, a new, fresh place that I can sit in. The other day during performance of *Angels in America* Jeffrey *[Wright]*, who plays Belize, fell asleep in his dressing room. Usually, the scene opens, the hospital bed starts sliding on, and I see him walking towards me. That day my bed came onstage and I didn't see him and I thought, "Oh, he's late. All right, I'm going to turn around and I'm going to futz with these get-well cards from my friends on the table behind me." So, I did that and then the bed finished rolling on and I futzed a little longer. Then I said to myself, "Okay, he's probably there right now holding that pose of his, so I better turn around." But he wasn't there. "La Vie en Rose" was playing and the stage manager let it run all the way to the end, for a minute and fifteen seconds. I sat there thinking, "By the end of the song he's going to come in." But he didn't come in. Then the universe changed. "What universe am I in?" I didn't even have to ask the question. I just suddenly knew. I am Prior, alone in this hospital room. I became more and more alone. One of the understudies who was watching said, "You seemed to get thinner and frailer. It was absolutely heartbreaking." I think it worked so well because the exact thing that was going on with Prior was genuinely going on with me. I really was just sitting there thinking, "I am so alone. Please someone come and visit me. Please!" I used everything I had to close in on myself and be increasingly alone in this hospital room. Of course, at the same time I was sitting there in that universe, all alone, I was thinking, "What would a really great actor do?" Yet, all the time, I was doing exactly what I should have been doing, being all alone. It was an amazing moment.

When Jeffrey came onstage, three minutes later, my job became "calm him down because he's going to be really upset." I knew what was going on in that specific universe; I had my wits about me and I was in control. I looked him in his eyes, willing him, "Everything is all right. Let's just have fun in the scene." That calmed him down and we did the scene. It was rocky, but we found some really nice places in it, and in the end the audience didn't know anything had gone wrong. It's funny because now when I do the scene, it seems to sort of lack the heartbreaking beginning it had that matinee. But it's one of those things that I think just happens once.

Right now I am working on doing *Millennium* eight times a week. Every night I get to carve out the performance again, going from moment to moment making each as exquisite as possible. I go to the areas where I feel weakest and try to clean them up. In the scene in the nurse's office, I'm working on that long list of symptoms to make each one absolutely specific without dwelling on them in any way. Each symptom has its own inner life, and I am working on making them deeper and more concrete. Prior is thinking, and when people think and talk, each thing is expressed very specifically. He doesn't have to go down to retrieve them, they come up. On the other hand, the actor does have to go down to retrieve them, so I'm working on making them so specific that I can do it with no pauses and, in a funny way, lighter.

At the beginning of the hospital-room scene with Belize, I have a very large, emotional mishigas about wanting Louis to come back. It's written as an explosion, and I have to come from a place that is kind of neutral and leap into the middle of this very upsetting thing. Lately, I've discovered that the way to do that is to be very much in touch with Belize and to stay with him as much as possible. It's hard to see him because I'm blocked turned out to the audience, while he's massaging cream into my back. I'm an actor who really likes to see the other actor. That's why I had a lot of trouble in the mutual dream scene, when Harper and I are looking into the mirror. The mirror isn't really there so I never really get to look at her, and that is very hard for me. That gives me trouble doing monologues in auditions. I am grounded by other people.

Those are some of the things that I'm working on in performance. During a rehearsal period I work on new areas of myself that I want to carve out. For instance, it took me at least six years to master the most extraordinary acting exercise I ever did. I was working on a scene with an actress named Annie, in Olympia Dukakis's acting class in graduate school. Annie was having some trouble, and Olympia went over and stood with her. We started doing the scene again. I said my first line and Olympia said to Annie, "Oh! What he just said makes me feel good. It makes me want to so something like this. What does that make you feel like? What do *you* feel like doing?" Annie told her and Olympia said, "Okay, let's do that." They did and then Annie gave her next line. Then I said my next line and Olympia asked her, "Oh! What does that make you feel? What does that make you want to do?" She took Annie through each step of the scene in this way, slowing down time to give her the opportunity to assess out what I made her feel and what her feeling made her want to do. The action and activity of the scene became specific to Annie and much more dramatically alive. It was really extraordinary. It was so incredibly meaningful to me that it's sort of what my rehearsal process became like for many, many years.

Other actors used to complain because as we were working on a scene, I was talking to myself. "Oh! Oh! That makes me want to . . . Okay . . . ," and I would figure out where their line put me, and then I would respond. Maybe I would respond three or four times, say the same line three or four times as a way of figuring out where it was coming from. "No, that really wasn't it. . . . No, that wasn't it either. . . . It's this!" The other actors would be like, "Come on, can't you just do the scene?" What I was discovering over those years was precisely that skill of being able to hear a line and go right to the place in my body or the place in myself where the response was coming from. But first I had to take their line into my body in order to find where my response came from. It took me a long time to get facile at that. Now I usually do that before the rehearsal period. When I first get a script, I'll read it and I'll go through that process in my apartment by myself.

I really don't like going into the first reading without feeling like I could have all of my lines within three days. I don't like having the script in hand when I stand up. I can't read and act at the same time. So I have to have the words in my head when I'm still sitting at the table.

This poses problems at auditions, so I try to go into them with the words already in my head. I had an intense audition for Edgar in *King Lear* a year and a half ago. Even before I went there, I had to make very serious decisions about what was going on with the character. They had me do four scenes, and one of them was Mad Tom. What is he talking about? I spent a lot of time figuring that out, and finally it was the phonetics that gave me the answer. He says, "Away! The foul fiend follows me." Why the foul fiend? Why is it foul? Why does Shakespeare have Mad Tom choose those exact words? *F, f, f:* all those fricatives. Are they allusions to his *f*ather? Then later, when Gloucester, his father, enters in the scene, he screams, "It's the *f*oul *f*iend," and that answered the question. Then you just play the scene and let the audience figure it out. You know what's going on and you just let the character have his time without indicating to the audience that the reason I'm saying these fricatives is because it's about the father. It's not a lecture. It's a life. That was a lot of decision making just for an audition, but I got the part.

Early in rehearsals we were working on the scene on the beach where Mad Tom is in the hovel. The audience knows that there's someone scary inside, so I wanted a spectacular, scary entrance. I asked if the opening to the hovel could be designed so that by springing off my feet I could literally come flying out. The stage was raked, and for a moment I was suspended in air, which the director punctuated with a flash of lightning. It was great. However, after you've made an entrance like that, you've got to back it up with the rest of your performance. My performance became about making big choices. My approach to the Mad Tom character was mandated by that leap.

Edgar was very different. When Edgar wasn't

feigning madness, to the degree that he feigns—I mean, who really understands how much he feigns madness and how much is an expression of his anguish—I made choices for him in a much narrower space. I think I got into a little trouble there. I was a much better Mad Tom than I was a heroic Edgar. I don't have a heroic body so it was harder for me to find my body for Edgar. Unfortunately, the costume designer put me in a raw silk peasant thing for the battle at the end. I got my brother's blood on my costume every performance so they had to wash it every night. Well, raw silk never stops shrinking, and by the middle of the second week I looked like an aerobics instructor when I came onstage. That sort of killed the heroics. The audience thought I looked silly and I lost control of them, at least during the sword fight. I could feel that loss and the scene became a hundred times more difficult.

This brings up the fact that you have to make both kinds of choices all the time: the big leap and the narrow. Sometimes I stay more within the narrow confines of my comfort zone, and I allow something to evolve out of that, sort of inside. Or, I can make a really out-there choice and then work toward filling that. But if I'm making the big, out-there choice, my body for the character always comes out of that. In fact, big leap or narrow, I always have to figure out how I can use my body.

Prior was a part where I had a lot of trouble figuring what my body was. It was one of those times when you don't really know what you're missing until you get it. When it came to me is when I realized that Prior is a queen, in the gay sense, and so everything loosened up. All my joints became a little more fluid and I became a little more statuesque. My hips went off to the side a tiny bit and my hand gestures became a little more fluid, and

that's when I realized, "Oh, here's my body. This will now give me more information." For instance, it immediately changed the first few moments of the scene after the funeral and those first lines about death: "Ooooh, cemetery humor. I don't want to miss that." It changed that gesture. But Prior's very complicated, and what happens to him is that when he's charming and clever he has a queen's body, and when he's serious or angry, his body closes up and he has the body of his father. These things turn on a dime as demand necessitates. I've rediscovered Prior's humor and his body every time I rerehearsed *Angels in America*. Every time, in every production. New directors, new Louises, new blocking—things change with each production. Thank God! The only thing that doesn't change is the words. However, there comes a point in each rehearsal process when I realize Prior is a queen all over again! So, I have to figure it out again, and it's all personalized.

Everything is personalized. You personalize character. You personalize actions. You personalize activities. What I mean by personalizing is that I'm always looking for the place in myself that it comes from. The more complexly I allow that place to be alive, the higher the degree of life that I can bring to the character or action or activity. Olympia used to say, "You are an incredibly multifaceted jewel, and when you play a character, you're only showing one or two or three of your facets." For example, in Churchill's *Serious Money,* I played Grimes, a grasping, aggressive, cockney bond salesman, working-class background, who has clawed his way to the top. He is incredibly dangerous, like a rottweiler, and very, very different from me. Olympia or Ron would say, "Now that's character." So, I wouldn't behave in this way. I'm too much of a chicken to play the stock market every day.

But Grimes isn't a chicken. Suddenly, that cowardice gets relieved from me. Stephen-as-Grimes gets to have that courage. I figure out that this particular courage is the courage of recklessness. I see from the words that he's exhilarated. "Fuck everything, fuck my life, fuck the future, buy them at fifty-five!" Stephen Spinella gets to have the exhilarating experience of being able to do that without the possible concomitant consequences in my real life, though these consequences exist for the character, Grimes. This is now personalization talking. I use the part of me that would be exhilarated by recklessness to create that courage or sheer willfulness or balls to be able to make those spot buys on the stock market. You give yourself the character's opportunity . . . or your opportunity is the character's life.

All of these things, character, personalization, shaping the moments of scenes, are like the lessons in *Zen and the Art of Archery*. You spend your life figuring acting out because it's always changing. You can never do it the same way twice. One of my acting teachers used to say, "You learn how to act all over again every time you play a new role." And she's absolutely right.

I'm interested in that sublime moment that happens between the person who's looking at the piece and the person who's doing the piece. When the character is so immediate, each moment so impeccably clear, the audience is invited inside of what is going on and they are with you. That, to me, is sublime. That's what makes a three-and-a-half-hour play seem like twenty minutes. At the end I suddenly find myself, and it's as though I've been in a dream. Or even better than a dream, in a vivid, enchanted reality. That is theater to me: the real and the enchanted simultaneously.

DANA IVEY

Dana Ivey is a superbly trained actor, justifiably proud of her ability to craft material. In her creation of Daisy Werthan in Driving Miss Daisy *and Melanie in* Quartermaine's Terms, *both Obie Award–winning performances, or in* Sunday in the Park with George *and* Heartbreak House, *both Tony-nominated performances, she augmented her craft and imaginative life with finely honed observations drawn from life. She sees her craft, however, as a backup to her creativity.*

She considers the source of her greatest creativity to be her unconscious mind. The question is, how to access it? Dana Ivey asserts that the entrance to that realm begins when one is no longer afraid to make a fool of oneself. If she is too watchful and afraid of being judged, then she won't allow herself to go beyond her limitations. She suggests that pushing and shoving at the boundaries of physical and vocal gestures and making a series of increasingly successful stabs at the truth of the scene marshals the energy required to open up to unguarded emotion.

Then there comes a time when perceptive people begin to sense the urges and darkness that lurk beneath their familiar personas. When this time arrives, each artist must make a choice whether to open to "the uncontrolled wildness that resides beneath the surface." Dana Ivey's skillful performance in The Color Purple *is an example of an actor's having crafted the narrative, found the character's inner logic, and then releasing herself to explore uncharted, inner territory. Dana Ivey sees this as a choice with a consequence: once opened, the unconscious can never be closed without ill effect. She has made her choice, and in her unconscious she finds the source of her most profound creativity.*

"I PROBABLY WOULD HAVE BEEN A GOOD EXPLORER. I LOVE FINDING UNDISCOVERED COUNTRIES."

Before we began *Sleepless in Seattle,* I based my character work on some ideas that Nora Ephron gave me, East Side matron images. However, when it came to shooting, what I came up with was a little bit different from what she wanted. I had to go back and reschedule her comments in my head and find the way it made sense to me to express them. Maybe more nouveau riche; not as elegant and real, not as still as my original idea. It was minutes between takes, so you just do it. You make the adjustment and play, seeing what comes out. You don't mull it over in a corner, getting your emotions all prepared. Sometimes that works and sometimes it's important, but nine times out of ten it's common sense, and you go right into the scene and start playing tennis, serving the ball. The ability to do that has to do with having an innate facility for mimicry and taking on characters that I've exhibited since I was a child. Of course, the main thing that you have to learn is not to be afraid to make a fool of yourself. You have to try something, and if it doesn't work, or if the director says no, you simply try something else.

The willingness to make a fool of yourself in order to do what you have to do is an essential aspect of acting, and it takes enormous courage. People very rarely look at that fact. An actor has to commit herself to an idea and be prepared to have people laugh at her and say, "What a fool you are! That doesn't work at all." Maybe you don't even get a chance to redeem yourself, but you have to take that chance. It's a very risky situation. And putting your personal self on the line is just part of the courage required. Then there is physical courage. Sometimes it's actually dangerous doing stuff. But mostly, I think, you need the kind of courage that permits you to unzip yourself and say, "Look, look at all my parts and how they fit together, and, God, I hope you like them. You might not like them, but I hope you like them 'cause if you don't like them, that's all I got." It's very scary dealing all the time with the courage to face possible rejection. And I don't mean just in an audition. I mean in every performance, in every moment that you're trying to be truthful and connect, to be someone that you want other people to accept and believe in. At every moment they may be scratching you off as a fool and a useless idiot. That happens, so it takes real courage to stay open in the face of all that makes you want to slam shut.

The thought of opening myself up to play, say, Medea is pretty horrific. I mean, I say I'd love to play it, but on the other hand, I don't know if I'd want to deal with that. For me to get into the truth of what Medea is, is almost to flirt with madness. It's an intriguing challenge, but I'm aware of how psychically painful and frightening it could be. It's fascinating because it's primordial and primitive and it would mean getting in touch with the dark shadow of self that we never want to acknowledge—but is there. If I acknowledge that, I can find all of the reasons within myself for what Medea did, and I can believe in it and support it. It's just finding a new value system. It requires a kind of psychic courage to take the chance of making a choice out of that chaos.

However, in order to do that you have to understand what it means. This is a metaphysical question. You must appreciate the fact that the unconscious has, if you want to personify it, a dark self. It is a repository of all that is dark and may exist to sabotage us. It exists to keep our lighter self, the heavenly part of ourselves, from triumphing. It is a deep, chaotic power that exists within all of us to a greater and lesser degree. I use it in my work a lot. It's kind of like riding a dragon, I think. If you're a creator, you have to acknowledge it, make friends with it, and begin to use it, because ultimately it is the creative power. You have to be very, very strong to ride it because it's dangerous in its power. As I said, it's like a dragon or some kind of steed that you ride, and it takes a lot to hold on to the reins and keep it going where you want it to go. You have to stay in control or that way lies madness. But once you have acknowledged it and made friends with it, you can no longer shut it out. You have to welcome its power in your life. It brings in a lot of excellent unconscious material, but it wants credit. If you try to shut it out, it will find a way to sabotage you and drag you down. This is all very poorly paraphrased Jung, but it's something that I've been conscious of in my work. It is an enormous power but it's like riding a whirlwind, and I have to be incredibly clear about where I'm going in order to stay in control.

At twenty I don't think I was even aware of it. Mastery of the ride developed with meditation, finding out who I really am, what my true power is, what I am made up of, and therefore what I have to call upon. Unless we are mad or aberrant in some profound way, the awareness of this demon within probably doesn't come to us unless we have developed enough strength to deal with it. That is a saving grace. As we grow older and develop some sense of inner structure, then we begin to reveal this other part to ourselves. I don't really know and I can't even say when I first knew this or used it. It's been a developing sense.

It's hard to talk about because the experience is beyond language. Getting there is a lot of trial and error and much practical, common sense. It's not that you emerge full-blown from the head of Zeus in command of this brilliant choice. I can see a moment. Try it. Didn't quite make it. Try it maybe more this way. Oh, it's getting closer. That's what rehearsal is for. And every time you don't make it, you have to be willing to make a fool of yourself in front of other people. You have to say, "I'm trying to do this incredible, weird, horrible thing." Then you have to keep trying until you find it. Sometimes it involves difficulty: yelling, screaming, crying out, and pushing beyond whatever parameters presently define you. You push and push and discover whether or not you can go further. Frequently, you discover you can and then you push to the other side where it lives. You must try to get closer to it every time without allowing your own self-definition stop you from trying something that you may not know how to do at this moment.

How do you learn to do anything you don't know how to do? You have to try first. You have to just keep doing it until you get it, until it becomes a part of you, like the kinesthetic sense of riding a bicycle. Once you have found it, you have found it forever and you can feel it there. But nobody can describe to you what that is because it's something you have to feel within yourself.

There are probably other ways of arriving at it, but frequently just pushing and shoving can get you there. Sometimes that can free you long enough that you can begin to allow the emotion to just be there. A lot of actors feel and feel, but their bodies and their voices are restricted to such an extent that the feelings can't be expressed. People are embarrassed to express themselves hugely, so sometimes it's good to force yourself to go around being huge in order to open the gates. Your body, already behaving hugely, will be there to support the inflow of emotion and inspiration and can go with it and react. Most people are so psychically repressed that they don't know how to allow that encounter. True, genuine, huge emotions do things to our bodies, and people aren't prepared for the enormity and suddenness of their expression. The false idea that acting is all emotion is part of the problem with the way it is taught in this country today. We're all one mechanism. Conversely, sometimes just by manipulating your body you will find emotion.

All creative people use whatever is going on in their lives in what they are creating at that moment whether they're aware of it or not. I'm not proud; I use any resource that comes along. I'll copy people. I'll remember something I had for breakfast that gives me a thought. You never know when the "Aha!" experience is going to strike and you're going to say, "Oh, yes! That's the way to make that work!" On the other hand I love technique and I've trained in it, first at Rollins College and then on a Fulbright at LAMDA. I am proud that I have a craft. If my intuition, which I've learned to trust a great deal, doesn't open the gates for me, then I have technical ways to batter them down. For instance, I can analyze the material in a more intellectual way. So I think of the craft as a backup for the moments when creativity may simply fail me. Sometimes it's vice versa. Sometimes, I don't understand and I hash away at it with all my intellectual or technical skills. Suddenly, a blessing will occur and then an "Aha!" experience will take place and I'm flooded with a kind of understanding that has nothing to do with intellect and that fills me in a very full, creative sense.

The characters I play are very real people to me. I don't think of them as characters. I can refer to them much the same as I would someone I know reasonably well. I like them. I have to like them if I'm going to be them and embrace them. People think I play a lot of hard, unlikable people, and yet I always find within them a value system that I can relate to. If there are things they do that I don't like, I find a way to understand them within their value system. That would be the only way I would know how to approach it. My character in *The Color Purple* was not a bad or evil person. She was not nice, but she was really a well-meaning person. There are prejudiced people in the South who wouldn't have been as nice as she was in her nicer moments with the kids. She was brought up in a climate of true fear. A woman like that would have been taught to be afraid of black men. Yet, in spite of that, she actually tries to reach out in the only way she knows how, which I find is a remarkable quality. She tries to go beyond what she doesn't even understand. Her prejudice is a fact, but she's a product of her time, and I'm not going to condemn her for that. I'm going to see that, as a product of her time, she is remarkable, because she tries somehow, even in a state of confusion, to go beyond.

I probably would have been a good explorer. I love finding undiscovered countries. The sense of actual discovery is exciting to me. I love seeking things out, putting them together, and coming up with the answers. The first role that comes to mind in terms of the spirit of exploration is Daisy in *Driving Miss Daisy*. Although I'd done a lot of character work when I was younger, Daisy involved meshing technical approaches to portraying age and diminishing capability with a real interior understanding of what was happening to this woman at given periods in her life. I'm also convinced that you have to have the right instincts to do it. There are so many nuances that people who aren't from the South simply don't get and can't be taught. I'm from Atlanta, Georgia, and I know those people and every place that was spoken of in that text. That understanding is what I tried to build on.

I discovered in the rehearsal process that I was getting too old too soon and leaving myself nowhere to go. I had to be very analytical at one stage and break the play down into sets of scenes of diminishing capacity: playing the first six scenes with one sense of energy and posture and the next five scenes with a different energy and posture. I had to be quite accurate about when to start changing, otherwise it became unclear. And, of course, I meshed it into my own experience. I had Guillain-Barré, which is a form of polyneuritis in which the motor and sensory nerves are useless because the ganglia are inflamed. It's very rare. I had it first when I was twenty-seven and then again at thirty-two. I couldn't walk and I had to go to Easter Seal to learn how. I'll never forget that experience. I was terribly aware of the sort of danger old people feel whose sense of balance is very weak. I was afraid of kids running around, I was terrified of being knocked over because I knew I couldn't get up again. When I finally could walk again, I had to use a cane. I used the feeling of helplessness and total physical inability in understanding Daisy's diminishment.

I drew on a wide variety of women in my life to make a conglomerate that then became very real to me as an individual. I had one grandmother whom I particularly copied from my childhood memory when I answered the telephone "Hello." That spoke about somebody who came from a generation that might be slightly suspicious of the telephone and other modern forms of communication. It wasn't a big acting moment of suspicion and discomfort, it was just a tone in her voice. In college I was taught to store up observed information that would someday be useful. This was an observation I'd made when I was small, and I finally got a chance to use it. So there were diverse things that I used in creating that character, and I approached her with all parts of my being: my mind, my own history, and my sense memory in my body.

I feel it's essential to understand that I am merely a part of the experience of the play, and if I don't understand its spine, or overview, then I'm not going to be absolutely clear in the way I serve it. Daisy is a major component of the story. You can't have a love story without two people, and she is one of the pair. It's like a Romeo and Juliet story. The most unlikely people in the world learn to love, respect, and admire the very person they would never assume that they could. The play is about the power of that kind of perfection. This was not a mystery, it was apparent from the first reading. My job was simply discovering how to facilitate it so that the audience could go on the journey with us.

As we rehearsed, we began to set up certain moments, almost like a second act cliff-hanger, even though it was a one-act play. A series of scenes added up to a transitional moment in their relationship. In previews as we ran it, I became increasingly aware of where those places were so that I could more efficiently and sparely set them up and then allow them to happen. From there, I became aware of the orchestration of the piece, which had been difficult to see in rehearsal when we worked on it specifically, bit by bit.

The question of whether it's the actor's or director's job to understand the structure of the play is an interesting one. If you're an actor who doesn't understand structure, then you're playing moments very fully, and it is up to the director to shape it, orchestrate it, and find the climax. Every play's got to have a shape, although less and less things do. But I believe strongly in understanding the shape because the play is, ultimately, a story and has to lead up to something. It pleases me to do so and I feel that I couldn't do the work unless I understood what my part in it is. Without seeing the shape of the play, I don't know how to serve it properly. It's not just discovering a moment but it's understanding what that moment means in relationship to forwarding the play. This is my particular take on it, and it may be just because, as I said before, I enjoy discovering and exploring. That's part of the fun. That's where I can truly say, "Aha!"

OLYMPIA DUKAKIS

Olympia Dukakis correlates why she acted at different stages of her career with how she acted and with the roles that became available to her. I have always been drawn to her acting, though the reasons for this attraction have also changed over the years. In the sixties I relished her gutsy earthiness, intense physicality, and sexuality in Peer Gynt at the Delacorte. In the seventies, her portrayal of Ella in Shepard's Curse of the Starving Class *was brutal and darkly judgmental. I admired the judgment as well as the architectural style of her acting. Olympia Dukakis taught me about the actor's power to delineate, and emotionally fulfill, reciprocal actions. Far from being predictable, this reciprocity was fraught with wildly human surprises, from the first moment of the play to the last. Years later, seeing her as Soot in Christopher Durang's* The Marriage of Bette and Boo, *I was astonished to see that the judgment she once might have leveled at this delusional character was absent. In this performance of delicate hilarity, compassion had taken its place. A change in her style had also taken place. While the throughline was absolutely clear, the supporting arches of her acting were softened into a seamlessly assured performance.*

Olympia Dukakis locates "the character's ballpark" first and then personalizes, finding places from her own life to inform her work. Without first doing this she would be "manipulated by her own history," never discovering the character's full range. But finding the ballpark of the character is not an objective exercise—it is interpretive. In fact, the same actor may arrive at different conclusions regarding a character at each phase of her life. Experience dictates interpretation. Interpretation is also affected by the unconscious currents of the actor's inner life. If one judges oneself harshly, then no matter how much compassion a character may require, she will be met with harsh judgment. Olympia Dukakis's varying takes on Mary Tyrone are a case in point.

Olympia Dukakis is at a point in her life when the urgent need to compete, or the compulsion to judge herself, no longer drive her or her acting. She is not held hostage by these unconscious undercurrents when finding the character. But the elements that arose at those times, gutsy sexuality, earthiness, judgment, harshness, delicacy and compassion, all remain available to her as colors she paints with, freely and truthfully.

She embraces the principles of sisterhood and the Great Mother, which find its way into her current performances. She talks at some length about her experimentation with a Sumerian mythic journey, "The Descent of Inanna," which has electrifying resonance for women in the world today.

In this interview Olympia speaks of her evolving self-definition and its analogue, her evolving acting. The reader is offered an unusual opportunity to understand the way in which the actor's personal and artistic imperatives are inextricably bound.

"WE ARE IN A LONG LINE OF WOMEN, AND THE ANCIENT MOTHERS COME AND THEY SMILE AT US."

I want the world of the play to move in on me. I'm not interested in what I've been doing and feeling and thinking, I'm interested in what difference the play is going to make in me. If the play's a whole new suit of clothing, why would I insist on thinking, feeling, walking, and behaving in my old clothes? The fun of it is to put on the new suit. But you've got to find out just what that suit is. How I've investigated that has changed over the years.

I think it is true of me that I'm a mindful, willful actress in the sense that it has been difficult for me to move freely in my work if I don't have a structure and order. The experience of the play's structure and its language draws me into its world. Then I can commit myself fully, without regard for what others may think or believe. My instincts, my persona, and my mythology are useful to me only once I've understood the ballpark. If I didn't work that way, then I would be totally manipulated by my own history and it would be anarchy.

Say, for example, that you have a character who is, on the simplest level, a very reality-based human being. This is her ballpark. You then identify the circumstances in her life that shaped her, so that you can build your "reality-based case." In any given situation when somebody else might behave more idealistically, this character behaves very realistically. For instance, look at the mother in *Moonstruck*. She is not sentimental in any way. She looks to see "What's real here; what's really going on?" or "Why do men chase women?" She doesn't scream, she doesn't yell. She feels betrayed. But what does she act on? She acts on her view of the world. Right away she tells that guy in the restaurant, "I'm too old for you." Not too many people in that moment would have handled that situation as she did. Some would have kidded themselves longer. She did not respond that way because she thought it was wrong. She said it simply because that's who she is.

I am aware that now I'm working in very nonlinear ways. I am aware that I'm working now even when I don't think I'm working. In large part that's because there's so much of my self that has become trustworthy. When I was younger, my work consisted of moving from one task to the other. Now I have no plan at all when I walk into rehearsal. When I read a script, I don't have a specific order in which I am going to ask specific things. It used to be important to me to identify the active elements of the play before I went into rehearsal. I needed to understand the conflict of the scene; what I want; what the other character wants; what the obstacles are; what my character element is; how I fit into the tapestry or design of the whole—all things that not only effect *what* the situation is, but delineate *how* the situation is played out by this specific character.

I finally believe—God knows after thirty years it should be true—that I'm never not going to take in who that character really is. I'm never not going to be concentrated and focused on what I need and want. I mean, I'm trained. I'm like a baker who's worked the recipe over and over and over. My craft is now part of me. That's not to say that at times I don't get into a situation and say, "Why don't we just sit down and talk this through very easily and be sure we know what we're saying." Or, sometimes I get into trouble and have to try to figure out

OLYMPIA DUKAKIS

what the matter is and I call on my technique to solve the problem.

Sometimes I become aware that my body wants to do something different from what my mind is working on, and I have to stop and assess the situation. I understand now that my body has all the information, so if my body, for whatever inexplicable reason, wants to do something, I totally trust that. When I go with my body, it takes me someplace else. It takes me someplace else in relationship to me. I absolutely love when my body goes first when I'm working on a play. I feel confident and solid in my work when that happens.

The interesting thing about the stages of your work are the changing reasons why you act, which, in turn, affect what you do in your acting. It influences the parts you get and the ones you seem to be ready for. At one point in my career, during *The Memorandum,* at the Public Theater, I was offstage with my hand on a doorknob, and I had no desire or need to go onstage. I wasn't scared. I was indifferent. It seemed to me that instead of going onstage I could have stayed in the wings. It was a very interesting time and I had to understand in a new way why I was acting.

In my twenties, my reasons for acting were entwined with my desire to be acknowledged. I shouldn't minimize this first phase because within me I had a desire to be great in a way that transcended the personal. I had this desire to play great parts and to walk on the stage and affect people profoundly. I wanted to act, to become good at having a craft. It was important to me to become skillful, but by the same token, these techniques and their structure were almost a way to keep myself together because I was so chaotic and had so much darkness coming out in my life.

At that time I was in Boston, part of a company of people who worked together and trained together. But when I came to New York, I realized that for me to get work, I needed to be better than other people. I got very competitive. I went onstage to be better than everybody. My strength was that I could be emotionally and physically daring onstage. So I did that and caught people's attention. Not too many women would leap from platforms or throw their bodies around. I competed physically and emotionally. Consequently, I reached a point where I stopped playing with people onstage. I stopped being part of the play. But then Peter Kass, who had been my acting teacher and knew me so well, said, "You don't have to worry about yourself anymore. You can risk letting go of it all, just step out there."

I have such wonderful stories and memories of Peter. We were doing *The Seagull* and I was playing Arkadina. I'd get to the point in act 3 where she says, "Am I so old and ugly that you can talk to me about other women without embarrassment?" and I would start crying and crying and never did finish the scene. Right before we opened, Peter was sitting there giving notes and asked, "Are there any questions?" And I said, "How do I finish the scene? I don't know how." Now, imagine the guts of this! He started to yell and scream at me that I had no courage because I wouldn't go forward. My reaction to this was very serious; I got very disoriented. A couple of years later, I said, "How could you take the chance of talking to me that way? You knew a lot of things were unraveling for me." And he said, "You know, it takes courage to be a teacher, too." He taught me that in this morass of who you are, you have some simple tools you can hold on to. You don't have to be at the mercy of your whole life onstage. You can focus your work. You can make it clear if you willfully embrace it, concentrate it, and permit nothing else to move in on it. If you value only this.

And I did that. I just did it. It became very important. And, as I said, time changes you. I was teaching, I'd had a couple of kids, and I had gotten stronger. My ability to tolerate myself was greater. Most people have strong feelings and they try to stop them, get rid of them, and judge themselves for having them in the first place. I was trying to let them live in me without manipulating or changing them. I had gone through a lot of therapy by that time, as well as bioenergetic therapy, which was about putting the body in positions that would release emotions. You know, sometimes when we look back and we talk about our pasts, they seem somewhat ludicrous. But at the time, that was an important exploration, and even now, looking back, I feel all of those efforts were inevitable.

That's when I went from being the competitor to the player. I was out there to play with other people instead of winning or judging. Years ago, when I was doing *Long Day's Journey* with my husband, my brother, Apollo, said to me, "Olympia, if an actor doesn't do what you think they're supposed to do, you remain invulnerable to him. You think, `They didn't do that right, they should do this.' Nine times out of ten, you may be right. So what? You're right, but you're alone." Well, I didn't want to be alone anymore, and it became important for me to come onstage to really play with the other actors.

I've played Mary Tyrone three times and I want to play her again now, because I've changed and I understand things that I didn't then. I want to share with the audience something I feel about women which I couldn't have done fifteen years ago. You know why I couldn't play it? Because I thought Mary was a hopeless failure. That's why I couldn't. I was puzzled that the director wanted to cast me in the role. At first I refused. I even suggested he cast my friend Jane Cronin instead. But he persisted and then I realized that I was preeminently prepared to play the part because I'd had a drug problem. I understood what it was to lose hope, to fall into despair, to lose faith in yourself. I understood what it was to not be in a state of grace and to feel untouched and unsupported by the universe. It's a terrible feeling, and that's where she's at. But the first time I played her, my judgment of her was very harsh.

The last time I played Mary I deeply responded to her feeling abandoned by the Virgin Mary, but now, after the last nine years of reading, acting, and writing on issues of women, I have a much deeper comprehension of what that abandonment is about for me and for other women today. She has been abandoned by the Ancient Mother. She is no longer in a line with women because we have been disconnected from any history or myth or any practice that has to do with being women. The knowledge of coming from the female protoplasm is gone and our feelings about our bodies are terrible. We are so separated from each other that we don't even know who to talk to. Access to Mary is not only psychological or through her personal history, it's carried in her DNA! My DNA! Something deeply mythic is tapped. Her son Edmund's journey is a linear, hero's journey. But a woman's journey is inward as she becomes aligned with those forces that are ancient in the world. This is Mary Tyrone's ballpark. For all of these reasons I want to play that part again.

This sense of sisterhood had changed for me when I came to play Soot in *The Marriage of Bette and Boo,* at the Public. Sisterhood. I had a sense that I knew Soot and understood where she was coming from. It hit me forcefully that what she was trying to do is to be happy. She was trying to make every day a happy day. Her husband would say these awful things and—oh, God!—she would wipe the slate clean. She'd get above it, perhaps a little far beyond, but he couldn't get her. She'd found her own way to survive and prevail. And, at the very end, she goes deaf so she no longer even hears his abuse! She found a way to maintain her wholeness, her spirit. I had great respect and regard for her, because I thought she was a person of great courage. Her husband was embittered all the time and could never rise above his own despair, agony, and sense of personal failure. My physical manifestation for Soot was that my head was always nodding. That happened naturally once my body lent itself to express Soot's ballpark, then I could be free within it. I had to shake my head to insure that I could keep getting above the pain.

Soot's spirit was very much like Winnie's in *Happy Days.* We produced *Happy Days* at the Whole Theater, in Montclair, New Jersey, which I helped to found. I loved doing this part every night. Winnie's the best in us. She gets up every day to try, somehow, to make it another happy day in the face of disaster. At times you think she's an idiot and that the only reason she can keep on going is that she's so stupid or because she wants to be loved. We judge her. But by the end of the play when she says, "Another happy day, so far," you feel that she is no fool.

After each performance I would come out and speak with the audience. I'd say, "That's my life," and I'd turn to them and say, "Isn't that what your life is? Isn't that what you get up every day to do? To try somehow to make your life and the lives of the people you love a little better every day? And don't you sometimes feel like you're an idiot? And don't you feel like you're failing? And don't you feel sometimes inspired? Sometimes don't things happen out of the blue and you think, 'Is this a sign? Does this mean something?' Maybe it is meaningful and important, but other people are looking at you and they're thinking, 'What a jerk!' " The audience knows all these things; they've just forgotten. In every play we say to them, "Okay, tonight we're all going to remember together *this* aspect about ourselves. We're also going to remember how treacherous our lives are. We're also going to remember how funny and stupid and silly we are, and we're going to laugh."

So I went from competing to playing, to being part of the purpose of the play for the audience. Besides the Whole Theater, I'm also very involved with a company called Voices of Earth. We are all women and we do performances that are totally improvised. Fifty or sixty minutes of living totally on the edge! Living on the edge is what I really love. We wanted to find ways to articulate the changes that happened historically for us as we went from a matrocentric to a patriarchal society. We committed ourselves to acknowledging what those changes mean to us in the present. By that I don't mean a return to anything, just an exploration of where we are today.

The first project we did we called *The Goddess Project*. We created poetic moments dramatizing the passages we experience from being virgins to becoming sexually active; from being sexually active to becoming mothers; from being mothers to becoming crones. We worked with these transitional times because they're essentially dramatic; conflict and obstacles exist whenever change is courted. We also did a minimal, simplistic dramatization of the Descent of Inanna, a Sumerian goddess myth. From the Descent of Inanna, we have taken a very specific scene that we use to dramatize the silencing of women and the split between what is dark, swampy, aggressive, and wild in women, and that which is acceptable for women to be and do.

Inanna, the Sumerian goddess of the world above, hears the call of her sister, Ereshkigal, the goddess of the underworld. Inanna is in great shape. She has tremendous powers that she's connived away from her father. This myth was generated after the patriarchy had begun in Sumer so that Inanna has to get her powers from the man. She's a great, powerful, sexy goddess, and when you read her words, they make you cry because we do not grow up in a world where women can talk about their bodies in this way. She is the fructifier of the world, not the perpetuator of original sin.

So, in the midst of all of her accomplishments in the world, she hears Ereshkigal's call of pain from the underworld. She descends because there is something she is missing: the knowledge of life and death. Now, this wasn't always the case; before the patriarchy the goddess represented death and rebirth, like Durga. But at the time of the telling of this myth, the aspects of woman were already divided. Ereshkigal is enraged because Inanna has betrayed her, rejecting her in order to succeed in the world above. She has agreed to relegate unreasonable aggression and the mysteries of death to the underworld. Ereshkigal has been abandoned. She is alone, immobilized, eating dirt, and full of resentment and rage—and you can find her within every woman. Girls learn progressively to stuff down those aspects of themselves that are unacceptable in the world. You cannot be a second-class citizen, be trashed and ridiculed at every age, and not experience this.

Ereshkigal says to the gatekeeper of the under-world, "Okay, Inanna wants to come here? She can come, but every day of her journey take one of her attributes away." Think of seven powers that make it possible for you to survive and prevail in a world that is run by men. One by one they're gone! At the end of the seventh day Inanna is a bloodied piece of meat which they have hung on the wall. Ereshkigal understands that in order for life to go forward things have to die and be destroyed. In or-der to grow we must give up some of the things that have enabled us to survive—even to prevail. This is indeed a dark mystery, but it is part of what women knew because they experienced it in their bodies.

And Ereshkigal sees Inanna, this piece of bloody red meat, and she feels she has gotten some measure of revenge. The pain and anger begin to unlock in Ereshki-gal. There is an outspokenness, a loudness, and a roar in her. She will say the truth directly without trying to ma-nipulate. She is not a steel magnolia, but a piece of steel. These androgynous creatures, born of the dirt from God's fingernails, come to witness Ereshkigal's vengeance and dilemma. Ereshkigal says, "Oh, woe to my outsides." And they repeat, "Woe to your outsides." And she cries, "Oh, woe to my insides," and they cry, "Woe to your insides." The more she is witnessed the more she releases. She has a rebirth, she is regenerated, and at that point she is willing to embrace her sister. At that moment the dual-ity of woman loses its strength and the potential for wholeness emerges.

I've explained all of that so that you can understand the improvisation we used to explore the myth. We ran workshops and we wanted to find ways for women to locate and release their Ereshkigal. We'd be in a circle, mumbling inside our heads, until we connected with a strong pain of victimization. The moment that you connected with the feeling, you sang whatever song you wanted to, and in the music we were together. I usually sing this Greek song that expresses deep, deep feelings. Then one of the women reaches a point where her rage is great and she says, "Okay, I'm on it." Somebody gets a chair and she sits down. We bring out a cloth and we wrap this woman around totally. She sits bound in the cloth and then begins.

Once, I did Ereshkigal and Joan MacIntosh did Inanna. I sat bound in the chair absolutely immobile, locked in the language in my head. What Ereshkigal does is she names the names of her accusers. The ones who most annihilate me, who make me feel like a helpless victim, are the men who say, "We're going to war. We're going to take your sons." I sat there in such rage and pain because my voice is not listened to. "You cocksuckers." There are no women involved in this decision. There are only these men, whom I watch helplessly on TV. "Ummm, ummm," mumbling inside the cloth. The audience can hear it, "Arrrr, uuuuuh, uuuuh, uuuuh," as you name your accusers. When I was ready, I said, "Okay," and I was unbound. Then what happens is the other three actors witnessed me. "What can I do? What can I do? I can't do anything!" "What can you do?" comes back at me. "What can you do?" they echoed. "All we can do is we tear our hair and beat our breasts! The women of Bosnia tear their hair and beat their breasts! The women in Somalia tear their hair and beat their breasts! And the world says, `It's just another woman crying. It's just another woman crying.' "

As you do this, you can see yourself and feel yourself coming back, and that begins to release you even more. You are in your body. Your Ereshkigal comes out. That's how it gets enacted and articulated in a way that is theatrical and clear. You should hear the gasps of the women when we start to wrap Ereshkigal up. People start to cry right away because, in their bodies, they experience being silenced. Each step in this theatrical process is being earned and discovered and explored and ridiculed by us, and then acknowledged. The space that we walk onto has in it the Great Mother's presence. By that I mean everything in us that connects us to what is essentially female in life. That is not an easy entrance. I find it hard every time. I feel frightened. I feel inadequate. I feel, how can I possibly be accepted? But, we are in a long line of women, and the Ancient Mothers come and they smile at us.

In this last thing I did for television, Maupin's *Tales of the City,* I played a woman who had been a man. This was such an interesting conglomeration of personas. It's like—I loved it!